CLEARING
THE AIR

CLEARING THE AIR

· · · ·

DANIEL SCHORR

Illustrated with photographs

Houghton Mifflin Company Boston

1977

Library of Congress Cataloging in Publication Data

Schorr, Daniel.
   Clearing the air.

   Includes bibliographical references and index.
   1. Schorr, Daniel. 2. Journalists—United States—
Biography. I. Title.
PN4874.S335A33 070'.92'4 [B]   77–22014
ISBN 0–395–25721–2

Printed in the United States of America

P 10 9 8 7 6 5 4 3 2

For Li, my wife, Jonathan, my son,
and Lisa, my daughter,
who, together and individually,
give meaning to my life

FOREWORD

WHEN I RESIGNED from CBS, I did not resign from professional journalism. This book, although concerned with personal experiences, is still conceived as a work of reporting. Indeed, discovering that information and recollections were sometimes clouded by institutional self-interest, I even found it necessary to do a certain amount of investigative reporting. The purpose, however, is not revenge against any person, organization or element of government; that would be un-journalistic. My hope is that this book rises above passions and feuds to illuminate some of the central conflicts involving government, the news media and society. This, I believe, is the function of a reporter.

Reporting, which has occupied all of my working life, has been not only a livelihood, but a frame of mind. This has meant that while others advocated, argued, worked in movements, ran for office, I observed and wrote about them all — aloof from the fray, rarely the joiner, never the petition signer.

It has been that way since a very early age. At twelve I started a four-page mimeographed monthly in the Bronx Jewish Center, where I was studying Hebrew. At thirteen, observing a suicide leap outside my family's apartment-house window, I interviewed the police, telephoned the Bronx *Home News* and earned my first five dollars as a reporter. In high school and college in New York, I worked on the Clinton *News* and *City College Campus* and as a "stringer" for metropolitan newspapers. My mother, considering journalism vaguely unrespectable, wanted me to be a lawyer; she knew she never had a chance. The only period in my life when I was not reporting was during my army service in World War II, when to my bitter disappointment, I failed to wangle an appointment to the staff of *Yank* or *Stars and Stripes*. After the war there was no time when I was not reporting for some news medium — a little Dutch news agency, American and British newspapers, magazines and, for almost a quarter of a century, radio and television.

The word "reporting" was always closely associated in my mind with the word "reality." The challenge was to discover the "real story" or to extract it from the mists of vagueness and pretense. In a more subjective sense — harder to explain — it made me feel real not to be involved. Participants took positions, got excited, shaped events for woe or weal, but ended up losing perspective on reality. I remained the untouched observer, seeing the whole picture because I was not in the picture. Admittedly, this attitude of noninvolvement may rationalize an abdication of responsibility, but the notion of being the invisible stranger always appealed to me.

Reporting for television was obviously incompatible with invisibility. Moreover, as a broadcaster from the power center of the nation's capital, at a time when media influence was becoming a controversial matter and a news story in itself, I found disengagement increasingly difficult to achieve. The new reality was that while we reporters scrutinized people, they were now also scrutinizing us, and not always appreciatively. It was something of a shock to discover that the Nixon White House took me seriously enough to have me investigated and that several Presidents criticized me by name. By my rules, the President wasn't supposed to notice us. Attacking the reporter was something like attacking the umpire; it just wasn't done.

Reporting meant, to me, getting to know things, or getting to understand better things already known. My keenest enjoyments, I must confess, came from finding out something that people in power didn't want known and telling people not in power something they should know. Under certain circumstances, either of those predilections can cause trouble. In combination, at a moment of heavy pressures, they can cause spectacular trouble — as I was to discover.

On February 18, 1976, a lifetime of reporting abruptly stopped, which meant that ultimate unreality began for me. I had caused to be published a House committee report on intelligence against the wishes of the CIA, the White House, the House of Representatives and my own employers. CBS, for reasons to be explored in these pages, took me off the air — not temporarily, as was then indicated, but forever. Unreality meant being turned from newsman into news story, from practitioner of the press into defender of the press — and sometimes target of the press. Being an issue had its interesting moments, but to one who had considered a press card as an exemption from controversy, it seemed like an intermission from normality. Normality was the press box, not the arena.

For seven months, from February to September 1976, I made speeches, gave interviews, tilted with critics, testified before a congressional committee and wondered when the strange dream would end. It ended when I turned to reporting in a new medium. Having committed myself to writing a book, I fixed up a working office in the attic of my home, engaged a staff of one and started on my most challenging assignment.

Once I had broken a coltish new electric typewriter of its tendency to race ahead of me, it clacked out words in a satisfying way. They were, moreover, words with one touch of reality that television could not impart; they stayed there, not melting with the twist of a dial. Also, no producers or directors hovered over me, advising how to tailor my words to their pictures, how to get in the "voice-over" or "music-under." There was no "shot list," with its second-by-second count of film scenes, dictating the length and content of what I should write. The new assignment was single-handed — more accurately, two-fingered — and the goal was to untangle five tumultuous years, to try to reduce confusion, controversy and misunderstanding to reality.

The search for a title that would suggest this job of reportage and not-so-instant analysis proved to be arduous. At an early stage, *Final Assignment* was the working title — suggested by myself, enthusiastically accepted by the publisher for its dramatic flair. On second thought, in a more recuperative frame of mind, I made urgent representations to change to something less terminal-sounding. Inspiration struck, and we settled on *Full Disclosure,* only to be apprised that we had run into the prior inspiration of my friend William Safire. Finally, we hit happily on *Clearing the Air,* all concerned agreeing that it had all the right connotations and was the best choice of all. The publishing process — jacket design, trade notices — was under way before I discovered, once again, that a friend — this time Edward P. Morgan — had used the title before, for a book published in 1963 and now out of print. Morgan, despite his strong nostalgic attachment to the title, expressed his generous understanding of the coincidence.

Writing this book provided an unexpected experience. I anticipated difficulty in fulfilling my resolution to make it high on information and perspective, low on gossip and rancor. This turned out to be surprisingly easy. Revisiting battlefields after the smoke had cleared, I found myself feeling unbelligerent. No longer embattled, I could discern some of my own errors, rash actions and distorted perceptions. Most of all, the clash of personalities faded in importance as larger issues came into focus. Neither Charles Colson nor Frank Stanton, Otis Pike nor William Colby, Richard Helms nor Fidel Castro, Richard M. Nixon nor William S. Paley, Bill Small nor myself seemed prime movers as much as figures swept along by a series of complex and interrelated conflicts involving secrecy and disclosure, government and television, the press and the public.

The play of these forces was the real story, a story that could not be adequately recounted from my limited perspective. There was only one course for a reporter: ask the others. At the expense of the agreed deadline for completion of the book, and the nerves of author and publisher, I suspended writing to embark on a series of interviews with former antagonists and other participants who could throw light into dark corners. The assurance to all of them was that the aim was reportorial — not to renew the war, but only to broaden the combat history. Their response was gratifying, and I am indebted to them for their generous and open-minded assistance.

Of those formerly in the White House, only ex-President Nixon failed to respond. Among his staff, interviews were conducted, in person or by telephone, with H. R. Haldeman, Charles Colson and

John Dean; Raymond Price, former speech writer; Kenneth W. Clawson, former communications director; Lawrence M. Higby, former staff assistant; and Tom DeCare, former assistant press officer.

CIA insights, background and assistance were provided by William E. Colby, former director; Ray Cline, former deputy director; Mitchell Rogovin, former counsel; Andrew Falkiewicz, former information officer; and the CIA's Freedom of Information unit, which expedited the release of requested material.

In Congress, information and clarification were provided by Senator Frank Church, former chairman of the Senate Intelligence Committee; Congressman Samuel Stratton, who sponsored the resolution to investigate the unauthorized publication of the Pike report; and former Congressman James Stanton, a member of the Pike committee.

Among current and past CBS officers, extensive taped interviews were conducted with William S. Paley, chairman of the board; Frank Stanton, former president; and Richard S. Salant, president of CBS News. Others who responded to inquiries were Arthur Taylor, former president; John A. Schneider, head of the CBS Broadcast Group; Bill Leonard, vice president in Washington; Sig Mickelson and Fred W. Friendly, former presidents of CBS News; Gordon Manning, former director of news; Sanford Socolow, head of the Washington bureau; Ed Fouhy, CBS News producer; Stanhope Gould, former associate producer; Herbert Mitgang, former editor; and correspondents Marvin Kalb, Robert Pierpoint and Dan Rather.

Additional information was provided by A. M. Rosenthal, A. H. Raskin and Roger Wilkins of the *New York Times;* Robert Rifkind of the law firm of Cravath, Swaine & Moore, representing CBS in an antitrust suit; Martin Mayer, the free-lance writer; and Kenneth Guido, counsel to Common Cause. Paul Hoch, of Berkeley, California, gave me the benefit of his erudition on the assassination of President Kennedy, and Professor W. David Slawson of Los Angeles, former member of the Warren Commission staff, provided guidance.

In a more personal way, William Safire offered invaluable material from his files as a Nixon speech writer, and equally invaluable counsel as an author and friend. David Wise gave me my first briefing on how to organize oneself to write a book. Morton Janklow, publishing matchmaker, made a good match for me and led my faltering feet to the altar.

Finally, this book owes much to three continuing collaborators. My wife, despite her own professional commitments, accomplished miracles of organizing the household to minimize interruption and also read draft manuscript with an unerring eye for loose thinking, faulty recollection and forgotten episodes. My editor, Joyce Hartman, punctured inflated rhetoric, forced me to parse with parsimony and stood as a rock of sound judgment and good taste. Deborah Herbst, for whom the title of "researcher" does not begin to cover the myriad forms of efficient and unobtrusive support she provided, invested the word "unstinting" with a new dimension of meaning. They each led me out of a great many factual errors and subjective excesses; any they did not lead me out of are my own fault.

DANIEL SCHORR

May 11, 1977
Washington, D.C.

CONTENTS

Illustrations follow p. 144

CLEARING THE AIR

I

THE ACCIDENTAL INVESTIGATOR

OMINOUS PORTENTS may have hung over August 25, 1972, but I missed them. As a general utility reporter for CBS News, I was called in on that date for one of my not infrequent temporary new assignments. This one had to do with the break-in at Democratic headquarters in the Watergate office building. In the next four years I would find myself pitted against the Nixon administration, against secret agencies in government, against Congress and — ultimately and sadly — against my own employer. I would find myself included in the fashionable group called "investigative reporter," and transferred to the less desirable class of *"investigated* reporter." None of this perilous passage seemed to fit my previous background and my advanced age.

On the threshold of my fifty-sixth birthday when this new career started, I had experience going back a great many years to a great many places. In the "postwar years," as we oldsters call them (for the Vietnam generation I have learned to say, "In the years after World War II"), I served a variety of print and electronic news organizations as a free-lance correspondent in the Low Countries. Unable to land a staff job with anybody, I was a stringer for everybody — the *New York Times,* the *Christian Science Monitor, Time, Newsweek,* CBS. Perhaps the insecurity of piecework payment, without fringe benefits, led me to be forever eager to come up with stories worthy of consideration.

In 1953, my on-the-scene radio reports from flood-stricken Holland attracted the attention of Edward R. Murrow, and I was invited by cable to join the staff of CBS News in Washington. I hesitated, for, though I enjoyed broadcasting, I considered it as a not-quite-serious sideline to newspaper journalism. Unable to realize my long-cherished dream of joining the *New York Times* staff, I cabled my acceptance to CBS News Director Wells Church and said farewell to the Low Countries and to stringerhood. In Paris, on my way to board the S.S. *America,* I had a taste of network high living. Bureau Chief David Schoenbrun invited me to an elegant lunch at a shrub-shrouded outdoor restaurant for the visiting president of CBS, Inc., Dr. Frank Stanton. Dr. Stanton talked of the cloudy future of net-work radio, and of his mission in Paris to buy a French automobile for the chairman, William S. Paley. The fourth person at lunch, puffing his pipe in reticence befitting his low station, was Schoen-brun's stringer, Blair Clark. In the mobile world of broadcasting, Clark would later rise to staff correspondent, and higher. Seven years later, when his Harvard classmate, John F. Kennedy, was elected President of the United States, Clark, in what few believed to be a coincidence, was named news director of CBS — becoming Schoen-brun's boss and mine.

My initial year-and-a-half stay in Washington, interrupted by trips to Latin America and Europe, was mainly divided between covering the State Department and the hectic activities of the department's nemesis, Senator Joseph McCarthy. I learned about the impact of television as ABC replaced its soap operas with live broadcasts of the Army-McCarthy hearings. And I learned about the manipulative uses of television as Senator McCarthy brandished papers and brow-beat witnesses, making it seem to millions of Americans that there was a vital national security question in who promoted an army dentist.

In 1955, I was sent to Moscow, instructed to try to parlay a one-week visa into a resident correspondenceship. Stalin was gone, but his memory lingered, and so did Senator McCarthy's. For two-and-a-quarter years I lived in Moscow hotels on CBS *per diem,* because my superiors refused to approve a formal budget for a Mos-cow bureau. As CBS News President Sig Mickelson ruefully confided on a flying trip to Moscow, "The CBS corporate people think it's too soon after the McCarthy red scare and network blacklisting to have a Moscow bureau officially entered in the CBS directory." Mickelson gave me to understand that there were irrational things in the big world of broadcasting outside the modest corner occupied by the News Division.

Under the circumstances, CBS seemed not at all displeased when I was periodically cut off the air from Moscow for defying censorship, and finally excluded from Russia altogether. If I had to be in trouble with a government, it was the right government. Back in the United States in 1958, waiting for a visa to return to Moscow that never came, I was invited to have lunch with CIA Director Allen Dulles and assess the situation in the Communist world.*

On a lecture tour, I found myself in the unaccustomed position of being lionized by conservatives. As one who had "stood up" to the Communists, I was feted along the way by the predominantly right-wing owners of CBS stations — especially that redoubtable patriot, Charles Crutchfield, of Station WBT-TV in Charlotte, North Carolina, who insisted that I stay in his house. Little did we know, as the dime novels say, that these admiring station owners would one day be demanding that I be fired.

There followed a medley of assignments of longer or shorter duration — the United Nations, Warsaw, Geneva, Paris, Havana, Germany and Eastern Europe, tours with Soviet Party Chief Nikita Khrushchev through Austria, France, Poland and the United States, and with President Eisenhower through Asia and South America.

My foreign reporting was sometimes attended by controversy that echoed through the corridors of government in Washington but did not seem to shake the news establishments I served. Hindsight has taught me that the early controversies lacked the ingredient of do-

*I must have made something of an impression. When I obtained portions of my CIA file in 1977 through a Freedom of Information application, I discovered that, in 1958, I had been under consideration for a job offer. The [deleted] office wanted me investigated, saying it wanted to "utilize SCHORR to do the evaluation of [deleted] scripts," having already turned down "approximately three to four previous candidates for this job." The job was never offered, possibly because of "derogatory information" from the FBI dating back to 1942: "Subject supports the Communist leadership of the New York Newspaper Guild and is either a member of the Communist Party or a close sympathizer." The New York Guild had indeed been under Communist leadership in its early days — which I opposed.

mestic political radioactivity that would later cause fallout behind my lines. These were some of the examples of stories that, at the time, caused trouble, but not between me and my employers:

Item: As early as 1948, my report from Indonesia for the *Christian Science Monitor* and *Time* of secret efforts by a United Nations committee to nudge the Dutch toward granting independence led the Netherlands to seize on the leak as a pretext to break off negotiations and resume its futile war against the nationalists. The furor in the U.N. Security Council embarrassed the State Department because the Dutch vented their suspicion that the American chairman of the U.N. Committee had been the source of the leak. The *Monitor* and *Time,* however, seemed more amused than worried about the anguish in Washington and at the U.N., and they had only praise for my work.

Item: In 1952, the Netherlands government, and Prince Bernhard personally, made strenuous efforts to get the *New York Times* to order me to halt an investigation of Queen Juliana's relationship with a faith healer. It was a relationship that led the unhappy Queen to believe in religious mysticism and, of more immediate concern to her government, in a neutralism that contradicted Holland's support of the North Atlantic alliance. *Times* executives refused to interfere. A situation that had The Hague in a state of agitation — with warnings that the Queen might be driven to abdication — left New York news executives unruffled. The episode had an anticlimactic ending when, persuaded by appeals of Dutch friends on sentimental grounds, I agreed myself to "kill" the article, which had been completed and sold to *Life.* That self-censorship contradicted some positions I would later take about "the public's right to know," which is another matter.

Item: In June 1957, President Eisenhower expressed irritation over the unprecedented hour-long "Face the Nation" interview with Soviet Chief Nikita Khrushchev in the Kremlin, which I had been instrumental in arranging as CBS News bureau chief. In these hesitant early days of post-Stalin coexistence, the White House resented our giving Khrushchev access to America's living rooms. In the interview, Khrushchev called for a "small step" toward disarmament, predicted that "your grandchildren in America will live under Socialism," and, incidentally, gave the first public indication of ideological disagreement with the Chinese Communists. At his news conference, President Eisenhower suggested the broadcast was a crass, unpatriotic act, terming CBS "a commercial firm trying to improve its commercial standing." But Chairman Paley said, in an internal memorandum, that the Khrushchev interview was "one of the most outstanding broadcasts ever carried on radio and television," and CBS President Stanton followed with a personal note about "a terrific job." However, hedging a little, CBS devoted an hour the following Sunday to critical comment on the Khrushchev interview — an unusual East-West variation on "equal time."

Item: In April 1959, the White House called a special briefing to deny and denounce my report from the NATO conference in Paris that Secretary of State John Foster Dulles was planning to resign. "Utterly irresponsible!" said Press Secretary James Hagerty. I heard no tremor from CBS, other than a cable asking whether I was sure of my story. Seven days later Dulles resigned.

Item: Stationed in 1960 in Bonn, Germany, I became involved — anonymously — in the presidential campaign by enabling CBS to contradict a statement by Vice President Nixon in his final television debate with Senator Kennedy. Kennedy had claimed that a "prestige poll" showed America's standing around the world sinking during the Eisenhower administration, and Nixon had suggested that the poll was nonexistent. My cable from Bonn, read on CBS broadcasts and widely quoted in newspapers, established that such a survey had been made by the United States Information Agency only two months earlier, and reflected a general belief abroad that the Soviet Union would be militarily stronger than the United States in a decade. I asked CBS to conceal the origin of the cable to help protect my source. That source is long out of government and, while still unwilling to disclose his identity, I can identify myself as the author of that anonymous story. Although it caused a stir at the time, it had no consequences for me, other than confidential congratulations, and apparently no adverse consequences for CBS in a year when Nixon lost.

Item: In 1962, President Kennedy, over the White House dinner table, asked his friend, CBS News Director Blair Clark, to get me out of Germany. He said I was being troublesome by reporting German criticism of his foreign policy. I had disclosed, for example, that Chancellor Konrad Adenauer had sent the President a "secret" letter, warning that concessions to the Russians could launch a wave of neutralism in West Germany. Later, in a closed meeting of German politicians in May 1962, Adenauer said relations with the United States were worse than at any time in his thirteen-year tenure and that he sometimes wondered whether President Kennedy considered West Germany his ally against the Soviet Union, or vice versa. Kennedy was "blowing off steam," said Clark, and he did not take the complaints from his old classmate seriously. The White House press secretary, Pierre Salinger, thought Kennedy serious enough. On a visit to Germany, Salinger told me of a phone call he had just received. President Kennedy told him that, while shaving, he had been listening to Schorr on the radio, and not liking what he heard. Still echoing in Salinger's ear was the acid Kennedy comment, "Pierre, you've been in Germany four days now, and our relations were never worse! Where are you going next?"

Seeking to offset the effects of Adenauer's hostility, and his incessant threats to go it alone with French President De Gaulle, President Kennedy came to Germany in 1963. Standing in the receiving line with Chancellor Adenauer, the President greeted me by saying, "Glad to meet you. I listen to you all the time." Thrown off balance by the smiling barb, I mumbled, "Thank you, Mr. President, I listen to you a lot, too." I would have welcomed the chance for another conversation to repair the inanity of my remark. It never came. In Berlin, when Kennedy made his "Ich bin ein Berliner" speech, I was doing live commentary from a German television studio. I was still in Germany when Kennedy went to Dallas five months later.

• •

Although my superiors were generally unconcerned about the domestic dust raised by foreign furors, there was one marked exception

— a crisis created in 1964 by special circumstances. It came to be known as "the Goldwater Affair."

From Munich I reported on the CBS Saturday News, during the weekend before the Republican convention in San Francisco, that Senator Barry Goldwater planned a trip to Germany immediately after his expected nomination, for a vacation as the guest of his friend, Lieutenant General William Quinn, commander of the U.S. Seventh Army. He would stay in Berchtesgaden, Hitler's erstwhile retreat, now an American army recreation center. He was expected to speak at a lakeside Evangelical Church seminar in Bavaria — his first postconvention speech. Also, I reported that German right-wingers, like Franz-Josef Strauss, were eager to make contact with him.

The report detonated in San Francisco with a megatonnage augmented by several factors I could not have anticipated. Supporters of William Scranton, Goldwater's rival for nomination, reproduced the text of my broadcast and circulated it to all the delegates they could reach. CBS Chairman Paley was in San Francisco, generally regarded, because of his friendship with President Eisenhower, as a Scranton adherent. Goldwater was nursing earlier grievances against CBS because of his inclusion in a documentary on the extreme rightwing and an unfavorable reference by Walter Cronkite on the Evening News. His eruption ("I don't think these people should be allowed to broadcast!") was heard across the Atlantic. So was the dismayed voice of Fred W. Friendly, undergoing his shakedown cruise as president of CBS News. His opening words in the first of several long and stormy overseas conversations were, "What are you doing to me?"

It was a vivid contrast to the optimistic Friendly I had seen only a month before. Suddenly promoted to president of CBS News, the flamboyant, imaginative producer who had made his mark as Murrow's alter ego and symbol of courage in "See It Now" and "CBS Reports" documentaries, had flown to Paris in June for lunch with correspondents summoned from all over Europe. He had talked glowingly of CBS News being ready to recover its dominance over

NBC. He had depicted a new era about to dawn in which CBS News would be linked to its correspondents in Europe by satellite, enabling us to report daily with splendid simultaneity.

Now Friendly spoke in anguish and anger, upbraiding me in terms that seemed out of proportion to one controversial story. Years later Friendly told me that he had been summoned to Chairman Paley's hotel suite. "I was talking to you with him sitting right there. That was the price I had to pay."

Friendly wanted a complete retraction, which, I said, was impossible to make. That Goldwater had planned this odd postnomination trip to Germany was a fact. That Berchtesgaden had been a favorite retreat of Hitler's was also a fact, and the unfavorable connotation was something that could have been anticipated. That Goldwater was to speak at a Bavarian seminar turned out not to be a fact — or, at least, no longer a fact; the organizers said that whoever had conveyed his tentative acceptance was now saying he had no such plan. That German right-wing groups were excited about the idea of the Goldwater visit was a fact. There was, admittedly, one sloppy and unfortunate sentence in my script in which I spoke of "a move by Senator Goldwater to link up" with the German rightwing. More accurately, it was a *German* move to try to link up with Goldwater. I told Friendly that I would go on the air with a "clarification" that would, in effect, apologize for that sentence. It was apparently far from enough to repair the damage.

In San Francisco, Senator Goldwater was proclaiming that he would never speak into a CBS microphone again. He had barred CBS from his hotel suite. A canceled Goldwater interview threatened to leave a gaping twelve-minute hole in a scheduled Sunday night preconvention special. Friendly (I learned twelve years later) called to his hotel room three top assistants — Bill Leonard, Ernest Leiser and Herbert Mitgang. According to Mitgang, who subsequently resigned, partly over this controversy, Friendly opened the session with the angry statement, "Dan Schorr has given me a clubfoot at this convention!" He went on to say that he was considering recalling me from Germany to be discharged or reprimanded, and asked for the views of his associates. Leonard and Leiser were noncommittal.

Mitgang opposed any discipline, saying, "You would be telling everybody, including the Goldwater people, that you're caving in under pressure." Friendly snapped, "What do you know about broadcasting?" — a remark that Mitgang found pregnant with meaning.

Twelve years later Friendly told me that he had been reacting to Paley's pressure, and had never really intended to fire me. "Paley sat at my side in our viewing room for four straight days — I could hardly watch the convention — repeating, 'Have you fired Schorr yet?' And I kept telling him that it would destroy the morale of the whole correspondents' corps if a guy got fired for one mistake."

Friendly did not fire me. He sent me a "confidential" cable of reprimand. And, during that summer and fall, he insisted on personally clearing any report I made from Germany alluding to American politics. No radio or television script that mentioned Senator Goldwater survived his blue pencil. When I returned to New York in the fall for a showdown, Friendly said, "I saved your job." I replied, "If it had to be saved, it isn't worth saving." At this tense point, the CBS News chief interrupted our argument to attend to other business.

Wandering down to the basement cafeteria, I ran into Walter Cronkite, who seemed to know, or sense, that a confrontation was in progress. He asked if I would mind some unsolicited advice, based on his own experience. "You may recall," he said wryly, "that I recently had a problem with management."

All America knew of the "Cronkite problem." That August, because of sagging ratings against Huntley and Brinkley on NBC, he had been replaced in the anchor booth of the Atlantic City Democratic convention by the duo of Roger Mudd and Bob Trout. Friendly had taken the pained responsibility for what turned out to be a panicky Paley decision. Cronkite, who had swallowed the humiliation and stayed on, said to me, "I thought of resigning last summer, but then I decided that it doesn't make sense to quit because of the action of some executive who may be gone in the next shakeup a week from now."

It struck me that Cronkite had a point, that CBS News correspondents seemed a lot more durable than CBS News executives. In eleven years I had answered to news executives Wells Church, Sig Mickelson, Edward P. Morgan, John Day, Blair Clark, Gordon Manning, Richard Salant and Fred Friendly. It took more than a week, but less than two years, before Friendly was out in his own confrontation over allocation of time for news coverage. I took Cronkite's advice to hold my peace, unaware that my real problem was someone more durable than a transitory news executive—the founder and chairman.

Back in Germany, I faced an epilogue to the Goldwater incident. His presidential hopes buried in the Johnson landslide, the senator flew to Germany in April 1965, commenting on arrival in Stuttgart that this was "the same trip that I canceled last year after a reporter loused it up." On hand, as *Newsweek* noted, was "the louser-upper." As though in retribution, I had to come with camera crew from my headquarters in Bonn to cover the delayed visit. I had no interview. In point of fact, the senator ignored me completely and has not spoken to me since, but the incident was not allowed to die.

It lingered on in books by Senator Goldwater and General Quinn's daughter, Sally. In his 1970 book, *The Conscience of a Majority,* Goldwater reviewed the incident at length and concluded that CBS had acted out of consideration for its own "political preference," trying to "influence the rejection of a particular candidate." Sally Quinn, in her book about her unhappy CBS career, *We're Going to Make You a Star,* complained that, as a result of the publicity over her father's invitation to Goldwater, President Johnson vetoed his promotion, dashed his hopes of becoming Army Chief of Staff and caused "a brilliant military career to go down the drain because of vindictive politics."

As late as 1977, Senator Goldwater was still nursing his grudge. Appearing on Dinah Shore's television program, he startled her by saying that I had "violated the law" in releasing the suppressed report of the House Intelligence Committee and should be tried for espionage, then reverted to 1964 to charge that I had told "the damnedest lie" about his trip to Germany. He snapped, "Schorr has never apologized to me and I won't talk to him." His epithet for me, "son-of-a-bitch," was "blipped" out of the tape. The "Dinah!" show producer felt obliged, because of the Federal Communications Commission rule requiring an opportunity to reply to personal attacks, to invite me to appear on a subsequent program. I noted that I had apologized for the one sentence about his German trip that I had acknowledged to be unwarranted, but still considered it strange that the senator would have wanted to "start his career as a presidential nominee by going to Germany."

It is depressing to me that Senator Goldwater, still seeing an imaginary CBS conspiracy, is unwilling at this late date to reflect on the wisdom and public impact of his original plan to fly to Bavaria immediately after nomination. As to General Quinn, I doubt that President Johnson needed any news report to cast a baleful eye on a general who would play host to his newly nominated opponent. It strikes me as another example of blaming the messenger for the news. It was an ill-advised vacation plan in which the prospective host and guest both seemed insensitive to the symbolism and the probable reaction.

My problem was CBS reaction. This was the first big black mark on my record. I had embarrassed the organization—and, worst of all, the chairman — with a political party and a candidate. An earlier object lesson had been there to read in Paley's dismissal in 1961 of Howard K. Smith, Murrow's successor as anchorman on "CBS Reports." Smith had refused to back down from the strong civil rights statement he proposed to make in the summation of a documentary from Birmingham. Paley said the statement was too editorial; Smith said it was no more editorial than comments he had made as a foreign correspondent. Smith did not prevail. After his departure, CBS News correspondents were circularized for their views on standards of objectivity. I replied that no rule could ever be written.

"I know," I wrote, "that if I refer in a broadcast to 'Crusty old Chancellor Adenauer,' that will be regarded as vivid writing. And if I refer to 'Crusty old General Eisenhower,' I'll soon be hearing about it. Objectivity varies with geography. Everything is just more sensitive when it gets close to home."

Smith had learned, the hard way, that provocative comments from Birmingham, Alabama, are somehow different from provocative comments from Cairo, Egypt. And I was only starting to learn that, in a medium sensitive to the regional passions of customer stations and the pressures of politicians, trouble with the Soviet Communist Party is one thing and trouble with the American Republican Party is another.

• •

In 1966, I returned to the United States after a six-year stint in Germany and Eastern Europe. In the world of television, Europe, without a major war threat, was a dwindling story, and Friendly had long been urging me to come home. By the time I did, in May, he was no longer there to receive me, having resigned in February in a stormy conflict with CBS management. Salant, back at his old stand, confirmed the new assignment I had requested. Convinced that television was giving inadequate attention to a peaceful social revolution, I asked to cover all the programs signified by the Johnsonian slogan of "The Great Society."

In Washington, at the half-century mark in my life, I was ready to hang up my foreign correspondent's trench coat forever and settle down to becoming re-Americanized. I bought the first property I had ever owned—a Georgetown town house. It did not long remain a bachelor pad. The long-resisted idea of marriage overcame me when I met, on my new beat, a brilliant and beautiful woman, Lisbeth Bamberger, an expert on the organization of health services in the War on Poverty. I started my own on-the-job crash training in poverty and pollution, Medicare and Medicaid, education and segregation. The stories I worked on were what I called "people problems," which seemed, as things go in Washington, relatively uncontroversial, relatively unpolitical. In August 1971, with the Nixon wage-price freeze, my assignment was expanded to include economic stabilization.

Being home also meant my introduction to the great game of presidential politics. I had been abroad, as it happened, during every presidential year since 1944. Now, I learned, one dropped one's "beat" when tapped for the big team — the political conventions. The conventions are television's Olympic Games — climactic quadrennial competitions, conferring gold medals on network news organizations in the form of ratings and prestige, vaulting new stars into the firmament.

From the conventions emerged Walter Cronkite in 1952, Huntley and Brinkley in 1956, John Chancellor in 1968. With so much at stake, the networks devote to the conventions months — nay, years — of planning, mints of money and armies of personnel. Long before the opening gavel, the convention city becomes the relocated nerve center of the network — the anchor point for news broadcasts, the gathering place for senior correspondents, producers, news executives, and corporate executives intent on a little discreet lobbying with the politicians.

Immersed in the convention swirl, the news decision-makers lose the global perspective that New York and Washington provide. When a major story breaks elsewhere during convention time, the networks have difficulty in grasping it and adjusting to unexpected requirements on overstrained resources. In no other part of the news industry do the top executives allow one event so much to obscure their overall perspective.

So it was, in 1968, that news executives in Chicago slowly raised their heads from the vast coverage problems of the riot-beleaguered Democratic convention to become aware of a Soviet invasion of Czechoslovakia on August 20, six days before the convention. Finally, a harrassed news director, Gordon Manning, beset with appeals from the foreign desk to augment the one correspondent in Czechoslovakia — Peter Kalischer — looked around him at a convention planning session and recalled that I had worked in Czechoslovakia in my East European days. Manning told me to drop my convention assignment and fly immediately to Prague any way I could get there.

Preparing to quit Mayor Daley's riot police for Brezhnev's tanks, I ran into columnist Art Buchwald on my way to my room to pack.

"Hey, Schorr," he said, "I'll buy you a cup of coffee!"

"Don't have time," I replied. "I'm leaving for Czechoslovakia."

"Chicken!" Buchwald sneered.

In 1972, the story overshadowed on television by the conventions was a story, ironically, that related directly to the conventions. While senior news people were preoccupied in Miami Beach, junior news people were left behind in Washington to follow developments after the June 17 Watergate break-in. CBS executives were already installed — some in rented villas in Key Biscayne, neighbors of President Nixon and his friend, Charles "Bebe" Rebozo — when I arrived in Miami Beach on the Fourth of July. My first assignment was to work with Walter Cronkite and others taping a documentary for children called "What's a Convention All About?"

We did not ignore Watergate in Miami Beach, of course, but tended to treat it as a reaction story — the impact on the two conventions. At the Democratic convention in July, Chairman Lawrence O'Brien, whose telephone was the principal target of the Watergate bugging, told about his $1,000,000 damage suit against the Nixon campaign organization, the five arrested suspects, and "others yet to be named."*At the Republican convention in August, Nixon Campaign Finance Chairman Maurice Stans, a target of the General Accounting Office, denied any wrongdoing.

But while the networks were locked in their electronic competition in Miami Beach, print journalists had started probing the "third-rate burglary" in Washington. There was, of course, the Washington *Post* with Bob Woodward and Carl Bernstein, but also the Washington *Star,* the *New York Times,* the Los Angeles *Times, Time* and *Newsweek.* Before the conventions were over, they had developed the first important cracks in the Watergate cover-up — the links to White House consultants E. Howard Hunt and Gordon Liddy; the Nixon campaign funds "laundered" through a Mexican bank; the hundred-

---

*We missed the most direct "local angle" of the Watergate story. Between the two Watergate break-ins, E. Howard Hunt stayed on the floor reserved for O'Brien and his staff in Miami Beach's Fontainebleau Hotel. Helen Berthelot, office manager of the Democratic National Committee, complained to the hotel management about the renting out of the reserved space, but she attached no significance to Hunt's name. Alfred Baldwin III, the ex-FBI agent who was monitoring the Watergate tap, had learned that O'Brien had gone to Miami, and obtained his direct-dial number at the Fontainebleau. In a memorandum introduced in 1974 at the Watergate cover-up trial, Hunt disclosed that he had pressed "an alternate plan to bug O'Brien's Fontainebleau convention suite, before occupancy, a low-risk, high-gain operation which was rejected." If Hunt's advice had been taken, there might have been no Watergate case, or there might have been, instead, a "Fontainebleau case."

dollar bills found on the suspects; the records destroyed at campaign headquarters. John Mitchell had resigned as campaign chairman and Hugh Sloan as treasurer.

On August 23, President Nixon accepted renomination without mentioning by name either Senator McGovern, his opponent, or Watergate. The network correspondents assigned to the podium, including myself, sought to draw him to the barrier that held us back, but unlike 1968, when he lingered after his acceptance speech to chat with television correspondents, this time Nixon was having no interviews. He walked off the podium, ignoring us. Vice President Agnew, in his acceptance speech, trumpeted "the sound, tested leadership of Richard Nixon." And so ended the Republican convention, more a television program than a deliberation. It actually followed a secret TV script, which we took some pleasure in exposing — complete with minute-by-minute cues for balloons, spontaneous demonstrations, and rehearsed ad libs, for example, in the script for actor John Wayne, "Don't get settled down for a speech 'cause speech-making isn't my business." But, finally, the Miami Beach spectacular was over, releasing us to return to the world.

Friday, August 25, was a sultry, listless day in Washington, a day for dropping in at the office to catch up with the mail and gossip. The *Post* was reporting that Dwayne Andreas, the Minnesota businessman whose $25,000 Nixon contribution had ended up in the Watergate fund, had just received a federal bank charter with unusual speed. My bureau chief, William J. Small, who had been with me on the convention podium, said it was time for us to start concentrating on the mushrooming situation that we had just about abdicated to the newspapers during the convention summer. He suggested that I make Watergate my full-time assignment.

I expressed reluctance, suggesting — with something less than prescience — that the story would probably not go much further because President Nixon would surely be able to keep the lid on it. I also said that Watergate seemed a crime story, a young reporter's story, and a better newspaper than television story. I had some sense of the drudgery the print reporters were enduring, trying to dredge up leads and clues, and I had little stomach for it.

Small said that, notwithstanding my lack of enthusiasm, he wanted me to do Watergate, at least for the time being. And so, notwithstanding, I started doing Watergate.

II

STAND-UPS AND STAKE-OUTS

TELEVISION LUMBERS into a complicated situation like King Kong, altering the landscape by its sheer weight and force. Brushing aside complexities and seizing upon a few concrete images, it often provides its own version of events, simplified and sometimes modified. Insatiably demanding to be shown something, it tends to neglect the thinkers and pursue the doers. When the real news is invisible — as intangible as an idea — television news makes do with symbolic pictures and contrived graphics. If it cannot find the relevant picture, it will settle for almost any picture to "voice over." An involved story about farm price supports will be told over any waving field of grain, an urban problem over any city crowd scene, an inflation story over any supermarket. This is often in blithe disregard of the fact that the gum chewing supermarket clerk, the sound of the tractor, the almost familiar face in the city crowd may distract attention from the information ostensibly being conveyed.

The consequence of television's picture passion is more serious when it affects the ability of the public, mainly dependent on this medium for its information, to learn, in time, of significant developments. Denying "picture opportunities" becomes the objective of those wishing to keep a story out of the public eye — almost literally — and creating such opportunities becomes the need of those who want the story told. In that sense, television becomes not merely the witness to a contest, but the arena for the contest, and perhaps the arbiter.

From the perspective of a television newsroom just trying to do its job and put on a livelier, more visual news show than the other networks, it works like this: A reporter offers a story, based on some acquired information. The producer asks, "What do we see?" If there is no ready answer, the story, however important in substance, may end up as a condensed paragraph in Walter Cronkite's script, helping to sustain his "Magic Number." That is the figure, written into the daily line-up of the Evening News, representing the irreducible total number of minutes — usually about six — that Cronkite must appear on camera during the Evening News in order to establish him as more than a mechanical switcher from one story to another.

Watergate, in the early days before the 1972 election, was a classic example of a story in search of pictures. Time and time again, to meet the needs of various news shows and specials, I took our cameras through the sixth-floor office of the Democratic National Committee to show where the door had been taped, where the suspects had been captured at gunpoint by the plainclothes police as they crouched behind the glass partition, where the files had been rifled to photograph spectacularly uninteresting papers, where an inoperative bug had been placed on the telephone of Lawrence O'Brien, and a more successful bug on the phone of Spencer Oliver, Democratic liaison officer with state committees (which mainly picked up accounts of the liaisons of several secretaries). Nobody has declared that office a national monument, but the Institute of Medicine of the National Academy of Sciences, the current occupant, politely shoos away thousands of tourists with a leaflet telling them that, yes, this is the place, but please take the leaflet in lieu of a tour because there's work going on.

There was a limit, however, to how often this scene could be used; the story soon spread far beyond the dimensions of the burglary itself. To the question "What do we see?" there are two television answers. One is the "stand-up," which, as the name suggests, refers to the correspondent facing the camera and telling the story — whenever possible, against a recognizable backdrop. Lacking the conventional backdrops of the Pentagon, the Capitol or the White House (indeed, to have used the White House on a Watergate stand-up in those early days would have been a form of editorial statement), one had to fall back on the distinctive crenelated arc of the Watergate apartment house complex. It was a more pictorial, if less precise setting, than the nearby Watergate office building.

On any given day, the information I gathered from a variety of places — often in the CBS News office, sitting at the telephone — was reduced to a script, which I dutifully took to the Watergate to do my filmed stand-up — by that time, my only reason for being there. Watergate became for me the trademark that the Kremlin and the Berlin Wall had once been. The need for a stand-up location had the effect of fastening the name of the buildings onto what developed into a national trauma and an era of history far transcending the one manifestation that broke to the surface there. Oddly enough, my first file folder, two months after the break-in, was still labeled "Bugging." It was hard to remember when the site became the symbol, but it was the stand-up that did it. For the corporation managing the Watergate development, this attention turned into a nightmare of bad publicity until the operators decided to join what they could not lick and vaunted the "excitement of Watergate" in newspaper advertising and on match covers.

The other conventional answer to "What do we see?" is the "stake-out." Television's reflex reaction to a newspaper sensation is to camp out at the office or home of the personality named in the story, seeking an interview, a brusque "No comment!" or even a silent, but visible brush-off. I came to hate the stake-out as generally a prodigious waste of time that could be better spent digging out information, but television demanded it. I learned more than I ever cared to know about suburban Washington real estate and the exteriors of houses like those of White House Appointments Secretary Dwight Chapin in Bethesda, Maryland, and Presidential Counsel John Dean in Alexandria, Virginia, plus some associated skills like the art of communicating by walkie-talkie. Those who became targets of stake-outs found the confrontation fraught with public relations peril. Furtiveness and/or anger, natural reactions to an unnatural siege, tend to register badly. The principal stake-out targets, with application possibly reinforced by professional advice, developed considerable skill at facing their stake-outs. One could imagine H. R. Haldeman, John Ehrlichman and Charles Colson practicing in the mirror their beatific smiles and confident disavowals before venturing out to brave the cameras.

The Democrats, anxious to quicken the lagging response of the voters to Watergate, needed to organize a more dramatic "picture opportunity," and the legal process served their purpose. A stake-out with unusual potential loomed just as I launched into my new assignment. Leading figures in the story were commanded by subpoena to appear for depositions in the Democrats' damage suit, meaning that these elusive personalities were required to appear at fixed times at one fixed place, the schedule of which the plaintiffs gladly communicated to the press.

The place was the offices of the attorneys for the Democrats, Williams, Connolly & Califano, located, conveniently for the press, in a small building on 17th Street with a single entrance and a tiny lobby. Here came figures right off the front page of the Washington *Post,* Nixon lieutenants entering through gauntlets of shoulder-mounted cameras and microphone-bearing reporters, later emerging from their interrogations for a strained television ritual of challenging questions and unresponsive replies. The defendants did their best to radiate casual confidence and to suggest contempt for a charade that had taken them from the constructive work of reelecting the President. These stake-outs produced little information, but here were famous faces, a scene of activity and the easy makings of a daily episode for picture-starved television.

Maurice Stans, Nixon campaign finance chairman, set the standard for demeanor and passed the stake-out test with flying colors. Although funds from his office safe had been found in the pockets of the Watergate suspects, he emerged from two hours before Edward Bennett Williams and Joseph A. Califano, Jr., talking with the crispness of a champion accountant about "ironclad procedures" and "computer processes" that left him mystified as to how campaign money could have gotten mixed up with so unsavory an enterprise. E. Howard Hunt, on the other hand, fared badly by violating the rules of the TV ritual and trying to avoid the cameras. We initially knew only that he had been a White House consultant and a former CIA agent whose name had been found in suspects' address books. He could easily have dead-panned his way in and out of the deposition. Instead, succumbing to the reflex of a secret agent, he slipped into the building long before the cameras had arrived for the daily stake-out and, puzzlingly, failed to emerge when his interrogation was over.

After an hour had passed, I went up the elevator to ask Williams — incidentally, the owner of the building — whether the master spy had located some unknown exit or made his way across the rooftops. Williams suggested that, more likely, Hunt was still in the building, and that the best bet would be the fifth floor, housing two law firms whose members were on good terms with Hunt's lawyer. In the office of Hundley & Cacheris, deserted during lunch hour, I encountered a man in a light suit and impenetrable dark glasses, who seemed most unhappy to see me. Like Stanley coming upon Livingston, I opened, "Mr. Hunt, I presume? May I introduce myself?"

No introduction was needed, he said, since we had gone to the same college. That led to this confused colloquy:

"*You* went to City College?"

"No, *Brown!* Aren't you Irving R. Levine?"

"No, I'm Dan Schorr of CBS."

It was a surprising lapse for an intelligence professional,*but Hunt gave me no opportunity to explore his confusion between me and Levine, a Brown alumnus, who had been my NBC competitor in Moscow in 1956. He ducked into the elevator, joined by me just before the door closed. Together we emerged into the lobby, starting a mad scramble among the unprepared TV crews. Pursued by cameras and reporters, he raced around the corner to the Connecticut Avenue office of his lawyer, William Bittman, walked into an elevator without noticing an "out of service" sign, and was trapped. He

---

*Hunt displayed a frequent tendency to mix up his facts. His expressed reason for targeting Daniel Ellsberg was that Ellsberg had first given the Pentagon Papers to the Soviet Embassy. That never happened. Testifying before the Senate Watergate Committee, Hunt said that he thought former FBI agent Alfred Baldwin had acted as a double agent because he was the nephew of a Democratic governor of Connecticut; Governor Baldwin was a staunch Republican. Hunt went to great trouble to get a CIA wig, disguise and tape recorder to go to Providence for an interview with someone supposed to have inside information about Chappaquiddick, but who had no inside information at all.

pressed buttons frantically, held his Panama hat in front of his face, emitted tight-lipped "no comments" to questions, until finally, feeling sympathy with his intense discomfiture, I pointed out to him that the elevator wasn't going anywhere. Whereupon, he darted out into the street and ran another block to refuge in the Army-Navy Club. The whole episode was not very informative factually, but the hunt for Hunt was excellent television and, as the saying goes, went over like gangbusters on the Evening News.

The furtive impression left by Hunt created a problem for the following day's witness. President Nixon's special counsel, Charles Colson, a Brown fellow-alumnus and a friend of Hunt's, had been his sponsor in the White House. Colson sought to put distance between himself and Hunt. He denied any connection with "the Watergate incident." Many months later we would discover how narrow that denial was. Colson had been involved in, and sometimes directed, assignments to Hunt aimed at discrediting Senator Edward Kennedy, the late President Kennedy and Daniel Ellsberg. Using attack as his best defense, Colson seized his moment before the cameras to accuse me of having inaccurately reported that Hunt had a desk in his office. It turned out that Hunt had had a desk not in Colson's immediate office, but in another office under his jurisdiction. Hunt, when away, had often left Colson's extension for telephone messages.

These appearances before our cameras, however insubstantial, served to introduce the Watergate principals to the television audience. They helped to make a television event of a newspaper story. For the Democrats they served an important purpose. For the same reason, the Nixon camp deeply resented these command performances.

"How is Larry O'Brien's press corps?" asked John Mitchell scornfully as he arrived for his deposition on September 1. The former attorney general, who had resigned two months before as Nixon's campaign director, "for the happiness of my wife and daughter," declared that he had nothing to do with Watergate — the first of a series of disavowals that would make a devastating film montage when he was finally pinned down before the grand jury. But his purpose that day was a legal maneuver to try to stop the media parade. He balked at answering the Democratic lawyers' questions on the ground that his testimony might jeopardize the legal rights of the five Watergate suspects.

The court refused to halt the unhappy parade, and Mitchell returned to give his deposition to Williams and Califano. But Federal District Judge Charles R. Richey did order the contents of the depositions held secret under judicial seal. The testimony, as it later turned out, was unrevealing, but it would have provided grist for the preelection Watergate mill. The judicial seal also created a hazard for reporters. I ran into it in the course of developing my first story contributing substantial new Watergate information to what the printed press had been developing. I learned that Liddy and Hunt, previously linked to Watergate only through the suspects' address books, had been in the vicinity on the night of the break-in, and, when the five were arrested, had fled across the street to the Howard Johnson Motel room where the monitoring operation was being conducted. One point in my story was that this had played a part in Hunt's interrogation by the Democrats' lawyers. I wrote, "On all questions about his whereabouts that night, Hunt took the Fifth Amendment — refusal to answer on the ground of possible self-incrimination."

As usual, I turned in my script to be transmitted to the Cronkite office in New York before driving to the Watergate to film my stand-up. The filming was interrupted by a call over the camera crew's car radio, asking me to telephone New York. CBS News executives had scanned the script, and CBS News President Richard S. Salant wanted me to be aware of possible jeopardy. If this first leak from the sealed depositions caused Judge Richey to investigate and demand my source, it might not be possible to protect me from a jail sentence for contempt of court. CBS would provide every legal assistance, said Salant, but it was only fair to warn me of the danger and permit me to delete the perilous paragraph if I wished. I replied that I was fully aware of this risk, and it had to be accepted if the news was to be covered. Salant said that was the answer he had expected, and that CBS would go with the story as written. Judge Richey, to my relief, did not choose to go into the violation of his ban on any disclosure from the depositions.

Seeking further to dramatize Watergate as an election issue, O'Brien called a press conference to raise the ante in his suit from $1 million to $3 million, demanding further witnesses for depositions, such as White House Assistant John Ehrlichman, and charging a "political espionage conspiracy." On the strength of private information, O'Brien said there had actually been two break-ins at the Watergate and also an abortive earlier effort to plant a bug in Senator George McGovern's headquarters. I noted, in my "stand-up close" for the Cronkite show on September 7, "The Democrats obviously have an interest in keeping the Watergate case going as a campaign issue, but as long as they keep coming up with new material about the bugging . . . they won't have much trouble keeping it going."

Soon, I realized that this was basically wrong, an error of perception built on my own involvement in the story. As a developing story being told by journalists, it would have only shallow impact on the public. It lacked the drama of firsthand revelations and confrontations with participants required to penetrate the American consciousness. A news event was not yet a media event.

One dramatic touch was provided by former FBI agent Alfred Baldwin, who had been at the listening end of the Watergate tap across the street in the Howard Johnson. Baldwin was being kept under heavy wraps by Earl Silbert, the deputy U.S. attorney in charge of the prosecution. The Democrats had made contact with him through their private investigators and learned from him a lot more than the public knew at that point. Baldwin had written the wiretap summaries for the Nixon campaign committee, had seen the police arrive to capture the five burglars, had tried to warn them over an inoperative walkie-talkie, had seen Liddy and Hunt flee after the arrests. He was the "Deep Throat" for O'Brien's press conference revelations, which had not created as much excitement as the Democrats had hoped. Despite Silbert's warnings of silence, Baldwin became available for two interviews. After an extensive interview with the Los Angeles *Times,* he agreed to film an interview for CBS. He lived on the ocean-front in New London. The almost-deserted Connecticut beach lent a theatrical note to a narrative which took on the overtone of a confession. What struck me about his account was the banality of his involvement in high-level plotting. He recited his story like an FBI agent being debriefed on an undercover assignment. Indeed, it was from Baldwin that I first got a sense of one of the great evils of Watergate — the way the aura of law and order was given to a conspiracy against law and order. As a former FBI agent, went Baldwin's explanation, he had no way of knowing that orders from what appeared to be legal authority could be illegal. He had once been able to get through an airport security checkpost with an unlicensed pistol by a call to Nixon campaign headquarters. "I believed that we were working for the former attorney general, who was the top law man in the United States. So I couldn't question the legality of what was going on."

A Baldwin confused between what was government and what was conspiracy made a small stir on television, but, for the general public, Watergate remained an obscure event of Washington politics — "politics as usual," as Americans like to dismiss such things. On September 15, the "Watergate Seven" were indicted, and the trial was put off until after the election. As John Dean would testify in a Senate hearing ten months later, on that day he received congratulations from President Nixon as he confidently assured him that "nothing will come crashing down to our surprise."

Six days later, Judge Richey agreed to postpone the civil suit, and those irksome depositions, until after the criminal trial. The Democrats' counsel, Califano, came out of the Federal Courthouse with a statement ready for the staked-out cameras: "If the facts do not come out, we are just saying to the Republican Party and to Richard Nixon that you can bug and buy and burglarize your way into the White House." He was also saying, by implication, how desperately the Democrats needed the drama of a televised investigation. Califano appealed to Congress to step into the vacuum.

Two committees were already conducting tentative explorations. Senator Kennedy, as head of a judiciary subcommittee, had a staff lawyer, James Flug, conducting interviews and issuing subpoenas to prevent the destruction of documents. This planted the seed for the postelection Senate Watergate Committee, but Kennedy, partly because he felt vulnerable to counterattack over Chappaquiddick, decided to avoid the public role of Watergate investigation.

Less diffident was the aging but doughty Wright Patman of Texas, chairman of the House Banking Committee. When John J. Sirica, chief judge of the Federal District Court, ordered a gag on "witnesses and potential witnesses," Congressman Patman successfully demanded that he modify it on the ground that it might interfere with a congressional investigation. Patman asked his committee for subpoena power to summon resistant Nixon administration witnesses before his committee — and before cameras. This produced a titanic battle, fought largely in secret, with full awareness on both sides that the outcome would determine whether Watergate would be brought home to the American voters by public hearings before the election. In the Oval Office (the White House transcripts subsequently revealed), John Dean warned what would happen "if Patman pulls the strings off," and President Nixon instructed him, "You just try to button it up," adding that the House minority leader, Gerald Ford, "has really got to lead on this."

It would be disclosed, during his 1973 hearings for confirmation as Vice President, that Ford met twice with Republicans on the Banking Committee, but he denied that he had done so on Nixon's orders. In any event, all fourteen Republicans voted against the investigation. More surprising — and spelling doom for the investigation—so did six Democrats, providing the margin for Patman's twenty to fifteen defeat. On our program "Face the Nation" the following Sunday, Patman said he simply could not understand why the Democrats had voted as they had.

Patman might have understood better if he had known what was going on behind the scenes at the White House. William E. Timmons, congressional liaison officer, worked hard, John Dean later revealed, on wooing the Democratic votes that would tip the balance. Timmons said he was "working on the Southerners," four of whom ended up voting against the Watergate investigation under circumstances that suggested that their cooperation had not gone unrewarded. For example, one vote was obtained from Robert Stephens, of Athens, Georgia, and three days later the administration released a long-stalled $2,000,000 for a housing project in Athens. Timmons also was quoted by Dean as saying that former Attorney General John Mitchell is "gonna swing Brasco." Frank J. Brasco, the only northern Democrat to oppose Patman, made an emotional speech in the committee about the importance of safeguarding the legal rights of the Watergate defendants—which was precisely what Dean had outlined to President Nixon as the argument to be used against the investigation. Brasco himself was then under investigation in a bribery conspiracy, which the Justice Department held in abeyance until after the election. In July 1974, Brasco was finally convicted. One of the most overlooked stories of that period was the way the White House obtained the Democratic votes to prevent an open investigation of Watergate before the election.

One can only surmise what would have happened if Watergate had received a public airing before the election. A confidential report of Patman's committee, leaked to some of us reporters by frustrated staff members, indicated that Baldwin would have testified about the 200 telephone conversations his earphones monitored from Democratic headquarters; Stans and others would have been interrogated about the "laundering" of campaign funds through Mexico, Luxembourg, and other countries. Other witnesses would have been questioned about surveillance activities directed at Democratic candidates and members of Congress. America would have seen before the election some of what it finally saw in 1973 in the Senate Watergate hearings. To forestall such media exposure may well have been worth whatever pressure and promises the Nixon White House employed to deny Patman subpoena power. As a final gesture to call attention to Watergate, Patman asked Mitchell, Stans, Dean and Campaign Director Clark MacGregor to appear voluntarily at a hearing. None showed up, and, while cameras rolled, Patman lectured the witness table exhibiting their name plates. Said Patman, "President Nixon has pulled down an iron curtain of secrecy."

Almost desperately, Democratic nominee George McGovern bought a half-hour of television time on October 25 to tell voters they were missing the significance of Watergate. President Nixon, he said, was getting away with "an executive abuse of power." McGovern went on, "He has blocked any independent investigation. He has refused to answer questions from either the press or the people. He stays hidden in the White House, hoping you will mistake his silence for innocence." McGovern aides reported, wishfully, that in the final weeks of the campaign the Watergate issue was beginning to get through, but independent surveys indicated otherwise. In the media age, it would take more than campaign rhetoric to bring the issue to life.

One chance still remained. Common Cause, the citizens' lobby, had a suit pending, aimed at forcing the Nixon campaign organization to disclose its millions of dollars in anonymous contributions. Some of that secret money had turned up in the Watergate investigation; its sources and uses seemed fertile fields for wider inquiry. It had been generally assumed that campaign contributions received before April 7, 1972, when a new law went into effect, were exempt from disclosure. At deadline time there had been a frantic spate of money flowing in from contributors with reasons to remain anonymous. But an energetic young Common Cause lawyer, Kenneth J. Guido, concluded, after research, that disclosure might still be required under the old, virtually unenforced Corrupt Practices Act, which still remained in effect. With Mitchell Rogovin, of the prestigious law firm of Arnold & Porter, Guido launched a suit for Common Cause that the Nixon campaign committee first shrugged off and then, after losing several preliminary rounds in court, began to take most seriously.

One consequence was another round of irksome depositions — by H. R. Haldeman, John Ehrlichman, Maurice Stans — even President Nixon's friend Bebe Rebozo and his secretary, Rose Mary Woods — providing targets for inquisition in private and for television stake-outs in public. One such deposition, on October 25, had an unexpected consequence. Hugh Sloan, Jr., former campaign treasurer, happened to be scheduled for questioning on the morning that the Washington *Post,* in its most sensational Woodward-Bernstein scoop to date, represented Sloan as having named Haldeman before the grand jury as one of those controlling a secret political fund. I was on hand outside the converted mansion on 19th Street where Arnold & Porter has its offices when Sloan arrived. Through his lawyer, James Stoner, he denied the *Post* story, denied having given any such testimony, and, after the deposition, repeated the denial before a CBS camera. As recorded in the book and motion picture *All the President's Men,* this created a crisis for Woodward and Bernstein, and for the *Post.* It was what Benjamin Bradlee, executive editor, later recalled as his "lowest moment in Watergate." He recollected to Woodward and Bernstein that he had looked at Sloan and Stoner, "those bastards on the television, walking down the street, turning right into the courtyard, and there's Dan, big, dangerous Dan Schorr, whom I've only known for thirty years, really tucking it to them and winding up tucking it to us." Normally, the television stake-out tries to catch up with the newspaper scoop. This time it undid it. When I lunched with Woodward and Bernstein two days later at our favorite French restaurant, they seemed a little chastened, but not resentful. They were basically right about Haldeman — only premature in saying that Sloan had already testified.

More menacing to the Nixon camp than the depositions in the Common Cause suit was the prospect of a trial. Federal District Judge Joseph C. Waddy scheduled it for October 31, a week before the election, and refused to postpone it. Though there was no chance of a verdict before the election, the danger was the event that could crystallize media attention — the trial, with high officials on the witness stand, sketched by network artists, pursued by cameras outside the courthouse—all adding up to that dreaded television pageant of Watergate that could finally electrify the voters. The Court of Appeals refused to stay the trial, and so did the Nixon-appointed chief justice of the Supreme Court, Warren Burger, when a last-minute "emergency appeal" was brought to him.

During the months of legal proceedings, the Nixon campaign committee had been arguing a "fundamental right" under the Constitution to make anonymous contributions, developing the theory that such a right derived from free speech and the right of association. But, with the threat of a preelection trial and the attendant television spectacular, lawyers were shunted aside and the "fundamental right" forgotten. The Nixon campaign organization offered Common Cause an out-of-court settlement. It would release names and figures for some $5 million in secret contributions — though not the sensitive ones involved in that mad scramble just before April 7. Common Cause accepted the half loaf. Out came tumbling word of $1 million in contributions from Chicago insurance man Clement Stone and $800,000 from Pittsburgh steel magnate Richard Scaife. Out came a list of large contributions linked to Nixon ambassadorial appointments, and other embarrassments. But they were only embarrassments of words and numbers, to be quickly reported and quickly forgotten. John Gardner of Common Cause called it "a victory for the American people." But President Nixon had had his victory, too. He had escaped a preelection media Watergate event.

•   •

The Nixon camp had successfully staved off the threat of a Watergate television event before the election. What it could not avert was a *journalistic* event on television. The distinction is important. A television event — regardless of whether spontaneous or contrived — is an occurrence of its own, with its own participants, following its own course. It ranges from a Senate hearing on organized crime to a landing on the moon, from a presidential inauguration to the killing of the supposed assassin of a President. As indicated by the examples, it can be dramatic, memorable and drive deeply into the American psyche. It displays, in its most vivid form, the potency of television as a creator, and sometimes a manipulator, of emotions, attitudes and opinion.

A journalistic event is much less gripping. It is the presentation of information in more than routine fashion — at greater length, with greater investment of effort — because journalists have determined that such special treatment is warranted. It can take several forms — a discussion among correspondents, interviews with specialists, an illustrated documentary, a "special" scheduled in prime time or, by the grace of the gods of television, in time preempted from amusements. It can also form part of the daily news broadcast — what is called an "enterpriser," which is a longer and deeper look at a situation than the routine calendar of news events would dictate.

In early October, the idea arose for a Watergate "enterpriser" on the CBS Evening News. CBS News had not, comparatively speaking, been neglecting Watergate; it had, in fact, given it much more attention than the other commercial networks.* My companions of many stake-outs, Carl Stern of NBC and Sam Donaldson of ABC, were reporting boredom and resistance to Watergate stories by their superiors. But Walter Cronkite, pleased with reaction to some earlier in-depth reports on complex situations — the sale of grain to Russia, a housing mortgage scandal, the failure of welfare reform — was shopping for ideas for more "enterprisers." At a dinner with CBS correspondents, producers, and executives at Washington's International Club, Cronkite asked for suggestions for subjects. Producer Edward Fouhy proposed Watergate. Others, including myself, supported the suggestion, saying that, as with the Russian wheat deal, the story had been reported piecemeal, but its full dimensions left obscure for the general television audience.

Stanhope Gould, a free-wheeling but perceptive producer who had handled the Russian wheat sequence, was assigned to a new Watergate project. Gould came to Washington, trailing assistants and researchers. The first step was to advise the White House of what was being planned and to offer the opportunity for any and all of the Nixon lieutenants involved to tell their side of the story. There was a collective refusal, on the ground that the matter was before the courts. In informal task-force discussions, we acknowledged that we might not be able to develop much new information, but we would try to assemble available information in a way that would make the fragmented Watergate story comprehensive and comprehensible.

I suggested, in an October 17 memorandum, dividing the situation into four main areas — the bugging, the "dirty tricks" of Donald Segretti and others, the trail of secret money, and "the masterminds." My memo said, "I think we'll end up with the conclusion

---

*In quantitative terms almost twice as much as either NBC or ABC, according to Edwin Diamond in the summer 1973 issue of the *Columbia Journalism Review.* His count for the seven weeks before the election was CBS — 71 minutes, 9 seconds; ABC — 42 minutes, 26 seconds; NBC — 41 minutes, 21 seconds.

that the thing lapped very close to the Oval Office, but that there is no evidence that the President himself gave specific orders or had specific knowledge. To that we'll have to add that the people involved were close to and loyal to the President, caught up in the desire for a crushing landslide victory, and believing they were serving his interests, if not his wishes. From all of this one ugly fact emerges — a kind of extra-legal shadow government, existing side by side with the constitutional government."

As foreseen, it was hard to illustrate the story. Gould set graphic artists to work contriving animations and charts. He sent one mission to Texas, trying to shoot film of an oil company airplane that had flown bags of money to Washington for the Nixon campaign. Specific parts of the story were allocated to different correspondents and reporters. Mine was mainly the Watergate break-in itself, and the story of campaign financing. There was thought of trying to put together one big "blockbuster," but when that added up to more than the whole twenty-two minutes of news on the Cronkite show, it was divided into two parts. CBS News executives were, naturally, aware of the project, but left it to the producer-correspondent team to work without interference.

Friday morning, October 27, in New York, Gould completed the assembling of Part I — almost fourteen-and-a-half minutes long. It was screened at a meeting in the office of Richard Salant. It went into great detail on the Watergate bugging and break-in, and disruptive activities directed against the Democrats. Cronkite's script spoke of "charges of a high-level campaign of political sabotage and espionage apparently unparalleled in American history." Eastern metropolitan newspapers had said as much, but not Walter Cronkite in America's living rooms.

There were some more than casual viewers in various places in New York and Washington that Friday evening when Part I — the most extensive report on Watergate yet to be shown on television — was "rolled" into the Cronkite show from a video-tape machine in New York, a copy running simultaneously on a second machine in case of a tape break. In the CBS Washington bureau, some of us who had labored on the project for two weeks gathered in the newsroom at 6:30 P.M. to watch the "first feed" of the Cronkite show (which is fed on the network a second time at 7:00 P.M. for stations that prefer the later time). In the White House, I later learned, video-tape recorders turned in the monitoring office managed by Morton Allin under the supervision of Patrick J. Buchanan.* Charles Colson, who was still in his office, was alerted to watch the report about which the White House had heard rumors. On the thirty-fifth floor of CBS corporate headquarters in New York, President Frank Stanton (so he told me much later) watched over a drink with Aline Saarinen of NBC, the widow of the architect of the CBS building. At the end Mrs. Saarinen said they must be tearing their hair out at NBC over the CBS coup. Stanton went next door to call on the private telephone to the apartment of William S. Paley. He suggested that the chairman watch at seven o'clock.

At the end, Cronkite announced, "In our next report — the money behind the Watergate affair." Gould assembled the second part — fourteen minutes long — over the weekend in New York, and it was ready to be aired on Monday. On Monday, something came unstuck. The afternoon line-up failed to list Part II. Later, we were advised in Washington that it would have to be drastically reduced in size and each part would have to be revised. The next morning, without warning, a proposed new script for my portion came over the teletype from New York, sent by Sanford Socolow, deputy news director; I telephoned him to say that I would cut my script to any required length, but under no condition would accept dictation about its content and wording. He apologized, saying that he had only intended a suggestion.

There were all the signs of tumult in New York, but no sign of what had caused it. On Tuesday evening, we gathered in the newsroom again to see what had happened to Watergate Part II. The main points were still there, but it was about half the original length. Some listeners called in protest or praise of our extensive analysis of

---

*The elaborate system of taping and analyzing television programs made it possible to provide speedy summaries to President Nixon and his aides, and to retrieve earlier broadcasts for screening. Once Buchanan playfully took me to the backroom to spring me on the staff member he called his "Schorr watcher" and to enjoy the gasp of someone who had followed me closely on television, but had never seen me in person.

Watergate. A few asked why the second part had been delayed. We were not able to enlighten them.

On election night, November 7, I was assigned to Nixon election headquarters at the Shoreham Hotel, watching the mounting landslide that reflected how little Watergate had mattered, and hearing the President's curiously restrained victory speech.

A few weeks later, at a cocktail party, I ran into Henry Cashen, an assistant to Colson. Expansive in triumph, he waggled a finger at me. "Well, Mr. Schorr, we didn't stop your goddamn Watergate spectacular, but we sure cut you down a bit, didn't we?"

It was my first indication that outside pressure might have been involved in throwing CBS off stride at a climactic moment after so steady a march.

III

WHITE HOUSE AND BLACK ROCK

PRESIDENT NIXON liked to watch sports on television, but not the news. To keep him posted on how he was faring in the media, a special news summary was put on his desk each morning, prepared overnight by a staff of four. On Saturday, October 28, 1972, preparing to fly to Cleveland for a campaign swing, the President read a summary that started out cheerily, noting favorable reaction to the previous day's announcement by Henry Kissinger that "peace is at hand" in Vietnam. Next, a Sindlinger poll estimating Nixon-McGovern at a ratio of 64–22 in the campaign's closing phase was getting a good play.

Further down Nixon found this unpleasant item: "CBS apparently decided the rest of the nation has suffered greatly for the past month w/out [without] receiving the *Post* and the *Times,* so it provided a 15-minute rehash of Watergate . . ." After a detailed digest of the "rehash," the news summary, dropping its customary just-the-facts detachment, commented, "This observer recalls in 3 2/3 years no shoddier, more irresponsible and unwarranted use of 'precious' network time than this report."

As we in CBS News worked on the second installment, we were totally unaware that this Saturday marked a climax in a three-year largely subterranean cold war between the Nixon White House and the television networks — especially CBS. We had only witnessed the oratorical thunderbolts and legal challenges hurled at network television. Later, the Watergate and impeachment investigations churned up records that revealed outlines of a political conspiracy to discredit and intimidate television. This I supplemented by research and interviews, seeking, in the face of clouded and conflicting recollections, to get a fuller picture of the hidden war between the jittery giant of television and a President determined, as far as his image and political fortunes were concerned, to be the ruler of the airwaves.

By way of introduction to the contestants as they entered the ring with the beginning of President Nixon's term in 1969:

In this corner, there were the networks, starting to feel a little defensive about their news operations. In the "old days" of the fifties and sixties, news had been thrust forward as the good-guy, white-hat, public-interest side of a show-biz, violence-prone, sometimes shady-looking industry. To remove the taste of the 1958–1959 quiz-show scandal, CBS had expanded its news time, resurrecting "See It Now" as "CBS Reports," and NBC launched a series of "creative projects" in the field of news. Amid what Newton Minow had called "the vast wasteland of television," news was supposed to be the oasis. But news itself had become a subject of controversy in the increasingly polarized atmosphere of the Vietnam war, urban riots and political terrorism. During the Chicago Democratic convention in 1968, television news seemed to many as much a fomentor as a witness to violent protest. The little news appendage to the vast entertainment industry could no longer be used to justify the rest; *it* had to be itself justified, and without the obvious defense of profitability. Indeed, its brashness was sometimes perceived as endangering more important interests. Unlike a newspaper, whose principal product is news, whose main executives are involved in the news process, in television, news is a small sideline. Its top executives live in another world of ratings, entertainment specials, affiliates and the overarching awareness that the whole structure is built on something as evanescent as places on a dial which the Lord government has given and the Lord government could theoretically take away.

In the opposite corner, there was Richard M. Nixon, with a great penchant for trying to control his environment, from salad or soup

for White House dinners to the makeup of crowds at airport rallies.*
Manipulative by nature, he responded to the vast potential for manipulation in television, a medium that fascinated him. To television
he attributed both his greatest successes and greatest failures. Of the
1952 "Checkers" speech, which enabled him to turn back a tide of
scandal and force General Eisenhower to keep him as his running
mate, Nixon wrote in his book *Six Crises,* "If it hadn't been for that
broadcast, I would never have been around to run for the Presidency." When he lost to Senator Kennedy in 1960, he attributed his
defeat largely to the television debates. "I paid too much attention
to what I was going to say and too little to how I would look," he
lamented. "Again, what must be recognized is that television has
increasingly become the medium through which the great majority
of the voters get their news and develop their impressions of the
candidates."

To Nixon, the successful employment of television required access
under terms that he could manage. It was in the cards that, once in
office, he would use his powers and prerogatives to try to reach the
people, over the heads of critics and the political party system, by
presidential television. It is instructive to review Nixon's public actions against background that can be filled in from subsequent disclosures.

•   •

*On November 3, 1969, the President went on the air to summon "the Silent
Majority" to support continued war in Vietnam. His speech was examined
by specialists and journalists immediately afterward on all three networks —
and CBS was especially critical. Correspondent Marvin Kalb disagreed with
the President's characterization of a letter from Ho Chi Minh as intransigent,*

*Alexander P. Butterfield, the former Nixon assistant, told the House Judiciary Committee
that President Nixon wanted to be consulted on whether curtains were to be closed or open,
how state gifts would be arranged, the menus for social functions, and especially the entertainment. "He wanted a professional producer to come and actually produce the entertainment,
especially the entertainment which was for television."

William Safire recounts that, dissatisfied with the size of an airport crowd in Cleveland during
the 1968 campaign, Nixon issued orders to Haldeman, "There will be no more landing at
airports!" After deliberating about how to transmit that order, Haldeman finally sent instructions to campaign advance men, "There will be no more *unsuccessful* airport rallies."

saying it contained "some of the softest, most accommodating language found in a Communist document."*

The next day Dean Burch, newly installed chairman of the Federal Communications Commission, telephoned Frank Stanton of CBS — and later the heads of ABC and NBC — requesting transcripts of their analyses. Stanton, disclosing this, said Burch had specified he was acting at the request of the White House. Stanton termed it a "peculiar" way for the White House to get a routine transcript. Later, in response to a complaint of bias, Burch gave it as the unanimous view of the FCC that the commission could not investigate network analysis to determine what was true or biased, but it was a network's obligation to "scrupulously eschew slanting or rigging of the news."

About two weeks earlier, a White House memorandum had suggested an FCC "monitoring system," to start as soon as Burch became chairman, as a way of getting the networks to toe the line. The memorandum, now part of the Senate Watergate file, had a history.

Almost from the start of the Nixon administration, his subordinates became aware of his sensitivity to media criticism. Every week a report was compiled on "Little Lies," which were directed by "President's request" to specified staff or Cabinet members for rebuttal. An October 1969 memorandum contained a partial list of twenty-one such "President's requests" ranging all the way from "take appropriate action to counter biased TV coverage of the Administration over the Summer" to instructions that letters be sent to the editor of *Newsweek* "mentioning the President's tremendous reception in Miss. and last Sat. Miami Dolphin game."

When H. R. Haldeman, the President's chief of staff, realized that the countercriticism campaign was lagging behind the workload, he asked an assistant, Jeb Stuart Magruder, to study the problem. On October 17, Magruder came up with a memorandum titled "The Shotgun versus the Rifle." It concluded that the "shot-gun" of individual complaints to the media was "very unfruitful and wasteful of our time" and should be replaced by the "rifle" of "concentrated efforts . . . that will have more impact on the media." Magruder's first three recommendations were:

*Six years later David Eisenhower, who watched with his father-in-law that night, told me President Nixon had commented that Kalb could be right.

1. Begin an official monitoring system through the FCC as soon as Dean Burch is officially on board as Chairman . . .

2. Utilize the anti-trust division to investigate various media relating to anti-trust violations. Even the possible threat of anti-trust action I think would be effective in changing their views . . .

3. Utilizing the Internal Revenue Service as a method to look into the various organizations that we are most concerned about. Just a threat of an IRS investigation will probably turn their approach.

Magruder wrote that, unlike the Kennedy administration, "we seem to march on tip-toe into the political situation and are unwilling to use the power at hand to achieve our long term goals which is [*sic*] eight years of a Republican Administration."

The first occasion for target practice with the "rifle" was the critical analysis directly following President Nixon's Vietnam speech. In effect, it challenged his right to deliver an uncontradicted message to the huge audience he felt he had assembled by his preemption of amusement programs.* In addition to rattling the FCC saber, the President decided on a public counterattack. He had the most vitriolic of his speech writers, Patrick J. Buchanan, draft an address. According to William Safire, Nixon read it line by line, added a few lines to make it tougher and commented, "This really flicks the scab off, doesn't it?" The draft was given to Vice President Spiro T. Agnew to be delivered the following week.

•　　•

Before a Republican gathering in Des Moines on November 13, Agnew attacked the television networks as "a tiny and closed fraternity of privileged men, elected by no one, and enjoying a monopoly sanctioned and licensed by government." He asserted that the President had a right to "communicate directly with the people who elected him" without passing through "the prejudices of hostile critics."

*What outraged the White House most about instant analysis was explained by Patrick Buchanan in an interview with Elizabeth Drew on the public television network on May 4, 1972. He said, " . . . If, instead of trying to piggyback on the President's address, there was a report right after the President concluded which said, 'CBS commentators will have an analysis in a half hour,' then they wouldn't have had any audience. No one would have paid any attention to them. But they piggybacked behind the President's address to try to reconstruct in their own words, which the President made perfectly clear in *his* own words. And to me this is the problem, and I don't think it should go on, frankly."

Raising the question of whether his attack on the networks would be broadcast by them, he said that "is not my *decision, it is not* your *decision, it is* their *decision." The text had been made available in advance, and all three networks carried the speech, more than a half-hour, in full and live, replacing their entire 7:00 P.M., Eastern Time, daily news broadcasts.*

On November 20, Agnew made another speech, in Montgomery, Alabama, disclaiming any desire for censorship, but saying that "a broader spectrum of national opinion should be represented among the commentators of the network news."

Agnew clearly tapped a deep current among Americans — their addiction to television, and their concern that this addiction might have left them prey to manipulation; their admiration for the facile omniscience of the TV commentators, and their worry about the misuse of such omniscience. In the ensuing days, the networks received more than 150,000 communications, by letter, telegraph and telephone, and about two thirds of them supported Agnew. The Agnew speech pinned a label of "Eastern elitist" on television journalists that we have never since managed to shake off. The decision to carry the speech "live" was taken as a signal of network nervousness and defensiveness.

"The ominous character of the Vice President's attack," declared Frank Stanton in a speech on November 25, "derives directly from the fact that it is made upon the journalism of a medium licensed by the government of which he is a high-ranking officer."

But it was clearly *meant* to sound ominous. Although the networks proclaimed that they would not be intimidated, the next time President Nixon went on television — on December 15 to report on the progress of his peace plan for Vietnam — CBS did not follow with any immediate analysis. Instead there was a summary by correspondent Bruce Morton. It concluded, "He thanked the American people for their support of his November 3rd speech and said that he had completely dashed Hanoi's hopes of winning the war through divisions within the United States." Nixon's rhetoric was duly repeated, but not examined.

Score one for the Nixon doctrine of "presidential television." The file of the Senate Watergate Committee indicates a spurt of White

House antimedia activity in the next few months. On January 21, 1970, Jeb Magruder sent a memo to Haldeman saying that "we have a number of people here and in the RNC [Republican National Committee] who are supposed to monitor the media," and he urged that this be made a "priority situation." Haldeman's handwritten comment was, "I'll approve whatever will work — and am concerned with results — not methods." On February 4, Haldeman sent Magruder a "high priority" memo calling for "the mobilization of the Silent Majority." He said that "we have got to move now in every effective way we can to get them working to pound the magazines and the networks in counter-action to the obvious shift of the establishment to an attack on Viet Nam again." (In the odd lexicon of the White House, the "establishment" was the anti-Nixon establishment and "attack on Viet Nam" meant opposition to the war.)

•   •

In July 1970, the Republican National Committee filed a complaint with the FCC, demanding time to reply to a CBS program called "The Loyal Opposition," the first of a scheduled four broadcasts providing the Democratic National Committee an opportunity to counter the Nixon administration. In his first eighteen months in office, President Nixon had enjoyed as much television time as the combined totals of Presidents Eisenhower, Kennedy and Johnson in sixteen years. The FCC ruled in favor of the Republicans, holding that the initial Democratic broadcast had been a partisan attack rather than a reply to the President on specific issues. The FCC ruling was overturned by the U.S. Court of Appeals, but CBS did not resume "The Loyal Opposition."

"It was all done out of my office," Charles Colson told me in a December 1976 interview, "and it was a pretty good fight."

Colson would become famous as the keeper of the "enemy" lists, the Nixon loyalist who would figuratively walk over his grandmother, the sponsor of E. Howard Hunt, the manager of special assignments to "get something" on Senator Kennedy or the late President Kennedy, and, finally, a convicted defendant in a case related to Watergate. But, in July 1970, Colson had just been assigned by President Nixon to ride herd on the networks. He recalls that "I engineered the legal challenge to CBS" because the President was "upset about equal time the networks were giving to answering Presidential speeches."

In that same month, Senate files show, Nixon was looking at television in a larger and more ominous context. On June 5, he had called together the FBI's J. Edgar Hoover, the CIA's Richard Helms and the chiefs of other intelligence agencies to launch them on a secret project for domestic intelligence-gathering. The outcome was the short-lived "Huston Plan," providing presidential sanction for illegal wiretapping, break-ins and surveillance of Vietnam dissidents and left-wing organizations.* But there were more than student demonstrators on his mind that day. His "talking paper" for the meeting said that some were not willing to face up to the "new and grave crisis" represented in the "revolutionary activity" among young Americans. "This is particularly true," he said, "of the media and the academic community."

By the next month, according to a Magruder "Confidential/Eyes Only" memo to Haldeman, plans were in progress for an attack on television journalism by making "objectivity" a national issue. This, said Magruder, was a better idea than trying to discredit a correspondent individually "since the newscaster enjoys a very favorable image and will apologize for his remarks, claiming to be misquoted." Among the suggested tactics for the campaign were, "Plant a column with a syndicated colunist which raises the question of objectivity and ethics in the news media. Kevin Phillips would be a good choice . . . Arrange for an article on the subject in a major consumer magazine authored by Stewart Alsop, [William] Buckley or [James] Kilpatrick. Also, request Hobe Lewis [editor of *Reader's Digest*] to run a major article . . . Ask the Vice President to speak out on this issue . . . Have Dean Burch 'express concern' about press objectivity in response to a letter from a Congressman . . . Have outside groups

---

*The plan, named for Tom Charles Huston, a White House assistant who coordinated it, was approved by President Nixon on July 23, 1970. He claimed that he rescinded his approval five days later because of Hoover's opposition. However, the Senate Intelligence Committee found that the Huston Plan only "supplied Presidential authority for operations previously undertaken in secret without such authorization" and that many of the operations — including mail-opening and eavesdropping on electronic communications — continued after the formal revocation of the presidential approval.

petition the FCC and issue public 'statements of concern' over press objectivity."

Colson was mentioned as the one to handle the FCC assignment. He was already working on a related project — the Republicans' demand for air time to oppose "The Loyal Opposition." When the FCC ruled in their favor, Colson sent a memo on August 26 to Haldeman: "It is obvious that the other side is really being hurt as they begin to understand the FCC decisions. The Democratic National Committee is using every procedural move (and CBS is cooperating) to stay the decisions . . . I think it is time to generate again a PR [public relations] campaign against the Democrats and CBS."

Until that point the White House had been dealing with the networks at arm's length — by speeches, inspired attacks and maneuvers through the FCC. Now, conferring with President Nixon and Haldeman, Colson suggested that he meet the enemy face to face. Haldeman endorsed the idea and Nixon, in Colson's paraphrase, said, "Great! You're on!"

Colson proceeded to storm what Agnew had called the "privileged sanctuary" of the television networks in their New York skyscrapers. On September 23 he visited "Black Rock," the CBS headquarters on West 52nd Street. In "that big corner office with all the modern furniture and modern art," as Colson gleefully recalls it, Paley told him of being a long-time admirer and sometime golfing companion of President Nixon's. After twenty minutes of private conversation, says Colson, Paley pressed a buzzer and Frank Stanton entered, standing until the chairman asked him to sit down, speaking only when Paley addressed a question to him. (Both Paley and Stanton say that Stanton was present from the start. Paley says that Stanton spoke when he wished to. Stanton recalls that he was content to leave most of the talking to Paley, who seemed to be handling his end very well.)

Colson's writing, like his verbal recollections, tends to be selective, combative and subjective. In the Senate Watergate files is the "Eyes Only" memorandum he wrote Haldeman on September 25 about his three network encounters. It contained little about the ABC and

NBC sessions. Colson noted that the only ornament on the desk of Julian Goodman, president of NBC, was the Nixon Inaugural Medal. He reported that in the presence of ABC's Leonard Goldenson, his vice president, James Hagerty, former Eisenhower press secretary, said that "ABC is with us."

The brunt of the memorandum was about CBS. "To my surprise CBS did not deny that the news had been slanted against us. Paley merely said that every administration has felt that same way and that we have been slower in coming to them to complain than our predecessors. He, however, ordered Stanton, in my presence, to review the analysis [made by the White House of CBS news coverage] with me and if the news has not been balanced to see that the situation is immediately corrected . . . They told me anytime we had a complaint about slanted coverage for me to call them directly. Paley said that he would like to come down to Washington and spend time with me any time that I wanted. In short, they are very much afraid of us and trying very hard to prove they are 'good guys.' "

Colson reported agreement by all three networks that presidential access to TV should "in no way be restrained." He pictured them as "terribly nervous over the uncertain state of the law," fearful of what the FCC and Congress might do to them. "This all adds up," concluded the memo, "to the fact that they are damned nervous and scared and we should continue to take a very tough line, face to face and in other ways."

Colson's account has been challenged by the other participants — especially Paley and Stanton — as slanted, tendentious and designed to impress Haldeman with his tough-guy cowing of the networks. It reflects, however, the kind of information that was guiding the Nixon White House. Also, network executives seemed worried enough about Colson to spend a great deal of time thereafter listening to his complaints on the telephone.

In the next thirty months, Colson told me in our 1976 interview, he made about a call a month to Paley or Stanton — much more often than to ABC or NBC — to complain about a news broadcast. The first call was on October 8, complaining of "biased" CBS treatment of President Nixon's TV speech the previous evening announc-

ing the latest "major new offensive for peace in Vietnam." Colson
says he recorded all the conversations, these tapes now locked up
with the Nixon files under court order, but this one he took "by
accident because it got stuck in some of my papers." Not by accident,
he had it transcribed, and had a text before him when I interviewed
him.

Unbidden, Colson read snatches to support his premise of a craven
Paley, apologetic about his own news division and promising better
treatment of the Nixon administration. I am reluctant to repeat
selected quotations from a transcript made without Paley's knowledge.* The conversation was clearly meant to be private. Paley
opened it by saying, "I shouldn't be saying this to you, and I hope
I can talk to you as candidly as you talk to me." Colson replied to
Paley, even as his tape rolled, "You are talking to me completely off
the record." Without repeating the quotations, I had the impression
that Paley was sounding conciliatory but making no concrete commitments. He did not go beyond avowing admiration for President
Nixon, saying that CBS correspondents were only human, conceding
there may have been some bad journalism and promising anew to
review CBS news policies. In Colson's excerpts there was no indication of a Paley surrender. Neither was there, however, any ringing
defense of the CBS news team or a challenge to the propriety of
White House strictures. Paley may have thought he was acting as a
buffer for his news organization. Colson thought Paley was getting
softened up. And that is what Colson was reporting to his principals.

At the beginning of 1971, Colson proposed a round of summitry
— meetings between President Nixon and the heads of the three
networks. They were held without public announcement, in an informal setting. At the CBS session in March, Nixon and Paley sat with
their backs to the fireplace, in a circle of easy chairs that included
Haldeman, Colson, Stanton, John A. Schneider, CBS executive vice
president, and Robert Wood, president of the television network.
Haldeman, in a 1976 interview with me, recalled that the aim of the
session was to overcome "a lack of rapport between the Nixon presi-

---

*In 1977, Paley told me he did not know his conversations with Colson were recorded, but
he figured as much after the Nixon taping system became public knowledge in 1973.

dency and the network presidency." Colson looks back on that meeting fondly: "Nixon did it beautifully. He told the CBS people they were not there because they were involved with the news, but because they ran large corporations. He wanted to hear what their problems were because there were lots of policy issues that involved the federal government. Paley wanted to reminisce about golf and country clubs he had shared with Nixon in the old days. Nixon slid into the news coverage problem indirectly several times in that special way he has, saying things like, 'I know you can't control your newsrooms . . . Of course, I know they're all biased . . . They never liked me, and I guess that's the way it has to be.'

"Of course," Colson grinned, "that was like sticking a hot poker into Paley and Stanton."

Paley later told me that this was the only time he ever met with Nixon as President and that Colson's version of what happened is almost the opposite of the truth: "It was a rambling conversation, with very little said by us. At the end he [Nixon] said, 'I just want to warn you fellows that the freedom you have is terribly important to the health of our form of government and for the best interests of our people.' He made a sort of pro-broadcasting speech. And I said, 'Mr. President, you know that CBS has been fighting for its freedom, its absolute freedom, since the earliest days of broadcasting. But what you have said gives me great comfort. Thank you very much!' "

It may well have been that Paley missed a veiled warning that the networks would have to perform better by Nixon's standards if their freedom was to be preserved. Paley recollects that, on leaving the White House, he was complimented by two CBS executives for the way he replied to the President, one saying, "When he put that to you, we didn't know how you were going to answer it." They apparently thought Nixon had said something tough to answer.

Whatever understandings — or misunderstandings — came out of the summit session, Colson says that complaints over the White House–Black Rock hot line accelerated in 1971 with continued war in Vietnam, continued protest at home and the rising pressure gauge of the approaching presidential election. He found Paley more sympathetic to his complaints than Stanton. But the White House remained generally dissatisfied. Resentment continued to mount against the networks — CBS first. At the dinner of the White House Correspondents' Association in May, President Nixon quipped that Vice President Agnew had three television sets in his bedroom — one for ABC, one for NBC and one standing in the corner.

• •

On June 30, 1971, the House Commerce Committee voted, 25 to 13, to recommend that Frank Stanton of CBS be cited for contempt of Congress. Dr. Stanton had defied the committee's subpoena for unused portions of interviews and other materials connected with the production of a controversial CBS documentary, "The Selling of the Pentagon." Stanton maintained that the "work product" of a news organization was protected by the First Amendment to the Constitution. CBS summoned all its resources to the defense of Stanton and the principle he was fighting for. Managers of CBS affiliates, invited to a meeting at a hotel near John F. Kennedy Airport, were asked to intervene with their local members of Congress. During the debate on the House floor on July 13, Harley Staggers, chairman of the Commerce Committee, criticized what he called "the greatest lobbying effort that has ever been made on the Congress of the United States." By 226 to 181, the House voted that Stanton should not be held in contempt.

Olson told me, in our 1976 interview, of one facet of that lobbying effort, not known at the time. He said that Alexander Lankler, Maryland state chairman of the Republican Party, a lawyer retained by CBS, telephoned to ask White House help in changing Republican votes that were going to be cast against Stanton. Colson quotes Lankler, an old friend of his, as saying that it would be in the interest of the White House to help, that CBS was desperate about the gloomy prospects, and that intervention at this point "will build good relations with which you can get better treatment in the news."*

Colson did not tell Lankler that the White House, having just lost its fight in the Supreme Court to halt the publication of the Pentagon Papers, had no stomach for a new legal confrontation over freedom of the press. Colson asked Haldeman's authorization to tell the

---

*Lankler declined to give me his version of his discussions with Colson, saying that he was bound by his attorney-client relationship with CBS.

minority leader, Congressman Gerald Ford, that the White House wanted its supporters not to vote to cite Stanton for contempt. According to Colson, Haldeman, reluctant to help CBS out of it predicament, agreed and added, "Get something for it!" Colson maintains that his intervention saved Stanton from going to jail.

Three days later, he recalls, Stanton came to the White House with Lankler to express gratitude. The meeting lasted an hour and a half, and Colson had it taped. Purposefully for that record, says Colson, he loudly proclaimed that he was asking nothing from CBS in return for the White House assistance and that anything CBS chose to do would be purely voluntary. Subtly — or as subtly as feasible for Colson — he pointed Stanton toward the rankling old problem of CBS News' irreverent treatment of the President. This he did with a joking remark that the White House had almost changed its mind at the last minute about helping Stanton when the President's news summary on July 13, the morning of the House vote, came up with word of a broadcast by Robert Pierpoint on the CBS Morning News that "just cut us to shreds."*Stanton replied that he had heard the report on the air, almost cut himself shaving, and told his wife, "Of all the times to do that! That Pierpoint is sending me to jail!"

There was more of this not quite lighthearted banter. Colson chuckled that he could never hope for constant fairness from CBS, but maybe they could agree on an "occasional fairness doctrine." Stanton smiled appreciatively and said he wanted Colson to feel free to pick up the phone any time he felt he had reason to complain.

As recalled by Stanton in an interview, the meeting was arranged because Lankler suggested that "maybe you can get a better relationship with Colson now that this thing is all over," but Stanton denies that the purpose was to express gratitude. In fact, he doubts that Colson was of much help in staving off the contempt vote. "Gerry Ford kept telling me long before the eleventh hour that he was waiting for some signal from the White House and he couldn't get

*The July 13 presidential news summary took note of Pierpoint's broadcast the previous day, which reported that "RN was about to take a step he refused to take last year — sign the public employment bill." It quoted Pierpoint as saying that the economy was "in worse shape than RN and his advisers had expected at this time." That Colson recalls this as something that "just cut us to shreds" is a reflection of how thin-skinned the Nixon lieutenants were.

any . . . So, this talk of Colson saving us — maybe there were some votes he got for us, but I certainly never was aware of the fact that Colson saved my neck."

"Then you were not expressing gratitude?" I asked Stanton. "It was a courtesy call?"

"Oh, I won't deny that I probably said I appreciated any help that they might have given, because he said that they had helped . . . But my purpose was just to see him and to make sure that he understood that if there were any pitches he had, let me hear about them. But I wasn't there to make any commitments about anything. God, I wouldn't do that! That's silly!"

Stanton also said he knew that Lankler had been retained by CBS not for his legal expertise, but because of his Republican connections. In 1969, President Nixon had offered Lankler the chairmanship of the Federal Communications Commission, Stanton believed. "We needed somebody who could cultivate some of the Republican side of the Hill and the White House." Paley — who had reportedly viewed the whole confrontation over "outtakes" as unnecessary — told me in 1977 that he had known nothing of Lankler's role or the private palavers with Colson.

CBS could not be faulted for mobilizing every ally it could find in the fight to keep Stanton out of jail and defend a First Amendment principle. But it is astonishing to learn, long after the fact, that a network publicly resisting government pressures was privately making itself hostage to a hostile White House. Soon, CBS scrapped "The Loyal Opposition" broadcasts — after winning its court fight to continue them. That, said Stanton, was for scheduling reasons, not a sop to the Nixon White House. After their meeting, Colson did call Stanton more frequently with complaints — the first of them, by coincidence, about one of my broadcasts. When Nixon aides concluded that CBS was not delivering satisfactorily on what they construed as a deal, they began mulling over how to put the screws on the networks.

•   •

On April 14, 1972, Attorney General Richard Kleindienst filed antitrust suits against ABC, CBS and NBC, charging that they dominated the production of the entertainment programming broadcast on their networks. The networks opposed the suits on the ground of "improper motivation." CBS argued to the Federal District Court that the White House had used the Anti-Trust Division as "a perhaps unwitting instrumentality to get the media to change their supposed views." The Justice Department denied any political motivation, saying the issue had been under study for many years.

The issue of network production of its own entertainment shows had a long history in the Anti-Trust Division; its use as an antitrust weapon to intimidate the networks had a shorter history in the White House. This was one of the "rifles" in the 1969 Magruder arsenal of weapons to subdue the networks. The idea of an antinetwork suit was mentioned, in guarded terms, in the Oval Office on April 19, 1971. President Nixon, angry about the suit against ITT, demanded an end to all antitrust actions. John Ehrlichman reminded him of one exception he had wanted to make. The conversation went like this:

PRESIDENT: . . . I don't know whether ITT is good, bad, or indifferent. But there is [sic] not going to be any more anti-trust actions as long as I am in this chair.
EHRLICHMAN: Well, there's this one . . .
PRESIDENT: God damn it! We're going to stop it!
EHRLICHMAN: All right, there's this one that you are going to talk to John [Attorney General Mitchell] about tomorrow — on the networks.

His memory refreshed, the President said that "we wanted to do that at another time."

A few weeks after the suits were started, Nixon speech writer Buchanan said in a television interview that, faced with "a monopoly like this of a group of people with a single point of view and a single political ideology, who tend to continually freeze out opposing points of view and opposing information . . . you're going to find something done in the area of anti-trust action, I would think." Reminded that suits had already been filed, he added, "Well, that's just testing the theory, that's all."

In December, four months earlier, Herbert Klein, the White

House communications director, had visited the heads of the three networks in New York. Stanton of CBS recalled that Klein "casually expressed interest in the amount of prime time programming that was produced by the CBS Television Network." Leonard Goldenson of ABC said Klein mentioned the possibility of an antitrust suit, but gave the impression that the matter was "under control by the top officials of the White House." Julian Goodman of NBC said he inferred from Klein's remarks that "there were forces in the Administration who wanted to bring an antitrust suit for punitive reasons related to news coverage," but that other "forces" had so far been able to prevent it.

If the network chieftains perceived in Klein's casual conversation an implied blackmail threat from the White House against their news operations, there were several things they could have done immediately. One was to expose it and denounce it. That was, however, not the way the leaders of this regulated industry customarily dealt with the White House. The Klein conversations remained secret for more than two years — until the spring of 1974 when they were disclosed in affidavits to the Federal District Court, filed in the course of opposing the suits.

Judge Robert J. Kelleher agreed, in November 1974, that the suits didn't smell right. But to prove the political motivation would have required a search through White House documents. By that time the Nixon papers and tapes had been tied up by act of Congress. Judge Kelleher dismissed the actions "without prejudice," meaning that the suits could be started again without the Nixon taint of political intimidation. In December 1974, Attorney General William Saxbe did, in fact, file the suits again.

•   •

To the three-year effort to cow television, Watergate added a new dimension. The conspiracy against the news media became an extension of the cover-up conspiracy. In those three years, President Nixon had probed the soft spots and learned the weaknesses. On September 15, 1972, assured by the limited Watergate indictments that the cover-up was likely to hold through the election, the President brooded with Haldeman and John Dean about retaliation against "all of those who have tried to do us in." He spoke of his number-one target, the Washington *Post*. "The main thing is the *Post* is going to have damnable, damnable problems out of this one. They have a television station . . . and they're going to have to get it renewed."*

That same day, Frank Stanton was back in Charles Colson's office, being lectured by the man who claimed to have saved him from jail. Colson charged that CBS was showing more anti-Nixon bias than ever, and brandished the latest analysis of network coverage. Based on criteria of the White House's own devising, it showed CBS as broadcasting almost three times as much "pro-McGovern" as "pro-Nixon" material. The report for weekday coverage for the two weeks ending September 8 looked like this:

	"Pro-McGovern"	"Pro-Nixon"
CBS	64 min., 32 sec.	23 min., 26 sec.
NBC	38 min., 35 sec.	34 min., 50 sec.
ABC	34 min., 10 sec.	26 min., 40 sec.

For Stanton, only six months away from retirement, this was one more indignity to be swallowed. His hope of succeeding Paley had been dashed. Stanton's successor as president of CBS, Arthur Taylor, was already on board, learning the ropes. Stanton, now "vice-chairman" for his phase-out period, returned to New York with Colson's latest threats and did — nothing.

There was a good story in this incessant pressure, but it remained under corporate wraps. It was another phase of the Watergate abuse of power mentality — an attempt to intimidate a vast, licensed communications industry. Surely, CBS would have been the first to report White House threats against a regulated airline or a regulated telephone company. Dr. Stanton's view was that management had

*License challenges actually were mounted by Nixon supporters against Florida stations owned by the Post-Newsweek Company. Ed Ball, Republican finance chairman in Florida, was involved in the challenge to Station WJXT in Jacksonville, a CBS affiliate. A law firm associated with President Nixon's friend Bebe Rebozo worked on a challenge to WPLG in Miami, an ABC affiliate. Both were eventually dropped.

the responsibility of insulating the news people from the knowledge of such pressures lest *they* feel intimidated. The other side of the coin was the fear of escalating the cold war into open hostilities against an enemy who seemed to control the weapons of massive retaliation.

Knowing nothing of the empire under siege, we in our little news province proceeded to steer CBS into greater danger. At this of all times, we decided that Watergate needed more attention on television with an "enterpriser" on the Cronkite Evening News in the period before the election.

Colson was alerted on the morning of October 27 by a call from Attorney General Kleindienst. Kleindienst had heard a woman who knew Cronkite saying at a cocktail party the previous evening that Walter was working on a Watergate "special." Colson understood from Kleindienst that CBS was looking for a sponsor for the special and was not having much luck; it had already been turned down by Gulf Oil Company. Colson telephoned Stanton, his voice full of marine-officer sarcasm, reminding him of favors done, and accommodation supposedly promised. He demanded to know what preelection stab-in-the-back CBS was planning. He accused Cronkite of trying to "zing" President Nixon for having recently refused him an exclusive interview. Stanton replied that no special program was being planned, no sponsor was being sought, and no decision about whether to put on a news special could conceivably depend on the availability of a sponsor. Stanton did not choose to tell Colson that his intelligence was not entirely faulty — that what was in the works was not a special, but a large segment of the Evening News. Colson, feeling that he might have scotched something, spread the word through the White House that there would be no Watergate special.

Colson, working in his office that evening, had reason to be surprised when Cronkite came on the screen saying, "At first it was called the Watergate caper . . . " and announced that CBS News would try "to pull together the threads of this amazing story, quite unlike any in American history." This was deception, betrayal! To Colson it was an especially "crummy shot" because of its timing. It seemed deliberately calculated to divert attention from the Nixon "peace issue," launched the previous day with the Kissinger "peace is at hand" proclamation, and instead "play off" the McGovern Watergate speech of two days earlier.

On Saturday morning, Colson talked to President Nixon in the Oval Office for eleven minutes, before the President's departure on a campaign trip to Ohio. Then, Colson says, after trying unsuccessfully to reach Stanton, he got on the telephone with Paley and dressed him down for almost an hour in coldly biting terms. Why was CBS only going after the Republicans? Why wasn't it covering Democratic harassments of Republican rallies? Why had there been no spokesman for the White House on the broadcast? Why was Cronkite allowed to take out his grudge against Nixon for having refused him an interview — which the President had also refused to other networks? What motivated CBS to give so much time to this rehash of stale Washington *Post* lies? Was the second part, which Cronkite had announced, going to be more of the same? President Nixon was getting tired of trying to make peace with CBS. Nixon, in case Paley hadn't heard it, was going to be reelected overwhelmingly, and CBS should not expect any friendly hand from the President after the election. Colson says that Paley, apologetic, contrite, promised to "get into" the question of Part II. "He left me with the clear impression that there would be no second installment."

On Sunday, Colson telephoned Stanton, asking what what the plans were for Part II. Stanton says he replied that it could be expected Monday. An argument ensued about whether the first installment had been unfair, which Colson interrupted by saying, "Whether the report was fair or not, it should not have been broadcast at all."

On Monday morning, there was an extraordinary meeting in Paley's office — Richard S. Salant, president of CBS News, facing the chairman before the assembled upper hierarchy of the corporation. It had been the practice to leave Salant in ignorance of the more oppressive problems of CBS relations with the government. One justification was that the News Division should be shielded from intimidating pressures. Another reason was that, as head of a news organization, he might feel a conflict of interest if he heard something that would make news. Therefore, Salant had a peculiar insider-outsider role as he came before the corporate chieftains.

There was John Schneider, the wisecracking head of the CBS Broadcast Group, wearing on his belt the scalp of the previous news executive, Fred Friendly. There was Frank Stanton, Salant's friend and sponsor, but now on his way into retirement. There was the new corporate president, Arthur Taylor, still cautiously feeling his way in this unfamiliar world. And there was Paley, looking grim, saying nothing of any contact with the White House and talking at great length about his feelings that the Watergate report had not met his standards of balance and objectivity. Never had Paley devoted so much time and tenacity to a subject that was, on its surface, so minor in his scheme of things.

When Salant returned from Black Rock to his own CBS News building, a converted milk-bottling plant on West 57th Street, the producer of the "Watergate special," Stanhope Gould, was waiting in Sanford Socolow's little office off the central newsroom. Salant rolled his eyes, wiped his brow, and shook his head in pantomime of having been through a rough time. After lunch they would meet in Salant's office, screen Part II, and decide what to do. Wanting support, Gould stopped off at Cronkite's office and asked him, as the originator of the project, to attend the meeting. Cronkite said he would watch the screening on closed-circuit from the Evening News office. "That increased my foreboding," says Gould. Cronkite does not have a reputation for deep involvement in losing causes.

Grouped around Salant's desk, the news executives watched Part II on a monitor across the room. Its main elements were my analysis of Watergate financing ("What seems to emerge is a shadowy treasury paying for shadowy operations, under a small inside group of Nixon men") and Dan Rather's examination of the Nixon men ("They keep issuing general denials; they are depending on that, and silence, to make the allegations go away").

Salant cleared his throat and said that the report did not contain enough new information to warrant such lengthy treatment. He opened a file of previous Watergate broadcasts and read from one of mine to support his point that much of the information had been on previous programs. Gould argued that this was inevitable with any recapitulation. Salant persisted. At one point, as though with a twinge of self-doubt, he said, "I hope that this is an honest news decision, and that I'm not doing it because of pressure." He decided that the report must be drastically cut. Only Gould dissented. The project was turned over to Socolow for revision and retaping. It could no longer be completed for airing on schedule, but would be postponed until Tuesday. Cronkite was informed, and he agreed.

The "compromise" truncated version did not satisfy the White House. President Nixon's news summary dissected it at length, and noted that Cronkite had concluded with "an unlabeled commentary — one far more opinionated than his usual parting shots." Nixon was also told in his news summary that the likely reason for "the Cronkite crusades" was that there would be a separate presentation of Emmy news awards the following spring, to be broadcast by "none other than CBS."*

Paley also got furious all over again on Tuesday night. He now had the worst of both worlds. The CBS reputation for hard-hitting independence would be damaged by the knowledge of delay and excision in the Watergate report. The Nixon people, unplacated, would be returning for a second term aching for vengeance against his vulnerable empire.

This climactic moment in White House–Black Rock relations revealed something striking about CBS. Only CBS News, among the network news organizations, had taken it upon itself to raise Watergate from a newspaper story to a television story — and therefore a national story. Then, under Paley's pressure, CBS News had wobbled. But so great was the momentum, so strong the tradition that not even the chairman could stop it in its tracks altogether.

CBS was, however, deeply concerned about the attitude of the Nixon administration after the election. In mid-November, it sent its Republican lawyer, Alexander Lankler, to the White House for some

*The 1972–1973 Television Academy news and documentary awards were presented at a dinner in New York on May 22, 1973, broadcast by CBS. "Emmies" were presented to Cronkite, Rather, Joel Blocker and myself for contributions to an "outstanding achievement within a regularly scheduled news program." The White House was right about the prediction, if not the rationale.

fence-mending, but found Nixon's people in no mood for conciliation. Colson recalls telling him some rough things like, "Sandy, the
only way you'll improve relations with the administration is if you
dismantle CBS," and, "When we get through with your guys, they'll
be jumping off the thirty-second floor." In 1976, Colson acknowledged making such threats, but said he was not being quite serious.
He called it "pure deviltry, like when I said to John Caulfield, 'Okay,
damn it, blow up Brookings!' "*

To make sure that his message did not get softened in transmission, Colson called Stanton directly, spelling out a five-point plan of
administration action against the television networks. Stanton took
notes, in his precise printed letters, as Colson spoke:

1. Government going to subsidize CATV.
   [Cable television, which the networks were resisting.]
2. The re-runs — we mean it.
   [Limitation of the number of times a movie could be rerun on
   television, demanded by Hollywood, but opposed by the networks.]
3. Network-owned stations — renewal troubles.
   [Challenges to the licenses of network-owned stations.]
4. License the networks.
   [A proposal to bring not only television stations but the networks
   under direct regulation.]
5 Divest the company-owned stations from the networks.
   [Forcing the networks to give up the stations they own in the major
   cities.]
*Even if we don't succeed we'll hurt them — bring them to their knees
in the market-place, Wall Street and Madison Avenue.*

That meant that even the public knowledge of such a determined
administration campaign would have disastrous effects on financial
confidence in the networks. Colson insists that he had no such conversation with Stanton — or, in fact, any contact after the 1972 election. Stanton swore to it in an affidavit he filed in court in the

*Caulfield, a White House investigator working on the leak of the Pentagon Papers, testified
that he took quite seriously Colson's suggestion, in June 1971, that the way to get at the files
of Leslie Gelb, former Pentagon official who had joined the Brookings Institution, was to plant
a firebomb in the building and retrieve the documents during the commotion that followed.
Caulfield told John Dean about the "insane" assignment, and Dean flew to San Clemente to
warn John Ehrlichman, who ordered the project dropped.

antitrust suit. It seems inconceivable that he could have imagined the notes he wrote down while on the telephone.

• •

On December 18, 1972, Clay T. Whitehead, White House director of telecommunications policy, spoke in Indianapolis, proposing that local stations get longer licenses — five years instead of three — but also take action against the networks' "ideological plugola . . . elitist gossip in the guise of news analysis." Whitehead foresaw license renewal problems for stations that "fail to act to correct imbalance or consistent bias from the networks."

It was the boldest effort yet to drive a wedge between the networks and their affiliates — in effect, offering them greater security in return for their joining a crusade to censor the network news, threatening them with possible loss of their valuable properties if they refused to enlist.

The Whitehead speech sounded like a crystallization of Colson's threats. Colson was delighted to associate himself with it. He told me it was made, by coincidence, on a day when he was having lunch with Paley in the White House mess. "I never saw a guy more upset," says Colson. "He asked where that speech came from. I told him that I personally had taken it to President Nixon for clearance. For the rest of the lunch, Paley kept coming back to that speech." Colson seemed to enjoy Paley's discomfiture as he looked back on the meeting.

Paley has an astonishingly different recollection of that luncheon and recalls no reference whatsoever to the Whitehead speech. He had only gone to the White House because Colson had been "raving" about something on the telephone and Paley had asked him to calm down and promised to have lunch with him next time he was in Washington.

"He couldn't have been more friendly," said Paley. "It was a warm meeting. He told me he was going into private practice . . . The main thing is that he was trying to get me to recognize that we didn't have anybody on our staff that represented the conservative viewpoint. And we ought to have somebody. If we did, then a lot of our problems would disappear. And who did he have in mind? You can take one guess — Herb Klein. And I said, 'Look here, now, we're not going to pick up anybody because he's a conservative or a liberal or a Democrat or a Republican . . ."

Despite these Rashomon-like conflicts of recollection, there were portents in the air at that luncheon in the White House mess. Colson was preparing to leave the White House, and he was looking for a job for Klein, who was also on his way out. It was the last time that Paley and Colson would meet in ersatz affability to patch up a White House–Black Rock quarrel or to open a new one. The Whitehead speech would turn out to be the final offensive of the Nixon administration against the networks before being thrown itself on the defensive.

•   •

In the war between the Nixon forces and CBS, the second week of March 1973 looked like a front-line disengagement, with those two antagonists, Colson and Stanton, both retiring from combat. Colson resigned on March 10 to go into law practice, and on March 14 Paley organized a huge reception at the Corcoran Gallery, across 17th Street from the White House, to bid adieu to Stanton and formally introduce the new heir apparent, Arthur Taylor, the brilliant thirty-seven-year-old corporate manager who had come from International Paper Company, innocent of broadcasting background or vendettas with the White House.

Unknown to the outside world, it was a moment of deepening trouble in the White House. On March 13, the day before, the President had concluded with Haldeman and Dean that partial disclosure of Watergate events to head off exposure was just not feasible. (*President:* "The hangout road's going to have to be rejected.") There was worry about insiders with knowledge, especially Colson, who had just left for the outside. Nixon agreed to keep Colson in the status of a White House consultant — "without doing any consulting," said Dean, and just "for executive privilege protection," said Haldeman. An overriding fear was that presidential television was about to be overshadowed by congressional television. The Senate Watergate Committee was preparing for public hearings. (*President:* "Public hearings the first of May! Well, that will be a big show!")

It seemed the point in time for a little détente with television. John Ehrlichman was planning to attend Paley's reception and invited Arthur Taylor to come to the White House beforehand for a get-acquainted meeting. It was over coffee, and friendly. Ehrlichman said it could be no secret to Taylor that there had been a lot of trouble between the White House and the networks, and there was hope that things would go better in the future. All the White House asked was fairness, which it did not think it had received in the past. Taylor recalls, with pride, his response, "I can only promise you that you will get what you deserve. If you do good things, we will report them, and if you do bad things, we will report them."

Leaving Ehrlichman's office, Taylor was surprised to learn from Ehrlichman's secretary that Paley was also at the White House, visiting Haldeman. Paley had not mentioned any such appointment. Haldeman, whom I interviewed in 1976, recalled the session as cordial and very long — so long that Paley was a late host at his Corcoran Gallery reception. "We got along very well," said Haldeman. "We agreed that we should get to know each other better, and that there should be further meetings. I raised some complaints about CBS coverage. Paley indicated understanding of our complaints. I said we were concerned because CBS, more than other networks, was showing us in a distorted way. I may also have raised the question of instant analysis — we were certainly concerned about it. But I can't specifically remember if I did."

Paley also recalled the Haldeman cordiality, but not the complaints. "I saw this rather pleasant-looking guy. I sat there, and he wasn't the monster I thought he was going to be. And, for an hour and a half, it was sort of small talk and generalizing — no bitterness, no complaint, no sense of dissatisfaction. And I took it for granted that the reason for the meeting, therefore, was just to get to know me, and wanting to see me more, and maybe a relationship with me somehow might be a good thing for him . . . He was supposed to be a Teutonic dictator — everybody quaking in front of him — but I found him a very pleasant, nice quiet guy. Never raised his voice. He let me talk, he talked — as though all the things I'd heard about him must be wrong."

Paley said he habitually dictated a memorandum after any meeting where something critical or important was said. He had made no note of his hour-and-a-half meeting with Haldeman because he could not remember any criticism or complaint to record.

The new special relationship did not last long. In April, Paley took his wife for a trip to China, on the way telling CBS News Director Gordon Manning, their escort, how fascinating he had found Haldeman. In Peking on April 30, Manning received word from the U.S. Liaison Mission that President Nixon, drawing his wagons more tightly around him, had fired Haldeman, Ehrlichman and Dean. With Paley's praise for Haldeman still echoing in his ears, Manning took the dispatch down to the Paleys' hotel suite. Paley was astonished. Later Paley asked Manning, "How could this happen? These were all men trained in the law."*

"They lacked character," replied Manning.

Paley shook his head and said, "I suppose you're right."

It was six months to the day from the meeting in which Paley had risen in wrath against the News Division because the Cronkite show was making too much of Watergate.

●   ●

On June 6, 1973, with no advance notice to news correspondents, Paley announced that "henceforth CBS News will not provide news analyses immediately after Presidential appearances." Analysis of presidential statements would henceforth be included in later scheduled news programs. In addition, time would be provided, when appropriate, for opposition viewpoints.

What the Nixon White House had been demanding since November 1969, when he was riding high, had incredibly happened at a moment when his administration was in deep trouble — more desperately anxious than ever to avoid searching analysis, but hardly in a position to exert much pressure.

The Senate Watergate hearings were running live on television; Special Prosecutor Archibald Cox, appointed a month earlier, was dismantling the cover-up with the aid of plea-bargaining Jeb Magruder and John Dean; the break-in on the office of Daniel Ellsberg's

*Paley was mistaken about Haldeman, whose background was advertising.

psychiatrist had been exposed; FBI Director William Ruckelshaus had announced the White House–directed wiretaps on seventeen government officials and newsmen. Two weeks before, on May 22, President Nixon had issued a written statement admitting much, pleading a national security justification and complaining about "a climate of sensationalism." Since he was not currently finding it advantageous to present his case on television, there had been no recent case of instant analysis to present a problem.

CBS looked absurd when Nixon next did appear on television, on June 13. It was to announce "Phase Four" of his economic program, with an advance text and advance briefings for the press that made analysis simple and relatively uncontroversial. *Variety,* the trade paper, jeered that John Chancellor on NBC and Tom Jarriel on ABC had done "very nicely, thank you" in their analyses, while CBS, with "the best and the brightest on television," had returned to the "Sonny and Cher" show. I was asked to broadcast the CBS analysis of the economic program on the Cronkite show next day, but begged off saying that I was too busy with Watergate. What I did not say was that I had no wish to be the lead-off analyst under a new policy that appalled me.

In the news department, we winced as we read the widespread charges of "cop-out." Senator John Pastore, head of the Senate's communications subcommittee, called it "a mistake" in a speech that also warned, "Once you are silenced, or intimidated, or subverted, it is just a matter of time before other liberties disappear." Newspapers quoted anonymous CBS newsmen as speculating that Paley had yielded to administration pressures. The chairman told us in an internal memo that he was "astonished" to read this because his only aim was "better, fairer, more balanced" coverage.

The implication that our analysis had been less than fair was salt in our wounds. Further, Arthur Taylor was quoted in the *New York Times* as saying, about instant analysis, that TV commentators often "did it badly." Another hasty memo advised that Taylor had meant commentators on other networks, not us.

We shell-shocked veterans of instant analysis decided on the unusual step of writing our friend and boss, Dick Salant, to tell him how unhappy we were. We wrote that we deplored the implied lack of confidence in us. We asked why we had not been consulted before the decision. We said that opposition replies were no substitute for journalistic examination. Finally, we could not understand the timing of what looked to us like "capitulation to accumulated government pressures." The letter was signed by George Herman, Marvin Kalb, Roger Mudd and myself. Eric Sevareid, long opposed to instant analysis, did not sign. Dan Rather vacillated until, when he asked to sign, we told him it was too late.

Salant replied to us that the policy would be "kept under review." We continued to wonder about the reason for Paley's decision. True, correspondents' ad lib discussions had sometimes been sloppy and unrestrained. In the year-end review for 1971, Sevareid, Rather and Mike Wallace had exposed our fallibility by unqualifiedly predicting Senator Edmund Muskie's nomination for President. In one "post-Nixon analysis," Rather had unanalytically exploded that if he once more heard the Nixon line about "the lift of a driving dream," he — Rather — would jump off the Tallahatchie Bridge. There was considerable room for improvement in analysis, but we had heard no specific criticism. We could not, therefore, make out to what extent Paley was bending to White House pressure.

We heard that Salant had arrived at a meeting of corporate executives on June 6 to learn, with astonishment, of a decision already made. It had been one of those cut-and-dried board room scenarios. Paley had read the statement, and had called for E. Kidder Meade, Jr., his vice president for public relations, to come and get it ready for immediate release. When Salant was represented in newspaper reports as having opposed the decision, he issued a painful-sounding statement explaining, "I have fully participated in the consideration of that policy over a period of years" and "as it ultimately evolved, I was in agreement with it."

To us — and even to executives close to the summit — it was mysterious how such a policy came about. Most disturbing to news people was the sense that basic news policies were being made at levels far removed from news operations. News dangled like the tail of a conglomerate kite. The CBS decision-making process seemed as obscure as the decision-making in the Kremlin, and for roughly the same reason — a giant enterprise under a basically central control.

A mysterious decision could be mysteriously reversed. Arthur Taylor, the new number-two man in CBS, seemed anxious to counter his managerial reputation and to embrace the journalistic tradition. Like Stanton before him, he made speeches about freedom of the press and sought to identify himself with the CBS news team. At a dinner with the Washington news staff on October 16, I asked Taylor if the ban on instant analysis was "written in stone." He assured me it was not. He repeated our conversation to Paley, he later told me, as a way of reopening the question, arguing the harm that had been done to morale inside CBS, and especially to prestige outside. On November 12, five months after abolishing instant analysis — and, incidentally, a month after the resignation of Vice President Agnew, who had first used the term — Paley announced that it was being resurrected. It had turned out, he said, "a journalistic service of far greater value than we realized."

The Nixon White House, with more pressing preoccupations after the "Saturday night massacre" of Special Prosecutor Cox, Attorney General Elliot Richardson and his Deputy, William Ruckelshaus, launched no new harassments against CBS. The hot line between White House and Black Rock had fallen silent. Those who had principally manned it at both ends — Charles Colson and Frank Stanton, who had learned such passionate contempt for each other — were both gone.

The next time Colson would speak to a CBS president, it would be more gently. It would happen when Arthur Taylor was fired by Paley in October 1976. From Colson, whom Taylor had never met, and who was now out of jail, active in a group of reborn Christians, would come a telephone call.

"We are praying for you, Arthur," said the one-time Nixon hatchet man, scourge of the networks.

IV

"A REAL MEDIA ENEMY"

ALONG WITH its efforts to manipulate the television networks, the Nixon White House nurtured grudges against individuals — several of them, predictably, in CBS. I was one of those marked as a journalistic adversary long before Watergate — and long before I knew that I was considered as one. Assigned to cover Watergate, I found myself having the surrealistic experience of observing the unfolding of a drama of conspiracy and abuse of power and discovering myself on the stage in a walk-on part. Hostility toward the press was deeply embedded in the siege psychology associated with Watergate.

President Nixon liked to represent himself as oblivious to news comment. In a March 1971 television interview with Howard K. Smith, he said, "I have never taken on a member of the press personally." During the same month he told the author Allen Drury that he didn't care what commentators said about him. "That's what makes them mad! That's what infuriates 'em. I just don't care!" The passion with which he said it indicated the opposite, and so did the elaborate news summaries that his staff prepared for him. Having had an opportunity to study them, I found them replete with entries such as, "H. K. Smith noted . . . Brinkley's journal tells . . . Rather voice-over RN entering the hall to 'polite, light, brief applause.' " The summary told Nixon — in shorthand written as though for a television professional — every nuance of picture, language and general effect of what appeared on television about him.

When Nixon said he had never "taken on" a member of the press, he should have added "publicly." In a meeting with Henry Kissinger and White House assistants on November 5, 1969, according to one of those present, he had railed against critics of his Vietnam television speech — like Marvin Kalb — as "Rumanian spies," one of his standard pejorative phrases. The White House had ordered physical surveillance of Kalb — short-circuited by the refusal of J. Edgar Hoover to have the FBI carry it out. Kalb was also one of four journalists — along with thirteen government officials — who were wiretapped on White House orders between 1969 and 1971. Dan Rather was the subject of an attack by John Ehrlichman, meeting with Richard Salant at breakfast on April 29, 1971, in New York. Ehrlichman tartly suggested that Rather, whom he called "a hatchet man for the Democrats," should be transferred to Austin, Texas. He also denounced me for biased and unfair reporting of Nixon administration actions and programs.

The vehemence of the criticism surprised me when Salant later told me about it, although I had been aware of broadcasts that had not sat well with the Nixon White House. Presidential displeasure under any administration was not in itself unusual. With President Kennedy, it had been my reporting of German criticism of him. Johnson was the only President ever to telephone me directly — waking me once near midnight to call me "a prize son-of-a-bitch." He had been disgruntled about several of my broadcasts discussing the short-changing of his proclaimed social goals, but especially one about a secret budget meeting at the LBJ ranch during the New Year's weekend of 1968. On the CBS Morning News I reported that John Gardner, Secretary of HEW, had left the ranch the previous night without waiting to witness the signature of new welfare legislation. He was distressed about President Johnson's deal with Congressman Wilbur Mills, chairman of the Ways and Means Committee, accepting restrictions on welfare payments in return for support of higher taxes to pay for the Vietnam war. Minutes after the broadcast, Mills subsequently told me with amusement, the President called him at his home in Searcy, Arkansas, to disavow responsibility for the leak.*

---

*When Gardner resigned from the Cabinet three weeks after my broadcast, one Johnson aide, Douglass Cater, went so far as to charge that my report had provoked Gardner's decision.

The Nixon administration started under what seemed like favorable auguries. My assignment on January 20, 1969, was the rotunda of the Capitol, interviewing celebrities as they returned from hearing the inaugural address to help fill the television stage-wait before the commencement of the parade. Democratic leaders commented approvingly on phrases like "lower our voices" and "Black and White together." Speculation started about a "new Nixon," compassionate in victory. A few days later, President Nixon landed on my journalistic planet, giving further indication of humane purpose. In speeches to civil servants at the Departments of Agriculture and Health, Education and Welfare, he announced, as one of his first goals, the elimination of malnutrition. To my surprise, he even had praise for a controversial CBS documentary, "Hunger in America."

Whatever the new administration's social goals, it soon became evident that Nixon aides were wary and tense about their press contacts. It was as though they had come from the wilderness into a hostile, liberal-tainted capital, eyeing the press and civil service from behind ramparts. They seemed less inclined than their predecessors to argue and more inclined to brood about journalistic offenses, real or fancied. A manifestation of the siege mentality was secretive in-group humor. The Nixon palace guard would talk of certain journalists with an initial "P" inserted in their names. It was "Dan P. Rather," "Sander P. Vanocur" and "Daniel P. Schorr." When someone finally broke the code for me, I learned that "P" stood for "Prick."

Patrick Buchanan perpetrated what was considered a hilarious practical joke for insiders in September 1969, when he fabricated a memorandum from Herbert Klein to President Nixon, proposing a series of background sessions with certain commentators, "all influential and susceptible to the Presidential charm." The list included Columnist Jack Anderson, Peter Lisagor of the Chicago *Daily News,* Max Frankel of the *New York Times* and Marvin Kalb of CBS. At the top of the list stood, "Jack Chancellor, Dan Schorr." The point

---

Gardner told me that this only showed how little was understood in the Johnson circle of the real strains between guns and social progress that had made it impossible for him to go on.

of the joke, as William Safire wrote, was that it was "opposite to the President's thinking about each individual."

How I became so early a Nixon un-favorite is hard to judge. From a study of his news summaries and talks with some of his former assistants, I believe that these are some aspects of my news coverage that attracted disapproving White House attention:

— the Administration's retreat on school desegregation, the defeat of HEW Secretary Robert Finch at the hands of Attorney General Mitchell on civil rights policy, and the Supreme Court's rebuff to the administration's bid to postpone integration.

— President Nixon's bowing to pressure from organized medicine and vetoing Finch's appointment of the reform-minded Dr. John Knowles as Assistant Secretary for Health.

— The fights over the nominations of Judges Clement Haynsworth and Harrold Carswell to the Supreme Court, and especially my interview with Senator Roman Hruska, leader of the pro-Carswell forces in the Senate, in which he defended representation for the mediocre.*

— The abrupt discharge in June 1970 of Education Commissioner James Allen, critic of the invasion of Cambodia, followed by protests in the Department of HEW and the hospitalization and replacement of Secretary Finch.

— The controversy over national health insurance, and especially my "CBS Reports" documentary in April 1970, "Don't Get Sick in America," which concluded that administration programs were inadequate to meet rising health needs and costs.

More overt signs of White House displeasure began to appear. HEW Secretary Elliot Richardson, after accepting my invitation to debate Senator Edward Kennedy on health insurance on television, later advised that he had been obliged by the White House to withdraw because I was the moderator. After I had arranged to film a story about Office of Education officials working on school redistricting to meet desegregation requirements, HEW Undersecretary John

*In a filmed interview in the Senate Television Gallery on March 16, 1970, I asked Hruska, ranking Republican on the Senate Judiciary Committee, how he responded to those who asserted that Carswell was a mediocre judge. While denying that Carswell was mediocre, Hruska made this surprising comment, "Even if he was mediocre, there are a lot of mediocre judges and people and lawyers. They are entitled to a little representation, aren't they, and a little chance? We can't have all Brandeises and Cardozos and Frankfurters and stuff like that there." The interview received considerable attention.

Veneman told me that permission had been revoked on orders from the White House, suspicious that the story would turn out critical of the Nixon administration. These were only preliminaries to an escalating series of clashes with the Nixon White House.

In June 1970, I reported that the administration, which had promised to have a food distribution program for the needy in operation in every county, had suppressed a report that found many counties running only paper programs. The report had been filed five months earlier by two West Point instructors commissioned by the White House to make the survey.

Senator Robert Dole, of Kansas, assigned to counter my broadcast, accused me in the Senate of "false and misleading statements." He said, "CBS viewers are, unfortunately, subjected to the biased views of Mr. Schorr. One can wonder if he is not less concerned about malnutrition in America than about constant harping at the administration's efforts to solve this nagging problem." Senator Dole sent his statement to my boss, Salant, with copies to Frank Stanton and to Thad Sandstrom, president of Station WIBW–TV, the CBS affiliate in Topeka. Salant replied to Dole, "I stand behind Mr. Schorr's report and behind his professional competence and objectivity." Salant also wrote me that it was too bad we had to waste time with such "nonsense," but that since Senator Dole worked hand-in-glove with the CBS affiliate in Topeka, "I have to anticipate letters from both him and our affiliate to all my bosses here at CBS."

In March 1971, I reported on the Cronkite show that Dr. James Fletcher, newly named NASA administrator, had once counseled President Nixon against the Safeguard Anti-Ballistic Missile system. Furthermore, my report said, Nixon had acknowledged room for doubt about the ABM and said it was one of the decisions, early in his administration, that he had been rushed into without sufficient preparation — somewhat like the Kennedy decision on the Bay of Pigs invasion. I did not give my source, but Dr. Fletcher himself, in the course of his disclaimers, disclosed that he had met me at lunch.

My broadcast came at a time when Dr. Fletcher was up for confirmation and the ABM was up for a new appropriation. Understandably, there was some embarrassment. Press Secretary Ron Ziegler called in White House correspondents to assert that the President "has not only never talked to Mr. Fletcher about the ABM Safeguard system, but has never at any time expressed any doubts about the ABM Safeguard system."

On the same day, President Nixon met with a group of newspaperwomen and used the occasion for his first public attack on me. He was not concerned with criticism, he said, but took "a very hard line" about inaccuracy. "Where something is inaccurate like Dan Schorr said yesterday or made a statement with regard to ABM that was totally without foundation in fact . . . that has to be corrected . . . You can't allow a little lie. Incidentally, when I call it a lie, that is unfair because, after all, the man just probably had the wrong information. I am always very charitable to my friends."

No longer could Nixon say, as he had told Howard K. Smith on television less than two weeks earlier, "I have never taken on a member of the press personally."

•   •

On August 17, 1971, addressing a dinner of the Knights of Columbus in New York City, President Nixon deplored Supreme Court rulings against government aid to parochial schools and promised them assistance. Praising some of his Catholic-educated associates — Transportation Secretary John Volpe, Attorney General Mitchell and "my very fine secretary," Rose Mary Woods—the President expressed sorrow that parochial schools were closing at the rate of one a day. "We must resolve to stop that trend and turn it around," he said. "You can count on my support to do that." Taking this as indication of some new step to rescue the parochial schools, the Catholic audience rose to its feet with a roar of applause.

The following day, Roger Mudd, substituting for the vacationing Walter Cronkite, screened the film of the Nixon speech for use on the Evening News and called me. To go with the Nixon film, he asked for a short report from Washington, explaining what steps the administration had in mind. Checking with HEW officials and leaders of the Catholic school organization in close touch with the administration, I discovered that there was no concrete program in sight. My broadcast had a somewhat more dramatic effect than intended when my taped report appeared on the screen just as the applause for Nixon was fading. There appeared to be "absolutely nothing in the works," I reported, and quoted a Catholic source as saying, "We can only assume the President's statement was for political or rhetorical effect."

The next morning, Alvin Snyder, a White House press officer, called to ask if I could meet that day with Patrick Buchanan and other officials at the White House because I did not "have all the facts" about administration plans to assist the parochial schools. Although pressed for time — it was the first week of the wage-price freeze, which had become my primary assignment — I decided that I could not ignore the invitation. In a one-hour meeting at the White House, I listened to a highly detailed account of formulas under consideration to aid private schools. My Catholic sources later analyzed the material and said they amounted to very little.

The following morning, Friday, August 20, I arrived at my office to find an FBI agent waiting for me. He flashed a badge to identify himself and said he had been assigned to interview me in connection with a "position of confidence and trust" for which I was being considered. He said he could not tell me what the position was. While he sat across my desk, notebook ready, my telephone began to ring with word of others being asked by the FBI for information about me — relatives, neighbors, colleagues, ex-bosses going back some twenty years and current bosses. I told the agent that I would not answer questions until advised of the job being offered, and I asked that the investigation be suspended because of the embarrassment it was causing me. He promised to relay my message.

I had trouble convincing my CBS superiors that I knew of no job offer. Salant said the head of the FBI office in New York, with whom he had previously dealt on personnel matters, had called him at home early in the morning saying the clearance had to be completed within three days because of an imminent announcement.

"Dick," I said, "I don't care what the FBI says. I know of no job."

A few hours later a CBS News vice president, Bill Leonard, called. "Don't get me wrong," he assured me. "Of course we believe you when you say there's no White House job. Just let me leave you with this thought — if money is the problem, then it needn't be."

"May I remind you of that when this silly business is behind us?" I asked.

That weekend I left with my family for our vacation in Aspen, Colorado, immensely puzzled. My bureau chief, Bill Small, who had almost thrown out an FBI agent seeking my personnel records, felt sure that the intention was harassment or intimidation. Perhaps egotistically, I considered the possibility that a government job offer might still be drifting my way through the bureaucratic pipeline. I thought back to a week that had started with my being plunged into a series of White House briefings on the wage-price freeze and going on television with lengthy explanations. I had also been on live television in jovial exchanges with Secretary of the Treasury John Connally, the new czar of economic stabilization. It seemed to me that such an independent soul, with a new agency to staff, might consider offering me a job despite White House antipathy. But in Aspen my telephone rang not with word of a government appointment, only with further word of FBI activity.

Back in Washington, I met Frederic V. Malek, the White House talent scout, at a dinner party in October. "Say," I asked, "if you're in charge of personnel recruitment at the White House, would you know why the FBI was investigating me a couple of months ago for a job?"

Malek almost dropped his fork. "You! No, I don't know. But I'll check first thing tomorrow and let you know." Malek never called. Mystified by the reasons for the investigation, I decided, in consultation with my CBS superiors, that we would not make a public issue of it. We speculated that a possible motive for the investigation was to lure me into a public accusation, which would inevitably place me in the adversary position to the administration that I was anxious to avoid. The story came out without our help, in a way that indicated it had been drawn into some Byzantine conflict inside the White House.

Colson, unknown to me at the time, had complained to Stanton in August about my parochial school broadcast. In early November he had a new complaint — that my reports of AFL-CIO disaffection with the operation of the wage-price freeze were threatening to undermine the President's economic program. Colson told Stanton specifically that on that very morning George Meany, as a result of my "incitement," had boycotted a meeting of the Industry-Labor-Public Federal Pay Board. Checking with Meany's office, I was told that he had merely arrived at the meeting late because of a doctor's appointment. The underlying truth, however, was that a labor showdown with the White House was coming, which I would witness later in the month when President Nixon, following a Colson game plan, flew to Bal Harbour, Florida, to face down Meany at his own convention. Colson's abrasive style and growing influence on Nixon were causing friction within the White House. One of his enemies in the official family apparently decided to embarrass him by a leak.

On November 10, a Washington *Post* reporter, Ken W. Clawson, known to be on good terms with the White House (which he would join three months later), called me to say he had learned of Colson's pressure against me with Stanton, and also about the earlier FBI investigation. I said it was CBS policy not to discuss this, but he assured me that he had the whole story. Next morning, the *Post* headlined on its front page, "FBI Probes Newsman Critical of President." Soon the story was on the news wires across the country.

Press Secretary Ron Ziegler, at his daily meeting with the press, stated that I had, for a short time, been considered, on the initiative of Malek's office, for a position "in the area of the environment." The Chicago *Tribune* had it from a White House source that the job was "in the $40,000-a-year range" and that my sponsor had been "a person of rank within the Administration." William Ruckelshaus, Environmental Protection Administrator, told questioners at a cocktail party, "Maybe it's my job they want Schorr for." Ziegler released a statement from the President that the matter had been "clumsily handled" and that in the future "such preliminary investigations will not be initiated without prior notification to the person being investigated."

Many remained unconvinced that there had been nothing more than a bureaucratic error. Senator Sam Ervin, whose constitutional rights subcommittee was planning hearings on freedom of the press, invited me to testify along with White House witnesses. Malek and Colson refused to appear. The President's counsel, John W. Dean III, also refusing to appear, sent a letter saying, "Despite some inaccurate conjecture to the contrary, the facts in this situation are quite simple. Mr. Schorr was being considered for a post that is presently filled and a routine job investigation was commenced without notifying Mr. Schorr." But Senator Ervin noted that this conflicted with the statement of another White House spokesman, quoted in that morning's Washington *Post*, that the position was assistant to Russell Train, chairman of the Council on Environmental Quality — a position not yet filled.*

There was also a letter from J. Edgar Hoover saying that the FBI investigation had been requested by "a member of the White House staff authorized to request federal personnel background investigations." Hoover said that during the one day of August 20, twenty-five persons had been interviewed about me before the investigation was discontinued at about 3:00 P.M. "The incomplete investigation of Mr. Schorr was entirely favorable concerning him," Hoover said, "and the results were furnished to the White House."

The hearing was, for me, like theater of the absurd. I acted out a scenario I had often watched — distributing copies of my statement to the staff and the press, taking my seat at the witness table facing Senators Ervin and Kennedy in a raised arc, nodding to the cameramen who were focusing on me, greeting my CBS News colleague, Bernard Shaw, who had been assigned to cover "the Schorr hearing." As though to underline the incongruity of the situation, Shaw came up to me to ask, jokingly, if I wished to mark the portions of my text on which he would cue the cameraman to "roll." I could not rid myself of self-consciousness as I started reading:

"I am Daniel Schorr, resident of Washington, D.C., a correspondent of CBS News for the past nineteen years . . ."

I recited all the facts I knew about the investigation, and said, "Job

---

*Train, induced by the White House to state that I was being considered because I had done "important work in the environmental field," later apologized to me for permitting the use of his name.

or no job, the launching of such an investigation without consent demonstrates an insensitivity to personal rights. An FBI investigation is not a neutral matter. It has an impact on one's life, on relations with employers, neighbors and friends. For me the effects, though I do not wish to exaggerate them, persist until today. I am still constantly asked whether my 'FBI shadow' is with me, whether it is safe to talk to me on the telephone, whether I am still 'in trouble with the FBI.'

"Let me say," I concluded, "that I do not think that many reporters will be directly intimidated. We are, on the whole, a pretty hardy lot. We generally cannot be deterred by Government, but only by our employers. And it is our employers who feel the real pressure — especially in the regulated broadcast industry, where networks can be subjected to pressure in many ways, and in indirect ways through the affiliates which give the networks existence."

Senator Ervin wound up the hearing by saying that the White House was guilty of "either stupidity or duplicity. These are the only alternatives I see."

The White House stuck to its guns, and speculation spread — as far as Russia. In Moscow, where I had been in trouble with the KGB in former years, the press found it fascinating that I should now be having trouble with its American counterpart. A front-page story in *Pravda* explained that I had been a victim of an epidemic of American snooping bred by a war psychosis. "Even the wildest fantasy could not imagine Schorr being in opposition to the capitalist system," said *Pravda*. "But in one of his reports, Schorr slipped up. He was critical of the USA aggression in Laos. Shortly after this the reporter noticed that he was being followed. One of his relatives informed him, from another city, that agents of the FBI were questioning all his relatives and friends. To make a long story short, Schorr decided to compromise and restrain his criticism of the government."

The *Pravda* story, written in terms that Soviet citizens could understand, was rivaled in fantasy by an explanation that came from the White House. Patrick Buchanan, interviewed on ABC's "Dick Cavett Show," said that it was "a prima facie case of bias" for me to be assigned by CBS to "explain the social policies of the Nixon administration to twenty million Americans." Cavett caught Buchanan off guard by asking why such an antiadministration bigot should have been considered for presidential appointment. Buchanan replied, "If you've got a guy that's hatcheting you on the air night after night, maybe you say to yourself, 'Why don't we offer the clown a job and give him a big fat paycheck and get him off so that we can get someone else on?' "

• •

Buchanan's interview, on March 22, 1973, was one of the last — and most flamboyant — efforts to maintain a little cover-up. The big cover-up was already under stress. Two days earlier, the first of the convicted Watergate defendants had defected. James McCord, losing hope for presidential clemency, facing prison and burning with resentment at those still free, wrote to Chief Judge John J. Sirica, charging pressure, perjury and payoffs to maintain silence.

The McCord bombshell found me, thanks to one of my clouded crystal balls, attending a symposium in Germany. I had covered the three-week Watergate trial in January, no more convinced than peppery Judge Sirica that the conspiracy was, as Prosecutor Earl Silbert told the jury, merely a matter of Gordon Liddy and his cohorts off "on an enterprise of their own" with misappropriated Nixon campaign money. Assuming, however, that there would be no break in the situation before a congressional investigation was mounted, I took my planned vacation, confidently advising our news editor that McCord's sentencing was not likely to provide more than a line or two for Cronkite's script.

Returning from Germany, I started on phase two of my Watergate assignment — the disintegrating cover-up, finding, here and there, a thread of my particular case woven into the fraying fabric. When, for example, L. Patrick Gray III came before the Senate Judiciary Committee in March for confirmation hearings as director of the FBI, a minor aside in his testimony was his continued insistence, based on his careful briefing, that the FBI's Schorr investigation had been conducted only because of "possible federal employment." More sensational was Gray's testimony — departing, to the consternation of the White House, from his briefing — that John Dean had monitored the FBI's investigation of Watergate and had "probably lied" about the extent of his involvement.

In subsequent months, a large part of my working life would be spent on the "Dean case," unaware at first of how much he knew about the "Schorr case." Until Watergate, John Wesley Dean III had been, for me, one of the more obscure names on the White House roster. The President's official lawyer traditionally had little to do with the press or public. I first became aware of him, in February 1972, simply as a name on a reassuring White House letter to Senator Ervin about the FBI investigation of me. The following August he was cast in a larger — but still faceless — role when President Nixon announced a report by his counsel that found nobody in the White House connected with "this bizarre incident" of Watergate. Now, identified by Gray as having scanned FBI reports for the White House, Dean began to loom as a tangible figure. McCord, called into executive session by the staff of the newly created Senate Watergate Committee, named Dean as involved in an obstruction of justice.

•   •

On April 14, word that John Mitchell had been seen leaving the White House roused me from a somnolent Saturday afternoon in shorts in my backyard. Minutes later I was racing out to National Airport to join a camera crew, hoping to interview him before he boarded a plane for New York. Mitchell was already seated as we piled aboard, seconds before the door closed. Once aloft, I stood in the aisle, leaning over him, the camera crew behind me. Champing on his pipe, he looked at me dourly.

"Mr. Mitchell," I said, "my assignment is to interview you, but I would rather not poke a microphone in your face while you're a captive. Why don't we agree to a brief interview when we arrive at La Guardia rather than have your privacy invaded during the flight?"

As he agreed to the interview, the corners of his mouth twitched into a wry smile. "And you've had some experience with invasion of privacy, haven't you, Dan? With that FBI thing . . ."

Mitchell, attorney general at the time of "that FBI thing," was the first insider to suggest it had involved not a job offer, but an invasion of privacy. From New York (the White House transcripts show) Mitchell called John Ehrlichman to make sure that President Nixon knew I had intercepted Mitchell for an interview. "And so he said to Schorr," Ehrlichman reported accurately to Nixon, "he didn't know anything about Watergate, and he didn't think anybody cared about Watergate, and he had just been down to the White House and he hadn't seen the President. That was all that he said."

Mitchell apparently said nothing to Ehrlichman of the tip he had given me about the White House–ordered FBI investigation. It was consistent with Mitchell's general contempt for the Nixon palace guard that he would be sarcastic about any impropriety that originated in the White House. This would later become the major theme of his public defense as he pointed to the "White House horrors" as the root of all evil in the Nixon administration and the real reason for the White House cover-up.

•   •

As Washington reeled from President Nixon's sudden announcement on April 17 of "major developments," few of us paid much attention to the line in his statement that none of his assistants, past or present, "should be given immunity from prosecution." This began to assume significance, two days later, when Dean issued his first statement, saying cryptically that anyone who thinks "I will become a scapegoat in the Watergate case . . . does not know me." It seemed clear that Dean was involved in some tumultuous, though still mysterious conflict in the White House.

My priority assignment — as several executives and producers brought emphatically to my attention — was not to analyze the cloudy situation, but to find the invisible John Dean and get him before a camera. A stake-out at his home in Alexandria was barren of results. A telephone tip from an anonymous informant embarked me on a hunt that turned into one of my less triumphant days as an investigative reporter. The informant said he had witnessed John Dean being introduced to someone at the Department of Health, Education and Welfare. On the theory that he was holed up in a temporary office there, I raced to my old stamping ground and combed the building, trailing a camera crew, looking for someone I had never seen. Eventually, puzzled officials of HEW turned up one John R. Deane III, a long-standing employee in the Office of Personnel and Training. My informant had apparently made a well-intentioned error in mistaking him for John W. Dean III. My detailed explanation, when I brought the camera crew back, did not save me from newsroom guffaws.

Unable to find Dean, I tried to find out what he was up to. It appeared that he was negotiating with the prosecutor, Earl Silbert, trying to avoid indictment in return for information incriminating others. His lawyer of record, Robert McCandless, available but uninformative, seemed little more than a public relations front. It took some digging to learn that Dean had another attorney, Charles Shaffer, a criminal lawyer with a Justice Department background, located in suburban Rockville, Maryland. It was Shaffer who was conducting the negotiations for Dean.

On May 7, I reported on the Cronkite show that Dean had been turned down in his bid for immunity. Silbert had concluded he had enough evidence from Jeb Magruder and other sources to enable him, without Dean's cooperation, to seek indictments against Dean himself and a series of higher-ups, up to Haldeman. I mentioned in my report that Shaffer, during the negotiations, had represented Dean as fearful of going to prison because "his boyish appearance might make him a target for molestation." Next morning McCandless telephoned to protest and to deny that any such fear motivated Dean's negotiations. On May 10, Dean issued a statement charging that efforts were being made to discredit and intimidate him.

Dean apparently reacted violently to my broadcast. He wrote, in *Blind Ambition,* that it left him "stunned, then angry." To McCandless, he called it "the dirtiest goddamn stunt I ever heard of." Oddly, there was no sign that he ever tried to find out whether Shaffer, in fact, had made such a representation about him. Dean viewed it as part of a White House campaign "designed to frighten me or impugn my motives." Concerned about image and credibility, Dean agreed with McCandless that it was time to emerge from hiding and counter adverse publicity with a television appearance.

On May 17, at Dean's home in Alexandria, Walter Cronkite filmed an interview with him, broadcast that night as a half-hour special. Dean ruled out discussion of "evidence," but volunteered some tid-bits to show the cynicism of his former superiors. For example, he said, there was a White House practice of assigning innocent persons to take the "heat" for the miscalculations of others. In August, the President had announced a Dean report "when I had not had any meetings with the President about this subject." Also, there had been "the incident regarding the FBI's investigation regarding Daniel Schorr, where ultimately an answer was put out that doesn't really meet with reality." Dean said that Malek had been told to say that his recruitment office had requested the investigation relative to a prospective job offer.

It was typical, said Dean, "of the type of razzle-dazzle they are able to put together. I'm not sure how many people believed that official story, but I'm sure that Daniel Schorr does not."

Once again I had bumped into myself covering the Watergate story. Dean had confirmed what Mitchell had hinted. The job offer and the bureaucratic error had been a lie. President Nixon's state-ment that such errors would be avoided in the future had been part of the cover-up. The FBI investigation had clearly been prompted by hostile motives.

•   •

The Senate Watergate hearings unearthed more of my buried White House story. John Dean, the gushing fount of Watergate knowledge, was also ready to spill more background about me. The issue came up during the second of his five days on the witness stand. The Caucus Room had settled down after crackling to the litany of his charges against the White House — wiretapping and burglary, per-jury and payoffs, cover-ups and clemency promises, and the fact that he had warned Nixon of "a cancer on the presidency." At my seat at the end of the press table, near the door, I sat back viewing the hearing with the double vision of the electronic reporter — seeing both the real event and the televised event. Occasionally, I would look down at a TV monitor to check how the hearing looked on the air, noting the close-ups of Dean, the senators, the frequent "cutaway" shots of the blond and impassive Maureen Dean, the audience reaction shots. I would need to have these in mind when I consulted the television producers about condensing the hours of tape into the daily "package" for the Cronkite show. Similarly, I enjoyed "double hearing." With one ear I listened to the sound in the Caucus Room. Through an earplug I heard Dean's voice coming back on television with a fraction of a second's delay. The earpiece also told me what the anchormen in the studio were adding to fill pauses and identify persons for the television audience.*

Dean's main charges out of the way, Senator Lowell Weicker raised a peripheral matter — the White House use of the FBI. Dean related how Lawrence M. Higby, a Haldeman assistant, had asked Hoover for a report about me, but Hoover, "to the dismay of the White House," had launched "a sort of full-field, wide open investigation," which left the White House "in a rather scrambling position to explain what happened."

During this colloquy, I became a "reaction shot." On my monitor I could see that the pool camera had picked me out at the press table and that I was on all the networks, not as a reporter, but as a subject. I puffed on my pipe and put on the deadest of deadpans I could summon up.

Dean said that Malek had been ordered to take the blame for the

---

*One beneficiary of information from the CBS broadcast was Dean himself. Dean had testified to a discussion of cover-up money with Herbert Kalmbach, President Nixon's personal lawyer, in the coffee shop of the Mayflower Hotel, where he said Kalmbach was staying. Dean was thrown into confusion when Senator Edward Gurney demonstrated from records that Kalmbach had stayed not at the Mayflower, but at the Statler Hilton. During a momentary pause I heard George Herman say on the air that there was a Mayflower coffee shop in the Statler Hilton, and this might explain the discrepancy. Seeing no reason why Dean should not know what the nationwide television audience had been told, I passed on the information to Dean's lawyers, enabling Dean to extricate himself, to the applause of the Caucus Room audience. In his book, Dean said that I thus "evened the score" for the "dirty deed" of my report on his immunity negotiations.

miscarried FBI investigation. Senator Herman Talmadge wanted to know: ordered by whom? Dean replied, "Mr. Haldeman, or the President."

On August 1, Haldeman was on the stand. When matters of greater moment had been disposed of, he was asked about the FBI investigation, and replied with great circumlocution. It was "in connection with something, apparently, I assume that arose at that time that generated a request for a background report on Mr. Schorr." He stressed that what had been wanted was not an investigation, but simply the FBI file on me. Senator Joseph Montoya asked Haldeman what made him think the FBI had such a file.

> HALDEMAN: They have a file on most people who are known pub-
>   licly, and the request was for whatever file they have.
> MONTOYA: You mean, the FBI has a file on every American that
>   is known publicly?
> HALDEMAN: I think they probably do. I have not been through their
>   files, so I can't verify that.

The camera was on me again for a reaction shot. The notion that massive FBI files might exist on Americans for no other crime than public prominence overwhelmed my assiduous effort at detachment. I shook my head in wonderment.

Higby, who had transmitted Haldeman's request to Hoover, told the committee it had been prompted by "a bad report that afternoon," August 19, 1971. Clearly the immediate cause of Nixon's anger had been my broadcast the previous evening indicating that his promise of federal aid to rescue the parochial schools was sheer rhetoric.

The episode was a microcosm of Watergate in all its four phases — the plot, the foul-up, the cover-up, the unraveling. The unraveling went further as this case joined the many instances of planned character assassination that entered into the impeachment investigation. The report of the House Judiciary Committee, supplemented by further interviews and FBI files obtained through a Freedom of Information request, enabled me to reconstruct the basic scenario of the investigation and the cover-up. The last gap in the narrative —

the presidential instruction that launched the FBI into action — was filled in for me by Haldeman in June 1977 as he was about to enter prison at the end of the five-year legal trail that had led from the Watergate building.

The jagged peaks of Wyoming's Grand Teton National Park served as the weird setting for the Nixon order. On August 19, 1971, the President had stopped for a statement on the parks program on his way to San Clemente after his Save-the-Catholic-Schools speech in New York. Nixon had been persuaded to make that speech, as a matter of political strategy, by Colson and Buchanan against the advice of John Ehrlichman, his chief domestic adviser. Haldeman was aware that my broadcast, exposing the rhetoric of a constitutionally unfulfillable promise, had infuriated Colson and Buchanan, one of whom — Haldeman could not remember which — telephoned Nixon in Wyoming to inflame him into retaliation.

A furious Nixon told Haldeman, "Get the FBI to pull the file on that son-of-a-bitch, Schorr." Haldeman relayed the instruction to his assistant, Lawrence Higby. Higby telephoned Hoover — who insisted on calling back as a precaution against an impostor — and said the White House wanted "a complete background on Daniel Schorr, CBS correspondent." Hoover apparently understood this to mean "background investigation," which is FBI language for clearance preliminary to a presidential appointment. There, apparently, came the major foul-up.

Hoover's first instruction, requiring a completed report by August 23 "without fail," said, "The President has requested extremely expedite applicant-type investigation of Schorr, who is being considered for presidential appointment, position not stated. Do not indicate White House interest to person contacted." The message, incredibly, was addressed to the FBI representative at the American Embassy in Bonn, Germany. It referred to a *Who's Who* biography listing me as CBS bureau chief in Germany. The FBI was evidently not aware that I had returned to the United States in 1966 and had been broadcasting from Washington for more than five years. Later telegrams to field offices advised, "Note: Schorr is now in U.S.," and, next day, "Investigation this morning indicates Schorr has been transferred back to the United States and is presently residing in Washington, D.C., with his family. He is apparently assigned to the CBS Washington Bureau."

One FBI memo advised that William Small, Washington bureau chief of CBS News, when contacted, had expressed shock, stating that he had "no indication that Schorr was being considered for any federal position." A further report quoted me as disclaiming knowledge of a prospective position. The FBI advised Higby of the strange situation it had encountered. An FBI memo said, "Higby . . . advised that in view of these developments, the FBI should discontinue the investigation until we hear further from Higby." Crisp telegrams went to field offices: "Discontinue investigation immediately," followed, after the weekend, by instructions quoting Higby: "The investigation should be cancelled; however, requested that all information developed by the Bureau to date concerning Schorr be furnished his office." Hoover wrote Higby enclosing "a summary memorandum containing the results of the investigation." (I have not been able to obtain or even locate that memorandum.)

When Colson telephoned Stanton to complain about my parochial school report, Stanton asked him, "Can you imagine what job they're considering Daniel Schorr for?" Colson recalls replying, "No, unless it's for ambassador to Siberia. That's got to be a mistake!" Unaware who had ordered the investigation, Colson called in John Scali, a White House communications assistant, and said, "This has the potential for a total disaster." Together they went to see Ron Ziegler, who, also surprised, started making inquiries.

As Colson describes it, Ziegler, having spoken to the FBI, hung up the phone, looking pale, and said, "It was Larry Higby! For the sake of the President, that must never leave this office!" Colson says he then called Haldeman, upbraiding him for stupidity, and telling him he had walked into a needless hornet's nest.

There was some anxious waiting for a public scandal, but it was almost three months before the first press inquiry came. On November 10, T. E. Bishop, assistant director of the FBI in charge of public information, got a call from Clawson of the Washington *Post*. "Clawson advised Bishop," said Bishop's memo, "that the FBI might not realize it, but the FBI had been 'used' by someone in the White House in connection with its investigation of Schorr . . . Clawson said that he had been informed by a source in the White House that Schorr was never being considered for appointment to a government position and that the individual who had made the request of the FBI was aware of this but had asked the FBI to conduct an investigation allegedly in connection with possible employment, but actually for the purpose of getting background information on Schorr in an expedite manner."

That afternoon Hoover, according to his own memo, was called by Haldeman, warning that "the Washington *Post* is cranking up a story" and suggesting they coordinate their response. Haldeman, the memo said, proposed to "slough it off over there, and, if they ask any questions, say they would not have anything to say as obviously information is sought on individuals at various times for various reasons such as appointments, routine checks, et cetera." Hoover agreed to go along.

When the story broke next day on the front page of the *Post*, Colson undertook to fashion a more elaborate cover-up. It involved, as he testified before the House Judiciary Committee, locating a specific and plausible job opening in the environmental area, which I had covered, and letting it be known that I had for a brief period been considered for appointment.* Colson said that he had discussed the plan with President Nixon and that the President had approved it. For the committee's counsel, John Doar, this represented a direct link to the impeachment investigation.

DOAR: . . . the President decided it?
COLSON: I think the President and I decided that that would be the best way we could work ourselves out of what looked like

---

*As one feature of the elaborate cover-up, Malek called in Ron Nessen, NBC correspondent, and offered him a job making films for the Council on Environmental Quality. "Five times in twenty minutes," Nessen told me, "Malek emphasized that this was the job for which Schorr had originally been considered. I left with the impression that Malek was not so much offering me a government job as trying to get me to spread the word that you had actually been under consideration for one — especially since I had been previously vetoed for a government job as politically unacceptable to the Nixon White House." Nessen eventually went to work for the Ford White House as press secretary three years later. Malek, after he had left the government, apologized to me for his role in the deception.

an embarrassing situation . . . We decided that this would be an appropriate way to dig ourselves out of a political hole. It may very well be that I said we ought to put this out and the President said "fine." It may be that he said to me, "Why don't you talk to Ziegler and see if we can give this as an answer."

Ziegler spent an hour before the press on November 11, blandly repeating the cover story and showing impatience when greeted with skepticism: "Maybe we could cut through some of these questions by my saying this: There was not an FBI investigation ordered by the White House on Mr. Schorr for any other purpose than the purpose which I have just described to you."*

The report of the House Judiciary Committee, in July 1974, said, "The President knew that Schorr had never been considered for any government position. The President approved the cover story."

Nixon also disclosed — on tape — that it was he who had ordered the FBI investigation. On June 4, 1973, he sat in the Oval Office, earphone on his head, listening to earlier tapes as he prepared his impeachment defense and making running observations to Alexander Haig, his new chief of staff, and Ziegler. He listened to himself suggesting on March 13 to John Dean that it should be maintained that he had used the FBI "only for national security purposes."

"Yeah," he said. "The only exception, of course, was that son-of-a-bitch, Schorr. But there — actually it *was* national security. (Laughs) We didn't say that. Oh, we didn't do anything. We just ran a name check on the son-of-a-bitch."

What would Haldeman have done if the investigation had not misfired and the FBI had come up with "dirt"? That, Haldeman told

*Unlike Ziegler, some played an unwitting part in the cover-up. The Nixon speech writer William Safire was the originator of the suggestion, which the President quickly adopted, to forbid future FBI investigations before the job candidate had been informed and had given consent. Safire wrote in *Before the Fall,* "I am not so easily duped; the secret of my self-delusion was a misplaced certainty that there was more stupidity than villainy at the top, and that was what misled a lot of us . . ." Patrick Buchanan, another speech writer, told me that President Nixon had "lied" to him about having a job in mind for me.

me in 1977, would have been up to President Nixon. "I assume it would not be to do something nice for me," I said.

"That's probably a fair assumption," Haldeman replied.

• •

John Dean, who had started the unraveling of the FBI episode in his second day on the witness stand, produced a more startling disclosure on the third day. As though routinely completing the record, Dean was identifying a series of documents that Senator Weicker had asked him to provide. They were part of the huge trove of paper that Dean, to help him barter for mercy, had removed from a White House with an almost unbelievable weakness for documenting its misdeeds. The weakness stemmed from President Nixon's preference for dealing with paper rather than persons.

I sat back at what seemed a moment of anticlimax, listening to the hearing with my eyes closed. Through my earplug a producer in the CBS control room said that this cataloguing of documents was a pretty dull show, and that at some point I would have to get on camera to explain what it was all about. Part of my paraphernalia included batteries taped under my jacket and a wireless microphone. These enabled me, when necessary, to rush from the room to a tiny roped-off enclosure in the hallway, where each of the networks had it own "unilateral" camera, ready to supplement the "pooled" coverage of the hearings with information and interviews.

This enclosure, where correspondents jostled elbow to elbow, trying to keep out of each other's pictures, was where live television turned when the hearing started late, as it usually did, or ended abruptly, as it sometimes did. The Ervin committee, more attentive to the Senate's needs than to television's, would recess suddenly to respond to a quorum call on the Senate floor. This left the correspondents to fill a gap with hastily gathered interviews, conversations with anchorpersons back in the studio and labored recapitulations. Once it became necessary to chat and interview our way through an intermission of an hour and thirty-five minutes. When possible, there was advance planning for how the next recess would be utilized. On this day it seemed clear that the television audience would need some explanation of the documents whose titles Dean was droning off and then handing to a clerk.

"The next is a copy of a memorandum of August 16, 1971, that was prepared for Mr. Haldeman, Mr. Ehrlichman and others at the White House by myself, which addresses itself to the general problem of dealing with political enemies . . ."

A stirring at the press table.

"The next is a document dated September 9, 1971. It is from Charles Colson to John Dean, in which Mr. Colson has checked in blue those he would give top priority on the enemies' list . . ."

Over my earplug came a message asking if I could find out more about these documents as quickly as possible. At the committee table I was told they would be distributed to the press as soon as they could be duplicated.

The August 16, 1971, memorandum was given out shortly after noon as the committee recessed for lunch. Hardly stopping to look at it, I stepped out the door into view of our camera, and said, "Let's go!" My colleagues of ABC and NBC were at my side, looking at *their* cameras. On the air, I explained that the memorandum was freshly received and that I was sharing it with the audience as I read it. Dean had titled it "Dealing with Our Political Enemies." It outlined a plan for using the machinery of government to harass the opponents of President Nixon. I read from the memorandum, "Stated a bit more bluntly — how we can use the available Federal machinery to screw our political enemies."

Hardly off the air, I was advised from our control room of protests from two CBS affiliates in the Bible Belt against the use of the word "screw" on the air. I asked to have them informed that I had no way of anticipating such language while reading a document from the White House.

A few minutes later we received another memorandum — the "top priority" list. Once again, with just enough time to notice that it listed numbers one to twenty, I went on the air. "No. 1. Picker, Arnold M., United Artists Corporation," and down through a series of Democratic politicos and fund-raisers. Then I heard myself telling the television audience, "No. 17. Schorr, Daniel. Columbia Broadcasting System, Washington. A real media enemy."

I remember that my first thought was that I must go on reading without any pause, or gasp or look of wild surmise. I made it through the last items, "Paul Newman, California. Radic-lib causes," and "McGrory, Mary. Daily hate-Nixon articles." Then I briskly gave the cue for return to George Herman and Nelson Benton in the CBS Washington studio. I do not know how well I carried off my effort to appear oblivious to the discovery of my name on an ominous-looking list, but I count this one of the most trying experiences in my television career.

Once off the air, I called the Cronkite show producers and suggested that the "enemies story" be handled separately from the rest of the day's package. Dean submitted more lists, and the number of "enemies" mounted to 490. But the list of the "top twenty," selected by Haldeman, Dean said, as the ones "who had incurred the President's special wrath," was the list on the front pages next day. I wondered whether my superiors would consider me disqualified from covering the Watergate story now that my name was a part of it. To my gratification, no such suggestion was made.

• •

The enemy lists had apparently been part of the planning for the Nixon second term. "I want the most comprehensive notes kept on all of those who tried to do us in," Nixon had told John Dean on September 15, 1972. "They are asking for it and they are going to get it . . . We have not used the power in the first four years, as you know . . . We haven't used the Bureau and we haven't used the Justice Department, but things are going to change now!"

"That's an exciting prospect!" the faithful John Dean had responded.

The enemy lists indicated what lay at the heart of the Watergate syndrome. The word "enemy" symbolized the hostility and paranoia of the Nixon White House. It introduced into the political lexicon a concept that signified not only political division, but irreconcilable ideological conflict.

In marking his American opponents as enemies, Nixon also provided a chilling preview of what he apparently hoped to accomplish in his second term. With White House agents installed like party commissars, government departments would be made "responsive" to the President's will. The government would be politicized into an instrument to reward friends and punish enemies. The "Plumbers," the private White House espionage agency, would be expanded into a large-scale White House intelligence and surveillance operation. President Nixon would, at last — he undoubtedly hoped — achieve control of his environment to insure that nothing could "come crashing down" to his surprise.

Nixon was thrown on the defensive before he could launch his offensive. The enemy lists remain a monument to a singular conspiracy to target the United States government against a President's real and fancied foes.

V

COLLISION COURSES

A HIGH-RATED STATUS on the Nixon enemy list was in one respect surprising — my position in television did not seem to warrant such consideration. Between the anchorpersons and the reporters — the stars and the supporting players — there is a sharp distinction. A reporter, unless in contact with the President as a White House correspondent, is unlikely to command his attention, favorable or otherwise. I often wondered what it was about my broadcasts that seemed to make me such a thorn in Nixon's side. To the extent that analysis of one's work is possible, I concluded that it stemmed from my newspaper background, and especially my background as a foreign correspondent — an urge to give the shapeless news a form and point that would bring it home to people far away. My years in the managed-news atmosphere of Eastern Europe made me especially avid for news that was being withheld. The magazine of journalism, *MORE,* observed that "Schorr probably functions more like a print reporter than any other network correspondent." It may well have been that a newspaperman's bluntness stood out amid television's blandness. I also had a newspaperman's antagonism to the stage-craft, image-making and slogan-selling to which television seemed so susceptible — the characteristics that made it so natural a medium for the manipulative Nixon. If this tended to bring me into conflict with a President, it also had the potential for bringing me into conflict — especially at a time of great stress — with the medium in which I worked.

From the start, I had been more a journalist *in* television than a

journalist *of* television. In 1953, when I left *New York Times* stringer-
dom in the Low Countries for CBS staffdom in Washington, there
was a standing joke between James Reston of the *New York Times*
and myself. Whenever we met, he would ask, "Had enough?" and
I would reply, "Pretty soon, Scotty, pretty soon!" It was a way of
underlining that I had ventured most hesitantly into electronic journalism and suggesting that, once having confirmed it was not serious
journalism, I would come home to the inkpot.*

For all the blemishes in broadcasting, there were also blandish-
ments. More than mere financial reward, there was ego reward —
telling the news more directly to more people than any newspaper
could assemble. The proportion of Americans — 70 percent at last
count — who relied on television for most of what they learned about
the world represented a giant classroom. In most reporters of the old
school there burns something of the teacher. Here lay the opportunity to initiate millions of Americans into the mysteries of post-Stalin
Russia, post-Hitler Germany and the postponed social problems of
America — with a vividness that print could not match.

In 1957, for example, Nikita Khrushchev, trying to make a comeback for East-West "coexistence" after the bloody suppression of the
Hungarian uprising, gave interviews to Reston of the *Times,* William
Randolph Hearst, Henry Shapiro of the United Press — and, on
"Face the Nation," to us of CBS Television. The hour-long filmed
interview contained little, in substance, that differed from Khrushchev's published views. While the film was on its way to New York,
I was asked by impatient editors what big news it contained, and
cabled back that there were no headlines because he had said it all
before. I had myself missed the real headline — that the new-style

*I would probably have never left print journalism had I not been rebuffed by the *Times.*
In 1952, Turner Catledge, the managing editor, after giving me a tryout in local reporting in
New York, promised me an early staff appointment, but had not come through nine months
later when I received the CBS offer. Catledge advised me to accept it. Five years later, Emanuel
R. Freedman, the *Times'* foreign editor, confessed to me at dinner that I had been the victim
of a temporary "freeze" on the hiring of Jews, instituted — with the approval of the publisher,
Arthur Hays Sulzberger — because of fear that the *Times* had too many Jewish reporters for
flexible deployment in a Middle East crisis. The policy was soon canceled, Freedman said, but
it was in force when my employment was being considered — with the result that Catledge
felt it only fair not to stand in the way of my CBS offer.

extroverted leader of the Communist world had never said it before in America's living rooms.

I derived — let me admit it — another important reward from reporting visibly on the air. My friend A. M. Rosenthal of the *New York Times* likes to recall what happened in April 1960, when it was announced that he had won the Pulitzer Prize for his sensitive and daring reporting from Poland. Being together in Geneva, we celebrated with a wine-lubricated lunch at the lake-front restaurant *Le Glôbe,* Abe exuberantly flourishing the European edition of the *Herald Tribune* with his name in headlines. At one point he whispered, "Don't look now, but those American tourists at the next table are about to come over and ask to meet the prize winner." A moment later they approached our table and, ignoring Abe, asked for my autograph. Abe swore that the next time he won the Pulitzer Prize he would shun all friends from television.

The manifest satisfactions of communication and recognition ebbed and flowed with my reservations about television. Trying to do newspaper-style reporting in a visual medium, seeking to transmit facts with the tools of fantasy, entailed compromises. One had to bend scripts to fit around sometimes barely relevant film. Trying to cram in more information than time permitted, I tended to read too fast and was frequently admonished to sacrifice a few facts for a less breathless pace. I chafed at the straitjacket of the conventional TV news story — a brief introduction voiced over silent film, a snippet of somebody speaking and a brief conclusion. The format left me with the feeling that I had merely "teased up" a story that remained to be told. A challenge to ingenuity was the process of writing a script that would convey the essential information (at least, the information I *thought* essential) while complying with a director's instructions to "hit" a certain name or place at the precisely ordered point to coincide with a picture. A new generation of television news professionals had learned how to provide a fair amount of information while going through this puzzle-solving. To an immigrant from the world of words, it was frustrating to try to present events in this fashion.

A greater problem arose from my fascination with stories that were *not* events. Most events on television are what the historian Daniel Boorstin calls "pseudo-events"; they are hearings, speeches, press conferences presented for self-serving or attention-getting purposes. I was more interested in the situations that evaded attention. They were such stories as the conflicts behind closed doors in the Pay Board, the Nixon administration's quiet revision of the statistical index of poverty to make the poor seem fewer, the lobbying of the auto industry to delay antipollution standards. They were not ideal television stories because they basically had to be told rather than shown. A story told by a reporter straight into the camera, without distracting film, is bitter medicine to television — to be taken in small doses. The time allotted on the Cronkite show for a straight "tell story," however important and exclusive, tended to range from forty-five seconds to a usual maximum of a minute and a half.

A thousand-word story reduced to two hundred words, stripped of nuances and qualifications, and then exposed to the magnifying effect of television, had an unavoidably explosive impact. The newspaper-style exclusive, condensed to a television "mini-scoop," could convey an unintended boldness almost to the point of provocation. The broadcast about the ABM in March 1971 that caused President Nixon to accuse me of "a little lie" was a minute and ten seconds. The parochial school story that brought the FBI down on me in August 1971 was under one minute. The raising of hackles went beyond government. In May 1971, when I was obliged to sum up with staccato brevity a conflict between the fishing industry and the Food and Drug Administration over the extent of pollution resulting from fishery canning practices, the Bumble Bee Seafoods Company felt moved to cancel its commercials on all CBS-affiliated stations because it considered me hostile to the fishery side of the argument. My bosses found that I had given the fisheries' position as fairly as I could in the few seconds available. The real problem was time. Any story on a controversial subject that is packed into so small a container tends to burst on an interested party like a hand grenade.

In the Watergate era, as the stakes grew higher and the nerves tauter, the mini-scoop became a more acute problem. On the Cronkite show on October 23, 1972, in little more than a minute I reported early internal friction over Watergate, including the warning of Patrick Gray, acting FBI director, to President Nixon that the conspiracy might have "more serious direct links to the White House than the President might know about." The President's news summary noted this broadcast with the observation, "CBS only net with Watergate story." Ziegler issued a denial of any such communication between Nixon and Gray — a denial that became inoperative ten months later when Gray testified in the Senate Watergate hearings about his telephone conversation with the President.

There was a succession of stories — brief, and irritating to the White House — about a secret list of campaign contributions kept by President Nixon's secretary, Rose Mary Woods; about the Nixon-ordered wiretapping and shadowing of his brother, Donald; about circumstancial evidence indicating that a motivation for the installation of the White House taping system may have been for its potential financial value.

The attention given to these bare-boned reports was gratifying, but sometimes a mixed blessing. The *New York Times* on July 5, 1973, gave a front-page headline to my broadcast disclosing plans to indict Haldeman, Ehrlichman, Mitchell and Dean and the fact that the prosecutors had discussed compiling the evidence against President Nixon "as a presentment to Congress, where the impeachment power rests." It was, I believe, the earliest indication that the prosecutors considered Nixon involved in the conspiracy and that the recourse would have to be impeachment rather than indictment. On the other hand, an overly condensed report about pending indictments on the CBS Morning News on February 28, 1974, created considerable misunderstanding. The indictments, I said, might list "as many as forty-one persons as defendants and co-conspirators." For those not listening closely, the distinction between defendants and unindicted co-conspirators was blurred, and my figure seemed woefully off the mark when the two indictments came out with a total of sixteen names. Not generally understood was the fact that an additional list of nineteen alleged co-conspirators had been with-held from the published indictment in the Watergate cover-up because Nixon was included among them.

As the tension mounted, there were other penalties of being in the spotlight — telephone calls not returned and frozen looks when I dropped in on some officials. A tribute I would gladly have waived was a memorandum circulated to members and staff of the Senate Watergate Committee by Sam Dash, the chief counsel, warning that I was trying to acquire an advance copy of the committee's final report and urging "very careful security." Obtaining parts, but not all of the draft report, I derived only small consolation from receiving a leaked copy of Dash's confidential memo about the danger of a leak.

•   •

To an unprecedented extent, the reporting of the Watergate situation became an issue in the situation and a factor crucial to its outcome. At the outset, in the fall of 1972, Judge Sirica tried to enforce a "gag" order on both sides of the criminal case, but relaxed it after a protest from Congress. In December, the judge shocked those covering the case by summarily sending John Lawrence, the Washington bureau chief of the Los Angeles *Times,* to jail for contempt, instead of following the usual practice of leaving him free pending appeal. The contempt citation arose from Lawrence's refusal to accede to Judge Sirica's order to supply the tape of an interview with Alfred Baldwin, the prosecution's star witness, to Howard Hunt's defense counsel, William Bittman. As Lawrence was led out of the courtroom to a jail cell before stunned spectators, Bittman turned to me and whispered, "You're next!" I was the only other newsman who had recorded an interview with Baldwin. Happily for him, Lawrence only remained in jail a few hours,*and, equally happily for me, Bittman never pursued his threat to me.

---

*Although most judges had already started their Christmas vacations, Lawrence's lawyers were lucky enough to find one Appeals Court judge, Harold Leventhal, still in his office upstairs from Judge Sirica's court. Leventhal ordered Lawrence's release pending appeal. The issue was soon resolved when Baldwin himself authorized release of the tape. Judge Leventhal told me he later asked Sirica, "Johnny, why did you send Lawrence to jail?" Sirica replied, "Because I knew you'd spring him in a couple of hours."

In 1973, as investigations started closing in on the White House, television's role began to dominate the backstage deliberations. No one better understood the stakes than President Nixon, who had for so long striven to establish his dominance over the tube. An early 1973 report of the Twentieth Century Fund on "Presidential Television" had warned that the medium could serve as a tool for Caesarism, that its increasing control by the Chief Executive "threatens to tilt the delicately balanced system in the direction of the President." Now Nixon anxiously saw the system starting to tilt away from the presidency toward Congress.

The White House transcripts, doctored though they were, reveal the incessant, almost obsessive discussions about whether the Senate hearings could be stalled, shunted into executive session, compressed into a single week, or at least be kept off prime time. On Saturday, April 14, when Nixon and the inner circle finally realized that a chain reaction of defection had started that could lead to disaster, with no volunteer scapegoats in sight, what dominated the President's last thoughts before sleep were not what would happen to him factually, but what would happen to him on television. Close to midnight, he was on the telephone with Haldeman.

"How bad is it if we go on television?" he asked. Haldeman consoled him. "I am not sure it is all that bad. In the first place, it is going to be in the daytime. In the second place, as of now, it is not going to be carried live by the networks . . . What will probably end up happening is that it will be carried on the public broadcasting, which has virtually no audience in the day time." Unplacated, Nixon explained what damage there would be even without live television. "What happens there," he told Haldeman, "is that every new break is carried for five or ten minutes in the evening news."

Contrary to Haldeman's optimistic prediction, live network television was on hand when Chairman Ervin banged his gavel on May 17 in the Senate Caucus Room, starting what he described as the task of dispelling "a black cloud of distrust over our entire society." The networks had vacillated until almost the last moment about how far they wanted to commit themselves to this contest. In the media age, coverage was no longer a neutral decision. What television covered could determine the nation's agenda; saturation coverage could decide the issue. I heard of discussion among CBS executives about possible "selective coverage" of principal hearings, or standing by to "go live" at dramatic moments, or trying to rotate coverage among the three commercial networks, leaving public television to do the humdrum "gavel to gavel" proceedings. I was at no point consulted, nor did I expect to be — such high-level decisions rarely involved working journalists. With the mounting excitement over promised revelations from John Dean, competitive pressures obliged the networks to agree on live coverage with pooled facilities, at least during the first phase of the hearings.

For a time it looked as though President Nixon's nemesis, Special Prosecutor Archibald Cox, might, ironically, come to his rescue. Cox, having failed to win the postponement of the Senate hearings pending the completion of his investigation, made an extraordinary appeal to Judge Sirica to require the testimony of Dean and any other witnesses granted partial immunity to be given outside camera range. Otherwise, he argued, future trials might be prejudiced. The chief judge was sufficiently attracted to the idea to call a courtroom hearing on the issue on June 8 and ask, "In what way is television necessary to fulfill the legislative function of the committee?" Counsel Dash replied that, at a time of crisis and loss of confidence in government, Congress needed strong support for remedial legislation — support that national television would help to arouse. Judge Sirica did not appear convinced, but concluded that he was prevented by the separation of powers doctrine from trying to set rules for a congressional hearing. Had he tried, and succeeded, in limiting television coverage of the hearings, he might have changed the course of history.

The thirty-seven days of televised hearings justified President Nixon's worst fear that television might tip the balance against him. In ten weeks America sat through two billion viewing hours of hearings — an average of thirty hours per household. Many Americans had not wanted to watch, and had demanded to have their soap operas back. Some came to accept the hearings as substitute soap operas. The correspondents on the scene — therefore regarded as responsible — received calls from listeners objecting to certain witnesses or grousing about dull moments, seeming to assume there was a scenario that television could repair. People chose their favorite characters on the Senate side of the table, and especially among the witnesses — the mocking Ehrlichman, the stonewalling Mitchell, the tearful Gordon Strachan and, most affecting of all, solemn John Dean with his blond wife behind him, murmuring devastation against the President of the United States.

The evidence, much of it developed by the committee out of camera range, was in itself important. The thirteen green-colored volumes of testimony resulted in three counts of perjury against Haldeman and one against Mitchell. Dash said that perhaps 90 percent of the material for the subsequent impeachment investigation came from his committee's files. The Senate committee, if it had done nothing else, would have left an imprint on history by its ferreting out of the Nixon tapes. This left the White House forever thereafter on the defensive, wrestling with the special prosecutor, resisting subpoenas, explaining mysterious gaps, releasing doctored transcripts, and eventually surrendering the "smoking gun" of the June 23, 1972, tape about enlisting the CIA in a cover-up plan — the final damning link in the tightening chain around the President.

The evidence developed by the Senate committee opened the door to impeachment, but it was the televising of the hearings that enabled Americans psychologically to cross that threshold and contemplate the unprecedented expulsion of a President from office. What penetrated the American psyche were not only the large allegations, but the small vignettes — undercover cops sent to dig for dirt, the smell of political blackmail, the miasma of hate and paranoia that seemed to emanate from the White House. Television brought these things home and played an important role in what turned out to be an irreversible process — not because anyone in television had planned it, but simply because television was *there.*

During this phase, the impact of television far overshadowed the impact of television journalism. The medium may have made the reporters hovering around the Caucus Room seem like featured players, but I am convinced that all our interviews, summaries and analyses added very little to the powerful effect of the hearings themselves. To some, we may have seemed like the symbols of what we were covering, bringing us both undeserved credit and blame. Morrie Ryskind, a syndicated columnist sympathetic to Nixon, angrily called me a member of "a kangaroo court," participating in a network "rivalry" intended to "get Nixon." He should have directed his chagrin at the impression the hearings themselves made on America and the unaccustomed impotence of presidential television in the face of congressional television.

When Nixon sought to turn television into his principal defensive weapon, reporters had a more important role to play. As the "tube" began to slip from his grasp, the President repeatedly tried to achieve a new "Checkers comeback" — a talk to the nation that would be so persuasive as to reverse his ebbing fortunes. Indeed, his confidence in his ability, through television, to reconstitute his Silent Majority and overwhelm the accumulating evidence may well have accounted for his complacent failure to destroy the damaging tapes or, as some of his advisers suggested, to go before the nation with a form of confession and appeal for forgiveness. He acted almost until the end as though he faced no reality so threatening that it could not be annihilated by a new reality created on television. The landscape of Watergate history is strewn with the bleak slogans of these attempted comebacks:

April 17, 1973: "I can report today that there have been major developments."

April 30 (announcing the Haldeman, Ehrlichman, Dean and Kleindienst resignations): "Justice will be pursued fairly, fully and impartially."

August 15 ("Address to the Nation"): "I pledge to you tonight that I will do all I can to insure that one of the results of Watergate is a new level of political decency and integrity in America . . ."

October 26 (after the "Saturday night massacre" in the Justice Department): "I would simply say that I intend to carry out, to the best of my ability, the responsibilities I was elected to carry out last November."

November 17 (before newspaper editors at Disney World in Florida): "People have got to know whether or not their President is a crook. Well, I am not a crook!"

January 30, 1974 (the State of the Union address): "I believe the time has come to bring that investigation and other investigations of this matter to an end. One year of Watergate is enough!"

April 29 (against the background of a document-crammed bookcase): "The materials I make public tomorrow will provide all the additional evidence needed to get Watergate behind us and get it behind us now."

The "Checkers" comeback syndrome seemed still to be operating when Nixon appeared on television in May 1977, a thousand days after his resignation. Interviewed by David Frost, the ex-President subordinated the facts of Watergate to the manipulation of emotion. He managed to express compassion for Haldeman and Ehrlichman while shifting blame to them. He managed to express contrition while denying guilt. He added one belated slogan to his litany:

May 4, 1977: "I let the American people down, and I have to carry that burden with me for the rest of my life."

While in office President Nixon was, paradoxically, adept at the use of television and a poor television performer. His mastery of the medium was intellectual rather than natural; he was a better director than an actor. Aside from his well-known problems with perspiration and five o'clock shadow, his gestures were stiff and studied and his manner reflected tension. He made embarrassing Freudian slips; for example, during his televised talk to newspaper editors at Disney World he said that Haldeman and Ehrlichman "are guilty until I have evidence that they are not guilty." His talents were in stagecraft — the timing of his broadcasts, their themes and scripts. He was attentive to theatrical effects — family pictures for one occasion, Lincoln portraits for another — and to camera angles and lighting. His consummate skill — at least for the unskeptical — was his way of investing his words with the aura of the presidency.

Presidents tend generally to identify their images with national image, demanding personal confidence as the price of governmental effectiveness. What President Nixon sought, however, was not simply a muting of foreign policy criticism for the sake of national unity, or support of domestic programs for the sake of economic stability, but acceptance of his personal conduct as President for the survival of the presidency.

For Nixon to be able to salvage his position, he needed — as never before — to have the medium temporarily to himself. Spellbinding required the unbroken spell, the unchallenged majesty of office. To offset this manipulation required — as never before — journalistic analysis to provide background and perspective. It was, however, extraordinarily difficult for a correspondent to go on television immediately after a President who was pleading for national unity and warning of international crisis. Did a reporter owe it to a polarized nation and a network under pressure to pull some punches?

We correspondents never talked about our feelings in this situation as we gathered for instant analysis in the studio of CBS News in Washington, busy with the business of smearing on makeup, fitting earplugs, testing microphones. As the moment neared for Nixon to appear from the White House, the lights were dimmed in the studio so that we could better observe him. An advance text was seldom available; we took our notes as Nixon spoke, kept our own counsel, referred to background on our clipboards and tried to think what we would say when the lights came up. Advance preparation rarely went beyond an indication from Roger Mudd, the usual anchorman, about the order of his first round of questions and word from the control room about how much time we would have after Nixon had finished.

On April 30, 1973, after President Nixon announced the White House resignations, we had thirteen minutes — Mudd, Dan Rather, Eric Sevareid and myself. I commented, "At this moment of high emotion, when the President spoke with a picture of his family near him, appealing for national unity and invoking the urgent needs of foreign affairs, and even the avoiding of nuclear war, it may be very hard to come down to the facts and substance of the Watergate case, and yet I conceive that to be our job." I proceeded then to point out questions that Nixon had left unanswered. Sevareid said that it was all "a very, very sad matter" and that President Nixon's assistants "couldn't keep functioning under this kind of cloud, however innocent they might turn out to be." President Nixon got an extensive synopsis of our discussion in his news summary next morning, with a reference to "the very critical Schorr."

On October 23 during a panel discussion following the unexpected announcement that the Nixon tapes would be turned over to Judge Sirica, Roger Mudd asked for an assessment of the President's prospects. I spoke of a volatile situation in which the White House seemed to be trying, by the last-minute release of tapes, to offset the adverse public reaction to the firing of Special Prosecutor Cox. "It may take another few weeks," I said, "before the public realizes that the tapes were not the only issue and, indeed, may not have been the most important issue. And the question now is: who wins the battle of public opinion? Is the public tired of impeachment talk? Do they want to let down and say, 'Okay, that's solved'? I would be the last one to predict what happens." Dan Rather said he considered the odds 60–40 that Nixon could ride it out because most Americans "are loath to even think of impeachment," though he added that the odds would change "if he isn't telling the truth."

On November 17, after Nixon's appearance before newspaper editors in Disney World, I joined Rather and Fred Graham for a fourteen-minute discussion (Paley having just reinstated CBS instant analysis). Analyzing Nixon's defense of his tax deduction for vice-presidential papers, I noted that, unlike President Johnson, whom he cited as a precedent, he may have taken his deduction after the expiration of the law authorizing such deductions.

I was aware that I was consistently more pointed in analysis than most of my colleagues, but I knew no other way to conduct myself. My superiors did not criticize me or admonish me to be more circumspect, but as the tension grew, I found myself being utilized less. In fact, after November 17, 1973, I never again appeared on television for immediate analysis of Nixon's Watergate arguments. My only other subsequent assignment in that role was on radio on April 29, 1974, when Nixon announced the release of the White House transcripts. I expressed myself as cautious about accepting these transcripts as the whole story. "Anyone with a judicious mind would wait to see the twelve hundred pages before reaching any conclusions," I said.

The "Watergate story" developed into the "impeachment story," and I was relegated more and more to the sidelines. Whatever problems had been created by my expressions on the air, I found myself under greater criticism for how I was expressing myself off the air.

•   •

I had long been accustomed to giving occasional lectures — on university campuses and elsewhere — and these had become a source of increasing friction within CBS. My remarks frequently bounced back by way of local newspapers, picked up by station managers as the basis for complaints to network executives. As early as September 1971, I told a social-work conference in Kennebunkport, Maine, that President Nixon tended to show more interest in international than domestic issues, that he struck me as "more concerned about America's global condition than America's human condition." The local affiliate complained, and Victor Lasky, the right-wing columnist, denounced me by writing, "Does everybody who watches the CBS Evening News really know the deep-seated political prejudices of some of its star reporters?" CBS News Director Gordon Manning brought the Lasky column to my attention with a jocular note asking if I would attend a cocktail party he was giving in Lasky's honor.

Reproof became less gentle as nerves tautened under the strain of Watergate. I have always allowed myself more latitude on the lecture platform than before the microphone in the belief that, off the air, I enjoy a citizen's right to express personal opinions. In lectures before the 1972 election, I unsettled some audiences by saying that I thought there was much more to Watergate than had so far been allowed to emerge. By the fall of 1973 I was describing what I considered an irreversible process that would probably make it impossible for President Nixon to complete his second term. Such remarks were frequently quoted in newspapers, and were forwarded to CBS with the angry comments of local station executives.

Furthermore, in question and answer periods, particularly on university campuses, my ambivalence about television tended to show. I made no effort to defend the temporary ban on instant analysis, saying that I was as surprised and as shocked as anybody by Paley's action. When asked what had happened to Cronkite's preelection Watergate special, I said anyone could draw conclusions from the facts that the second installment was broadcast late and was half as short as the first part.

At a dinner with Washington correspondents early in 1974, Richard Salant noted that there were heavy pressures on CBS, and asked correspondents to be more cautious in public speeches. I won no award for tact when I replied that a news organization exercising First Amendment rights could not appropriately try to limit the personal First Amendment rights of its personnel. At a cocktail party at the home of journalist Elizabeth Drew, a neighbor on Woodley Road, one of my bosses, John Schneider, asked me why I had to make so much trouble for CBS by lecturing, and didn't I earn enough money broadcasting? He asked, "Why the hell did you say all those things at Beaver College?" One of my problems was that, although I remembered having lectured in September 1972, at Pennsylvania's Beaver College — Joe Namath's alma mater — I could not recall precisely what I had said. Matters were getting very tense in CBS, and clearly a lower profile was desired.

• •

Every reporter involved in the stormy twilight of the Nixon presidency retains some special recollection of how it was. For me it was paper. In the last days, documents came pouring out in a torrent, to be swiftly read and reduced to television-size capsules. The Nixon White House had floated on paper; now it seemed to be sinking in it.

There was the final report of the Senate Watergate Committee, long on ponderous facts, short on conclusions, which the senators short-circuited in their rush to clear the stage for impeachment. Howard Baker, the ranking Republican on the Watergate Committee, had his separate report, its turgid prose suggesting but unable to prove that the CIA had been deeply involved in Watergate.

Most voluminous of all were the impeachment documents that rained from the House Judiciary Committee — thirty tan-covered books with chief counsel John Doar's assembled evidence. These had to be combed for fresh information. There were transcripts of hitherto undisclosed White House conversations and more faithful texts that exposed the fraud of the "White House transcripts." Some recorded episodes were reenacted, with CBS News correspondents "playing" President Nixon and other principals.

"Good evening," said Walter Cronkite at 11:30 P.M. on July 18. "Here in Washington it's like a cyclone. It swept through the courthouse and scattered its thousands of documents to the winds." We had a half-hour for hasty digests of hundreds of pages of documents about wiretaps, surveillance and other presidential abuses of power. We didn't quite make it — because of an error in calculation, the computer cut the program off the air at midnight with Cronkite in midsentence. That happens very seldom, and, when it does, it creates a control-room crisis that makes a national crisis momentarily pale by comparison.

In the first week of August, with the end near, network executives had more serious reason to worry.

Nixon had long tried to make television his creature and the news establishment his whipping boy. He had taken to provoking confrontations with the press, as though to tell Americans who was plotting to drive him from office. Back in May 1973, he had complained of "grossly misleading" news accounts; in August, that "some members of the press, perhaps some members of television," were exploiting Watergate to keep him from doing his job; in September, that "leers and sneers of commentators" were eroding confidence in the President; in October, that the networks called him "tyrant, dictator" and wanted him to resign or be impeached. He then began his baiting of television correspondents. When Robert Pierpoint of CBS, referring to his previous criticism of his treatment on television, asked what had angered him specifically, Nixon said, "Don't get the impression that you arouse my anger . . . You see, one can only be angry with those he respects." Before the National Association of Broadcasters in Houston in March 1974, he taunted Dan Rather of CBS: "Are you running for something?" As he entered the East Room of the White House for a news conference, he turned to Sidney Feders of CBS, who was acting as the "pool producer" for the three networks, and said, "Walter Cronkite isn't going to like what I say tonight — I hope!"

It looked like part of a build-up, at least a contingency plan to cast the news media as the villains if Nixon was forced out of office. The idea had already been rehearsed when his two assistants resigned in April. Haldeman's letter to the President had said that with "the flood of stories arising every day from all sources" it was "virtually impossible under these circumstances for me to carry on my regular responsibilities in the White House." Ehrlichman had blamed "unfounded charges or implication or whatever else the media carries," and had said, "I have to conclude that my present usefulness to you and the ability to discharge my duties have been impaired by these attacks, perhaps beyond repair."

On the morning of August 8, the nation wondered whether President Nixon would "tough it out" through impeachment or resign. Many of us, in television, wondered how he would stage-manage a resignation scene, whether the 1962 "no more Dick Nixon to kick around anymore" would be revived on such a scale as to turn a part of the nation in rage against us.

Events, however, began overtaking speculation. Speaker Carl Albert had called a meeting of bipartisan House leaders and network executives in his office to agree on ground rules for televising the impeachment debate. Unlike ABC and NBC, which sent news executives, CBS was represented by its corporate president, Arthur Taylor, who had flown from New York to become personally involved in this historic moment. With Sanford Socolow, Washington bureau chief, at his side, Taylor found himself embroiled in an angry debate in which the Speaker and John Rhodes, the minority leader, accused the networks of wanting to turn impeachment into a circus. There were arguments about whether mobile cameras could roam the aisles or would have to remain stationary, whether television could show the assembled Congressmen or be obliged to focus on the rostrum. Albert's staff had prepared a statement of "principles" to govern television's presence in the impeachment proceedings, but the heart went out of the argument when Speaker Albert, after receiving a message, said that the discussion might turn out to be superfluous: it looked as though President Nixon would be resigning that night. Socolow, a few minutes before, had guessed as much. He had been called from the room to be told that Ron Ziegler had phoned him as network pool chairman (the official contact for arranging television coverage of a White House event) but wanted to speak to him when he was back in his office, not while he was on Capitol Hill.

Taylor stopped to chat with me as he returned, with Socolow, to the CBS News building. His great concern now was that President Nixon, in announcing his resignation, might make a vicious attack on the news media — especially on CBS, which he regarded as his most implacable foe. Taylor even had concerns about the immediate security of CBS personnel at the White House because of the crowd gathering outside. He believed that 10 percent of any crowd was capable, under certain circumstances, of cruelty and violence, and he told Socolow, "Keep an eye on security — we're responsible for the safety of our CBS News people." His longer-range worry was that Nixon might polarize the nation on the subject of television, precipitating the long-feared American uprising against the news media. I agreed that everything we knew about Nixon justified such a fear.

Taylor took over the office of Socolow's assistant, Bill Headline. The three-story CBS News building at 2020 M Street had become the network's nerve center. Downstairs, in the studio, Cronkite was on the air. From another appropriated office, Bill Leonard, vice president of CBS News, acted as the ranking news executive, in contact by telephone with Salant and Small in New York. From them the line of communication should have gone upward to Schneider and Taylor at Black Rock. Taylor's presence on the scene marred the neatness of the diagram, and created some confusion about the command channels.

It had long ago been decided that, whenever the presidential crisis reached its climax, the schedule would be brushed aside and CBS News would be continuously on the air for the evening. Plans for that day had long been made. Since January there had been in preparation a Nixon "political obituary," a video-taped record of Watergate and the other scandals that had driven him from office. I had worked on it with Mark Harrington, a talented young producer from the special events unit in New York. Each few weeks it was updated for the latest developments. Now the thirty-five-minute video tape, with

Harrington's expertly edited highlights and my narration, was screened by Russ Bensley, the overall producer, who would direct that night's coverage from the control room. The "Nixon scandals," as the project was informally called, drew general plaudits that were conveyed to me by Harrington. Bensley's only concern, given the uncertainty about the night's events, was about being "locked" into a thirty-five-minute tape, and so he asked Harrington to prepare an alternate version that would divide the production into three installments for more flexible deployment.

I meanwhile returned to brooding about how Nixon would orchestrate his resignation, whether he would, indeed, make a demagogic attack on the news media. It occurred to me that being on the air continuously from the end of the Cronkite show at 7:00 P.M. and not knowing until nine o'clock what Nixon would say would mean two hours of enormous tension. I wrote out some tentative thoughts about what I might say if asked to participate in a panel discussion during that period.

The message that President Nixon seemed to be transmitting through Senators Barry Goldwater and Hugh Scott, who had seen him the evening before, I wrote, was that "the President's decision will be 'based on the national interest.' " My notes continued:

> The emphasis on "national interest" was clearly a way of setting the stage for the new decision. The President was, in effect, saying his original view had been that history could best be served by completing the painful process of impeachment, but that he now realized, as the process went on, the damage to the national interest.
>
> Assuming that Mr. Nixon has now decided to step down, there is also a vital "national interest" in how he chooses to explain his decision to the nation. He could do it in a way that would deepen confusion and bitternesss. Or he could do it in a way that would help, in his own 1969 words, to "bring us together." No one understands better than this reporter how great the temptation may be for a new version of "You don't have Dick Nixon to kick around anymore." It is easy to imagine his harking back to President Johnson's decision not to run for reelection and saying that he is the second President in succession to be forced out of office by the power of the news media.
>
> There is no doubt that Mr. Nixon's preoccupation with the press as

the source of his troubles runs deep and rests on genuine conviction. He may believe that the principal guilt lies not with him, but with the press. But if he chooses to emphasize that, he will be inciting those who still believe in him, and he will be enormously complicating the task of his successor. Whatever personal satisfaction he could gain from that final jab at his tormentors, he may consider what the national interest really requires of him tonight.

My notes were, by my own standards, shamelessly editorial in tone, and if I were to say anything like this on the air, it would have to be labeled "comment." Amid the chaos in the CBS News office, early in the afternoon, I noticed Taylor sitting alone at his borrowed desk, and sat down to resume our discussion of the morning. He told me that the problem was moot — he had now been assured that the Nixon resignation speech contained no attack on the news media. Relieved, he was planning to return to New York. It was the first indication I had heard anywhere of what the President would say that night. Indeed, there was at that point so much uncertainty about Nixon's intentions — and whether he was fully in control of himself — that we were instructed not to go beyond saying on the air that "President Nixon is *expected* to resign."

What Nixon would say that night was as impenetrable a secret as any in Washington's history. Nobody outside a few family intimates and insiders had any inkling at that moment of what he planned to say or not say. Whence had come Taylor's reassuring word that a rejected President would not turn on the afflicting news media? Long after the event, I sought the answer to that question and found it receding into a strange welter of contradictory accounts.

•   •

To discover when Nixon had made up his mind on the tenor of the speech, I went to Ray Price, who had drafted it. He said that the general conciliatory theme had persisted through all five drafts and had been in the President's mind from the time he had decided to resign. When that moment had come was hard to fix. "Mr. Nixon had been working for some time on how he was going to leave. Like any decision, you go uphill, you go downhill. You're sixty percent decided, then you're ninety percent decided. That's why you can't pinpoint the exact moment the decision was made. But, as to its substance, there never was anything other than just that one speech." The rumored "nonresignation speech" — in which Nixon would apologize for everything and throw himself on the mercy of the American people — had been a blind, a "make-work project" for Price's assistant, Ben Stein, to get him out of the way. The "real" speech had remained closely held until shortly before delivery, seen only by family members, Chief of Staff Alexander Haig, and Ron Ziegler.

How, then, did a significant clue to its nature get to Taylor early in the afternoon of August 8?

Taylor, now out of CBS, told me in his modest office in New York's RCA building late in 1976, "Let's see now . . . Sandy Socolow told me he had it from the White House — from Ken Clawson."

Clawson, former White House communications director, recovering from a stroke, told me in the basement study of his house in Washington's Virginia suburbs that he had been told of the general tenor of the speech in the morning by General Haig. "I had lunch with Socolow at the Sans Souci restaurant. Dan Rather was with us, as I recall it. I said that the President wasn't going to lambaste the media or anybody "

Rather told me that he had seen Clawson and Socolow at lunch at the Sans Souci, with another CBS person whose identity he had forgotten, but was himself having lunch at a separate table with Tom DeCare of the White House press office, who was speculating on the possibility that Nixon might "flip." Rather said he was left with the scary feeling that Nixon might just go berserk on the air.

Socolow told me that he did not have lunch at the Sans Souci, did not recall talking to Clawson at all that day, had no memory of knowing anything in advance about the Nixon speech or conveying any impression of it to Taylor. Furthermore, said Socolow, in a subsequent conversation, he had checked with Rather, who no longer remembered seeing him or Clawson at the Sans Souci.

Salant recalled receiving a call from Taylor in the morning expressing belief that a major part of Nixon's speech would be an attack on CBS and another call from Taylor in the afternoon with the reassurance that there would be no such assault. But Salant remembered Taylor attributing his information to his own "good contact in the administration." Salant had passed on the word to Socolow in Washington, so Socolow could not have been the original source. Salant had speculated at the time that Taylor's contact was his good friend William Simon, Secretary of the Treasury. Or perhaps it had been Ken Clawson, because subsequently Taylor had called Salant to recommend Clawson for a job with CBS News.

It was back to Clawson and Taylor again!

Clawson told me that he had been friendly with Taylor, who had come to his home for a party on the night of the 1973 Nixon inaugural. Indeed, said Clawson, Taylor had the reputation in the White House of being "one of us," having served on the Nixon campaign committee in Rhode Island in 1960 while at Brown University. Clawson, however, had no recollection of having talked to Taylor on the fateful day of the Nixon resignation — though his stroke could have blotted out memory of a telephone conversation. He still clearly remembered lunch with Socolow, though perhaps without Rather.

Taylor told me he did not remember having talked to Clawson that day — it conceivably could have happened without his remembering, but wasn't likely. If Salant said that Taylor referred to an administration source of his own, there is no reason, said Taylor, to challenge Salant's recollection. But, if Taylor talked to someone in the Nixon administration, he cannot remember having done so. His best recollection remains his original recollection that he heard it from Socolow, who mentioned having gotten it from Clawson.

Confusing? A piece of White House information vital to a television network filtered through the corporate capillaries that day, and no one seems able to establish how it entered the CBS bloodstream. August 8, 1974, was a day to remember — but, for some, not to remember too closely.

• •

The atmosphere at CBS was strained as "Nixon night" neared. While I was reading a news ticker, Socolow came over and urged me not to be "vindictive." When I objected that this sounded like a reflection on my professionalism, Socolow assured me I was not being singled out, but that this precautionary word was being passed to all correspondents.

About the same time, I became aware that advance line-ups listing correspondents who would participate in panel discussions and interviews did not include either Fred Graham, who had been covering recent Watergate courtroom proceedings, or myself. Nor did the line-up include the much-praised "political obituary." It was as though the events that had brought Nixon to this juncture had been suddenly deemed irrelevant to the dénouement. Graham and I were later permitted to broadcast specific stories on Nixon's legal and financial position after resignation, but neither of us was included in the more broad-ranging discussions about the significance of his resignation.

At nine o'clock, I listened to President Nixon from the control room. "It has become evident to me that I no longer have a strong enough political base in the Congress . . . because of the Watergate matter I might not have the support of the Congress that I would consider necessary . . ." He sounded like a British prime minister resigning for lack of support on a policy issue. I wondered who would point out that he had been, in a phrase once used by John Connally, "dis-elected" by the American people, that it was national "non-confidence" in his willingness to tell the truth, not parliamentary nonconfidence in his programs, that had finally driven him from office.

The "Checkers" speeches had not worked — including one more he was reportedly still thinking of trying just days before his resignation. The game was over, and it was not because of the "Plumbers" and the "Huston Plan" and the "dirty tricks." Americans would have accepted all that as justified by national security or condoned by politics as usual. If only he had confessed in time, and not continued relying on his ability to manipulate the American people! He had lost not because of what he had done, but because he could not be believed. Who would explain that?

Cronkite was saying on the air, "And so, Richard Milhous Nixon has resigned as the thirty-seventh President." Dan Rather rushed in from the White House to join the final instant analysis of President Nixon. "Aren't you coming into the studio?" he asked. I said I was not on this panel. "I can't believe it," he said.

Sevareid was now on the air saying, "On the whole, it seemed to me as effective, as magnanimous a speech as Mr. Nixon has ever made. And, I suppose there'd be many, even among his critics, who would say that perhaps, that few things in his presidency became him as much as the manner of leaving the presidency. Certainly no attacks on his enemies — none on the press, as we did have from Vice President Agnew a year ago when he resigned . . ."

"It certainly was a conciliatory speech," commented Cronkite.

Were my colleagues analyzing historic import or simply reflecting relief over some horror averted?

Dan Rather told me, more than two years later, that he had felt relief because of his earlier fear that Nixon might throw away his prepared speech and do something irrational.

On the air, Rather said, "Walter, I think it may very well go down, when history takes a look at it, as one of Richard Nixon's, if not his finest, hour . . . He did give — and I would agree with, Walter, what you said — he did give to this moment a touch of class. More than that, a touch of majesty . . ."

Only Roger Mudd, speaking from Capitol Hill, dissented from the chorus of thanksgiving: "Just from a pure congressional point of view, I really wouldn't think that was a very satisfactory speech. It did not deal with the realities of why he was leaving." He went on to say, ". . . there is still to be accounted for in the country, it seems to me, a sizable body of opinion that would rightfully ask: Is the President of the United States really to be beyond the law? That, if certain crimes were committed and certain laws were violated, then somebody ought to be punished for them . . ."

Rather said that most people would not want "to shoot at lifeboats," and concluded, "My own decision is: I don't think that the American people, nor the Congress in the end, will want to pursue Richard Nixon if it can possibly be avoided."

I would have spoken differently, but what concerned me more

than what my colleagues were saying was what was happening in the control room. Producer Bensley sat looking at a dozen monitors, giving him a selection of interviews and reports to be put on the air from the studio, Capitol Hill, New York, Chicago, or the West Coast. Behind him were medium-level executives, on the telephone with higher-level executives and making suggestions to Bensley in terms like "If it's nation-healing we want, why don't we have an interview with . . ." "A good nation-healing bit would be . . ." Nixon had stated in his speech, "The first essential is to begin healing the wounds of this nation." It was as though CBS was taking its cue from him. The network seemed to forget that this resignation under fire was not an inexplicable tragedy like the assassination of President Kennedy. If then it had accepted the role of consolation, now it assumed a mission of conciliation, grateful that Nixon had spared his television enemies.

I went home that night deeply disturbed, trying to sort out what part of my feelings were simply wounded ego at the minor role I had played at a historic moment — the climax of my Watergate story — and what part rested on a judgment that CBS had copped out, had succumbed to Nixon's last act of manipulation, had been so terrified about what he *might* do to us that the network let him stage-manage his own departure, consigning to some Orwellian memory hole the journalists, the film, the facts that would remind America of *why* he was going.

That weekend, as it happened, I was scheduled to go on vacation. As during previous summers, the Denver *Post*'s television critic, Barbara Haddad Ryan, met me for an interview at the Denver airport during a stopover en route to Aspen. She asked me about what she called "the strange performance" of CBS, about the marked difference between Mudd and Rather. I said it was "professionally unethical" to talk about colleagues individually, but I was willing to state, as a general view, that I saw the task of the journalist as information and analysis, not the fulfillment of any purpose, however laudable.

"It's wrong," I said, "to take on the role of nation-healers as it is to take on the role of nation-wounders. That is the job of others, and we report it. If history requires that we do analysis, we must do it even if some people don't want to hear it . . . It is not for us to join in *any* process of manipulation. The media were accused of manipulation against Nixon, which was not true. We should also not engage in manipulation *for* him . . ."

In her column, Mrs. Ryan surmised that "nation-mending" might have accounted for the "curious absence" of the CBS "senior Watergate correspondent" from the network's special programming.

• •

The more I brooded about the night of August 8 the more I felt that the issue was not the words of individual correspondents, but the way CBS coverage had been tilted away from straight journalism by management's code signals and "climate control" in the control room. It epitomized what had always troubled me most about television — the sense of unseen corporate hands at the levers whenever the company considered its own vital interests at stake.

Such an issue had almost led to a break between CBS and myself as early as February 1969. Salant, in a rare direct intervention in the news operation, ordered the Cronkite show to delete parts of my broadcast summarizing a study of television by President Johnson's National Commission on Violence. The study found that violence on television affected the attitudes of Americans and that some, after years of exposure, might be more likely to engage in violent behavior. The conclusion was obviously not welcome to the broadcasting industry, but it emerged from one of a series of studies on violence that I had been reporting as they appeared. Salant flared up when I told him that he should avoid interfering precisely because the subject was television; at one point he threatened to discharge me for having impugned his motives. The incident blew over, as most such incidents did. The Nixon resignation, however, was more than an incident.

On January 17, 1975, during a "bull session" with students at Duke University billed as "Press the Press," a long leading question was put to me. A student asked why CBS had "gone soft," why Watergate experts like myself had been so obviously brushed aside, why Sevareid and Rather had spoken so strangely. The question, coming so close to my own feelings, led me to vent my suspicions with unpremeditated candor. I said that CBS executives, fearing an attack on television, had been relieved to learn — by means not immediately clear to me — that there would be no such attack; in a kind of tacit truce, they had reciprocated by soft-pedaling Nixon's wrongs and establishing a general atmosphere of sweetness and light.

An inaccurate summary in the student newspaper, *Duke Chronicle,* caught the attention of Kevin Phillips, a one-time Nixon campaign assistant, who was editing a Washington news letter called *Media Report.* Phillips published a totally distorted version of my remarks, quoting me as saying, ". . . CBS wanted to establish a 'truce' and told commentators (Rather, Sevareid and Mudd) to go easy in their post-speech remarks." I had not mentioned any instructions nor named correspondents, but had spoken of management. Shortly thereafter, on February 5, Bill Small, now director of CBS News, came to Washington, invited Mudd and Sevareid to lunch and denounced me as having maligned them, thus deflecting a challenge to management into a feud among correspondents.

Since that day, Sevareid has not spoken to me. He rejected my offer to clarify the episode, writing me that he wanted no clarification, but "your personal apology and your public retraction of your remarks about me and the others in the place you made those remarks." When *New York* magazine, in a profile of me in June of that year, referred to the Duke speech, Sevareid enlisted Cronkite and Rather (Mudd refused to go along) in a letter to the magazine that charged "slander" and said, "The notion that executive orders at CBS News were handed down to 'go soft on Nixon' and that those of us who felt constrained from whipping an obviously beaten man behaved in response to such orders is false."

More serious was the CBS reaction. On Small's instructions, Socolow issued an unprecedented memorandum to me, stating, "We expect you in each instance in the future to obtain written permission for lecture, and other non-CBS activities, from me, or Bill Small or

Richard Salant. In the matter of public speaking appearances, we shall require texts of your proposed remarks before such written permission will be granted."

This meant, it was made clear, that I was forbidden to give newspaper interviews or engage in any ad lib public discussion. Astounded, I consulted a lawyer to learn if CBS could enforce such a gag rule. The answer turned out to be — yes, it could. I had waived my free-speech rights in signing the standard show-business contract containing a clause originally intended to keep "talent" from endorsing commercial products or appearing on other networks. The clause says that "artist's services shall be completely exclusive" and that "artist will not perform services of any nature . . . except with the prior consent of CBS."*

I canceled one lecture, and threatened half-seriously to announce in another that the text had been cleared by censors — like my broadcasts from Moscow. Finally, I asked for a meeting with Salant. To him I acknowledged indiscretion at Duke, and promised to be more restrained in the future, but said that I could not accept "prior restraint" on my personal utterances in public. Instead, I offered to provide him with tapes of all talks and interviews, leaving him to take whatever disciplinary measures he considered necessary. As often happened after a heart-to-heart talk with Salant, he lifted the "advance permission" order, returned the first tape I sent him and said that the incident was closed.

I had no illusion, however, that anything would ever be the same again, having broken the cardinal rule of avoiding public criticism of my employers. Resentment of my temerity went far beyond Salant's domain — to the corporation I had challenged. Television, for

---

*In an April 1975 speech — at Duke University, by ironic coincidence — Chief Judge David L. Bazelon of the U.S. Court of Appeals for the District of Columbia, asserted that such contractual provisions may be "contrary to public policy represented by the First Amendment and hence unenforceable." An "exclusivity" clause, he said, "can be used to prevent network reporters from disclosing news items which they have uncovered but which the network has decided not to report." The effect of such a provision, he continued, could be to maintain "the network's monopoly on the sources as well as the actual reporting of news, and thus the network may prevent the reporting of information it considers damaging to its economic or other interests."

complicated reasons arising from its sensitivity as a licensed and regulated medium, its reliance on the good will of its affiliates, its own internal tensions, seems unable to tolerate debate and criticism in its own ranks, directed toward itself.

Least of all could television open itself to an examination of corporate influences over news operations. John Schneider told me in 1977 that he had long resented my speeches reported to him as being critical of CBS, but he was vague about how the concerns of CBS, Inc., were conveyed to CBS News. He described his relationship to units subordinate to him in these elliptical phrases:

"Authoritarianism is not the way you get anything done. What you feel is pressure from peers and subordinates and superiors. What you're trying to do is to maintain leadership, but it has to be done harmoniously. There is institutional pressure that comes from beneath as well. What they expect of their leader can be an enormous amount of pressure. Maybe they want their leader to do something. The easiest way is to do nothing. But sometimes the apparatus won't permit that."

In 1977, Salant told me that he had made the decision about the policy to be followed for the Nixon resignation. Although he had been in close touch with Schneider, although he had talked to Taylor of the fear — later allayed — of a Nixon attack on television, Salant said that the decision was his own. It was he who had ordered the killing of the "political obituary" that reviewed the Nixon Watergate scandals. It was he who had given instructions to Bill Leonard in Washington to "emphasize continuity in government, not jump up and down in glee on Nixon's body, but concentrate on the transition." Unfortunately, Salant added, he should have known that on the rare occasions he issued instructions for coverage of a news event, they might be carried too far. "People went further than I intended," said Salant, apparently himself unhappy at what he had seen on CBS that night.

CBS never forgave me for criticizing the way it pulled its punches on Nixon. Nixon — in his manner — subsequently made a gesture of détente toward me. When the ex-President in September 1974 went to the hospital suffering from phlebitis, my son, Jonathan, then seven, asked me to mail an illustrated get-well card he had fashioned. It was signed, "Jonathan Schorr (son of Dan Schorr)."

Eventually, Jonathan received a reply from Nixon, expressing thanks. The letter concluded, "If only you and the other young people of your generation can grow up and mature without experiencing the horrors of war, my greatest goal during my years in the White House will have been achieved. Perhaps you will choose to follow in your father's footsteps, and, if you do, I trust I will live long enough to observe you on television."

Nixon later gave me permission to quote the personal letter to my son.* It was a graceful way to say that we were no longer adversaries. My adversary relationship within CBS turned out to be far more obdurate.

*Nixon himself referred to the correspondence in his television interview with David Frost. In a passage that was not broadcast, Nixon commented on the exchange: "Everybody knows that I don't like Schorr and Schorr doesn't like me. But I like kids and so does he."

VI

TRANSITION

MY FAMILY'S VACATION fell, with accidental symmetry, precisely between President Nixon's resignation and his pardon. The Colorado Rockies, with Aspen seminars and music festival concerts, tennis and hiking, provided a literal and figurative cooling off from the battles of Washington. Distance and altitude lent enchantment and detachment. As though from a remote planet, we watched President Ford, on August 28, telling a news conference that Nixon had suffered enough, and that a pardon would be considered when the legal process had run its course.

Presidential pardon was on the agenda for discussion next night when Herman and Sarah Wouk, summer residents of Aspen, held a dinner party — a gastronomic and logistical feat of kosher cuisine a hundred and fifty miles from the nearest source of kosher meat. Historian Henry Steele Commager thought that a pardon would have to wait until after a trial. Chief Judge David Bazelon of the U. S. Court of Appeals believed it could come at any time after indictment. Having done some recent research on the subject, I ventured the opinion that the President could grant a pardon at any time, but found no support.

On a crisp Sunday morning, three days later, browned and somewhat de-traumatized by three weeks in the restorative mountains, I took off with my wife and two children in our rented car for the Denver airport, headed for home and an uncertain professional future. As the car chugged up to Independence Pass, I turned on the radio and heard the breathlessly delivered bulletin that President

Ford had unexpectedly announced an unconditional pardon. My wife had to assure me that I was not suffering from some aberration of altitude. My five-year-old daughter, Lisa, who used to call the Watergate building "Watergate Breakin" because that was the way she had heard it since infancy, wanted now to know what a pardon was. Her older brother, Jonathan, asked, "What's Nixon being pardoned *for*, Daddy?" I said, "He's being pardoned for what he did, but because he's being pardoned, we may never know all he did."

In Washington, I worked at first on miscellaneous aspects of the transition. The Ford administration displayed a curious mixture of desire to bury the past and refusal to put it behind. At times, the new President seemed to be acting in the "we shall continue" spirit of carrying on after an assassination. The Democratic-controlled Congress, on the other hand, assumed a stern posture of keeper of the new post-Watergate morality.

President Ford tried to give Nixon back his tapes; Congress passed a law to block the move. The President tried to ease Nixon's return to private life with $850,000 in transition funds; Congress held indignant hearings, pointed with outrage to payments for a butler and maid, and cut the request in half. President Ford announced a program of limited clemency for Vietnam draft evaders and deserters; his congressional opponents scornfully compared that to the full and unconditional pardon for Nixon.

The pardon, precluding Nixon testimony under oath, left the Watergate investigation incomplete, and history cheated. For the next two years — and during his 1976 election campaign — Ford would defend the swift pardon, denying that any "deal" was involved. The evidence led me to conclude that Nixon had left office with good reason to believe the pardon would soon come — that he had orchestrated his own departure more skillfully and successfully than was generally believed.

A variety of "inside" accounts, fed by anonymous former Nixon aides with their own reputations to salvage, have created the legend of an emotionally crumbling Nixon who was gently eased out of the White House. His chief of staff, Alexander Haig, emerged in these stories as the strong unofficial "acting President," who held together the White House, and perhaps the country, until Nixon came to accept the inevitability of his resignation. There is reason to distrust that picture of Nixon, who tended to function at his coolest and best in crisis — indeed, sometimes seemed to derive stimulation from his own predicaments. His way of insulating himself from the reality of the threat he faced was to become immersed in the game plan for how to deal with it. His life was tactics. One of the tactics — which he espoused as a useful tool in international negotiation — was the appearance of irrationality, the threat of unpredictable behavior. He had admired its use by General De Gaulle.

President Ford's own testimony before a House Judiciary subcommittee in October 1974, intended to refute rumors of a pardon deal, provides clear indication of how Nixon obtained the tacit assurance he wanted.

On August 1, General Haig presented Vice President Ford with five possible courses of action that President Nixon might take. He could fight impeachment; he could try to negotiate a compromise arrangement for censure instead of impeachment; he could use the 25th Amendment to declare his "inability" to govern, stepping out temporarily and returning to office at his pleasure; he could pardon himself and resign; he could pardon the Watergate defendants and himself and resign. These were all courses that President Nixon still could take, and any of them would throw the country into tumult. That was made clear to the Vice President.

Haig mentioned one other possibility — "a pardon to the President should he resign." Ford was thus, in effect, being told that only by assuring a pardon could he induce Nixon to leave quietly. At this crucial point, Ford said he "inquired as to what was the President's pardon power." Haig, prepared for the question with a legal memorandum in hand, said there was "authority to grant a pardon even before any criminal action had been taken." Ford said he needed time to think, to talk to a lawyer, and "I also said I wanted to talk to my wife before giving any response." He seemed fully aware that he was faced with a momentous decision.

The next day the Vice President told Haig that, after thinking the matter over, he had decided he could not answer the question about a pardon. Furthermore, he wanted nothing he had said the previous day (whatever that might have been) to play any part in "whatever decision the President might make." Ford carefully explained to Haig why he had to take this position: the Vice President "should endeavor not to do or say anything which might affect his President's tenure in office." In other words, Ford could not be in the position of making a commitment that would advance him to the presidency. Haig said he was "in full agreement with that position."

One cannot learn, from Ford's account, what glances, what studied looks may have accompanied that exchange, but Haig was presumably able to tell Nixon that Ford understood the powers of pardon, had expressed no objection to using them, but for technical reasons could not make a formal commitment at that point. For a Nixon with no real bargaining power left, he had done pretty well! Perhaps America had been numbed by too many revelations of "smoking guns" to be struck by subtler understandings.

•   •

Pardoned, Nixon left America to wonder about the aspects of Watergate that remained unresolved because the special prosecutor had to drop the investigation for lack of sufficient evidence. Unresolved also was the question of what dark cave had spawned the White House's twisted little intelligence beast. The Nixon television interview with David Frost in May 1977 provided no clarification. These were some of the important questions that America was left to puzzle about:

1. Why Watergate? Astonishingly, although Watergate had given its name to an era of American history, there remained doubt about the reason for the original break-in. No one else took seriously what the burglars had been told — that it was to get evidence of Castro financing of the McGovern campaign. Persons as close to the planning as Jeb Magruder, John Dean and Charles Colson had denied to each other knowing the real motive. John Mitchell had acted as though he had reluctantly approved what President Nixon or Haldeman had wanted.

Certainly, the routine files of the Democratic National Committee and the chitchat of its employees would not have warranted the high-risk operation. Indications were that the principal target was Democratic Chairman Lawrence O'Brien, but for reasons that could only be surmised. Possibly it was because O'Brien, as a former consultant to Howard Hughes, was feared to have information about Nixon-Hughes connections, or alternately, because it was hoped to get adverse information about O'Brien.

2. Who obstructed justice? Howard Hunt had learned from Gordon Liddy, and passed on to the five Cuban American burglars, the promise of hush money, and mighty efforts were made to honor the pledge. It is not known — and Liddy has not said — who made the original commitment. Nor is it known who erased the eighteen and a half minutes of tape of the Nixon-Haldeman discussion of June 23. Only President Nixon, Rose Mary Woods and Stephen Bull, a Nixon aide, had access to the tape at the time; Woods and Bull entered denials. It has also not been established who was responsible for the apparently deliberate doctoring of the White House transcripts — words substituted for other words, whole damaging phrases and paragraphs excised — that President Nixon presented to the House Judiciary committee as "the whole story."

3. What was the secret exchequer? There were indications of a hidden treasury maintained for President Nixon aside from his campaign funds. The President had hinted at it when he told John Dean on March 21, 1973, that he could lay his hands on a million dollars in cash for payoff purposes. During his first month in office, in February 1969, he had given instructions through John Ehrlichman that "major contributions" should be raised outside Republican channels, to be handled through Bebe Rebozo so that "we can retain full control of their use." Money was sought from millionaires like J. Paul Getty, Howard Hughes and the Boston shipping operator Tom Pappas. Was there, in effect, a system of levying tribute from American tycoons, and perhaps from foreign governments? And if so, were any favors given in return?

4. What was the CIA connection? There had been indication of a CIA cover-up at the time of Watergate. Director Richard Helms had issued orders intended to impede the FBI's investigation. Although President Nixon did not get the CIA's full cooperation, he appeared to think the agency could be called upon for assistance. He told Haldeman, "We protected Helms from one helluva lot of things." Why did the CIA provide Howard Hunt with a psychological profile of Daniel Ellsberg, and, later, with spy gear? Why were so many of the Watergate participants formerly associated with the CIA's Cuban adventures?

Watergate had not been a single, compartmented aberration, but one manifestation of the abuse of power. The Huston Plan of 1970 for spying on antiwar dissidents suggested that, among the intelligence agencies, there existed known blueprints for illegality — physical surveillance, break-ins and electronic eavesdropping — which had been requisitioned by the Nixon White House for its political purposes. The blueprints remained and had perhaps been used for other purposes. It was as though just one layer of a little-known secret government had been peeled off the onion, leaving many more layers to be exposed. The Nixon pardon and President Ford's haste to end the "nightmare" of Watergate had halted the process of disclosure of how secret agencies of government had threatened the rights of Americans. Along with the administration, the cleansing of government was in a state of transition.

•   •

On a personal level, my own transition looked bleak. Perhaps once too often had I applied to my own industry the skepticism it wanted me to direct toward news targets; perhaps once too often had I permitted my criticism of CBS policy to become known "on the outside." There was no new show, no new documentary, no new assignment on the horizon. It was the way broadcasting traditionally dealt with the ill-regarded — by letting them sit around and handle random chores.

Without Watergate, I was back on "general assignment," which I found depressing. I heartily disliked being the available "body" when the news editor looked around the room for someone to go out with a camera crew for a trivial interview. In television news there are two ways to escape the general assignment fate. One is a "beat," a clearly demarcated area of coverage, normally associated with a "base," like the White House, Capitol, State Department or Pentagon, but sometimes simply a subject, like the environment, the economy — or Watergate. The other escape route is graduation to an "anchor spot," presiding over a daily, weekly or special broadcast. Seeking to smooth my own transition, though aware I was in disfavor, I decided to explore the possibilities.

In New York, I met with Bill Small. His long-standing ambivalence about me had perhaps been best illustrated by his remark as we descended wearily from the podium at the end of the Republican convention in Miami Beach in 1972, where he had worked closely with me as my producer, buttonholing politicians to be interviewed, wheedling air time from the control room, fetching sandwiches. As he had metamorphosed back to being my boss, he said, "Schorr, you're a son-of-a-bitch, and I only wish I had half a dozen sons-of-bitches like you." By the fall of 1974 he had seemingly changed his mind about the latter half of that observation. When I said that I wanted some steady assignment, he asked what I had in mind. Recalling that I had handled the economic beat during the Nixon wage-price freeze, I suggested that it might be worth reviving this assignment in the light of the new Ford antiinflation program. Small said he would think about it and, a few weeks later, announced the appointment of my friend George Herman to that position.

"Anchorman" was a role I had never considered for myself, partly because of my judgment that I lacked the youth, the smoothness, the middle American diction, the "performer quality" that television demanded; partly also because the work was freighted with the mechanical and show-business requirements that I liked least about television and was remote from direct contact with the breaking news that I liked most. Yet, "anchoring" was the easiest passport to recognition and the safest haven from exile to the "general assignment" pit. There were forms of anchoring that combined well with direct participation in the preparation. The best such outlet for developing one's own concepts, writing one's own script and doing one's own field work was "CBS Reports."

"CBS Reports" had been the reincarnation of the Murrow-Friendly "See It Now." Since the days of Murrow and Howard K.

Smith, the policy had been to have no permanent anchorman, but to have the programs narrated by the correspondents who had worked on them. Because of my enthusiasm for these documentaries, I had anchored more "CBS Reports" broadcasts than any other correspondent. In Europe, I had worked on programs about East Germany and the Adenauer years in West Germany, about Romania and Czechoslovakia. In the United States, I had narrated documentaries about air pollution, health insurance, school financing, child neglect and infant autism. They were part of what I had regarded as my true role — until Watergate had come along to make me an investigator of political crime.

Even with Watergate, I sought to make time for "CBS Reports." In progress, when President Nixon resigned, was a program, two years in the planning, whose concept I had helped to develop, dealing with the overuse of prescription drugs. Between Watergate assignments, I had flown to the West Coast to interview pharmacologists and health experts. Completion of the documentary needed a few weeks in New York screening the assembled film with the producer, agreeing on the structure, and writing the script.

In the wake of the Nixon resignation, Dan Rather had been removed from his White House assignment. Word of this leaked before CBS was ready to announce it. The shift became the subject of newspaper controversy, with suspicions being expressed that Rather had finally been sacrificed to the rancor of conservative CBS affiliates. Vigorously denying this, CBS asserted that Rather was being promoted to a long-planned new role — Murrow's heir as the permanent anchorman of "CBS Reports."

Since, in fact, there had been no long planning, hasty action was needed to lend credibility to the announcement. Frank Mankiewicz, who had been trying unsuccessfully to interest CBS in an interview he had filmed with Fidel Castro, was told that now CBS was interested — if it could quickly be made part of a "CBS Reports" program for Rather. Sylvia Chase, who had been working on a program on cancerous agents in water, was advised that the project was being transferred to Rather. I was told that my program on prescription drugs would be narrated by Rather — with due credit to me for my interviews.

I wrote a bitter protest to Burton Benjamin, the executive producer in charge of documentaries, an old friend with whom I had worked, in years past, on some of his own "Twentieth Century" productions. Benjamin replied that the decision had been "difficult," but said, "Had you sat at this side of the desk, you might have understood better: a new permanent reporter for 'CBS Reports.' Essential: get him involved at once. Otherwise, if we waited for new projects, we would not appear until March. Untenable for me and grist for the mill of those who claim this was a thinly veiled ploy to get him out of Washington."

I replied to Benjamin that I still considered the action to be "a small piece of larceny." Al Wasserman, the producer with whom I had been cooperating, telephoned me to say that he had protested, in vain, against the transfer of the project on which we had worked together for months and hoped that I would understand that he had no alternative but to complete it as ordered. Rather, when I next spoke to him, indicated his own embarrassment, asking me to understand that such decisions were beyond his control.

What was most discouraging to me was that no new CBS doors were opening and an existing one had closed. If I was to find anything in CBS worth doing, it would only be — as in the past — by seizing upon some story that accidentally crossed my path and hoping that it would develop into a regular beat.

VII

SON OF WATERGATE

IT WOULD BE NICE, for a literary touch, to say that I experienced a feeling of déjà vu early in October 1974, when I embarked on the temporary assignment that became the son of Watergate. Full disclosure requires me to say that, at the time, it looked like just one more project in matching a newspaper story. In the *New York Times,* Seymour Hersh had been running a series of exposés of clandestine CIA operations in Chile aimed against the late President, Salvador Allende. The Hershes had been at our home for dinner on a Sunday night — they were neighbors, their children the ages of our children — and Sy had been talking excitedly about the CIA coming under increasing scrutiny since Watergate, apparently no longer as immune to leaks as it had been for so many years. By coincidence, three days later, on October 2, Socolow, my bureau chief, said that Small would like me to work on developing a television version of the Hersh stories on Chile.

The information was in the Hersh stories, but the problem was how to tell for television what had happened in secret, far from the eye of any camera. Mark Harrington, who had worked with me on the ill-fated Nixon "political obituary," went off to research background film on anti-Allende demonstrations in Chile. I started looking for "talking heads" — persons who would be willing to appear on camera to say something about the operation, from involvement or simply knowledge. Telephone calls to CIA officers, active or retired, drew unanimous refusals.

Eventually I was lead to Ray Cline, who had recently resigned as

State Department chief of Intelligence and Research in a dispute with Secretary Henry Kissinger. Cline, who had previously been deputy director of the CIA, had not given interviews before, but said he was now prepared to make a public statement. In his office at the Georgetown University Center for Strategic and International Studies, Cline talked smoothly and articulately while the camera ground behind my shoulder. He said that in the State Department he had always opposed involvement in Chile, and the CIA had also resisted it, but the operation had been imposed on the agency by President Nixon and Secretary Kissinger. Cline charged that they had operated together "on an Olympian plane," carrying out a policy that only the two of them seemed to understand.

Nathaniel Davis, who had been in Chile as ambassador in 1973 when Allende fell, was an old friend from our earlier days in Moscow. His dark suits, narrow ties and air of rectitude concealed a lively independence of mind that had taken us on some interesting off-the-beaten-track trips in the Soviet Union, and later taken him into the Peace Corps. Davis would subsequently become assistant secretary of state for Africa, and when Kissinger saw me at the swearing-in ceremony, he joked to Davis, "If I had known Dan was your friend, I wouldn't have appointed you."*

Because I trusted Davis, I asked him to tell me, for my own information, how much truth there was to the *Times* stories about Chile. Over lunch at the dowdy Cosmos Club on Massachusetts Avenue, he said that the CIA was not involved in any of the strikes or demonstrations that had led to the coup against Allende, but only in trying to keep alive the democratic opposition to him.

The next morning, a Saturday, in response to my earlier request, I was telephoned from the White House and asked to stand by at home for a possible appointment with Kissinger. An hour later I was told to come quickly — he had a few minutes. In the cramped, blue-carpeted West Wing office of presidential security adviser, which he seemed to prefer to his palatial State Department suite, Kissinger paced back and forth, venting his anger about leaks.

---

*Kissinger later may have wished he *hadn't* appointed him. Davis resigned in 1975 in protest against CIA intervention in Angola and was shunted off to the embassy in Berne, Switzerland.

Hersh, on top of his original disclosures about Chile, had created a new stir with the report of a sharp Kissinger reprimand to David Popper, the current ambassador in Santiago, for having protested to government officials against the torture of political prisoners. He was helpless, said Kissinger, to tell the facts that would correct the impression the story had created — he had reprimanded Popper only for cutting across the delicate negotiations which the secretary himself had been conducting with Chilean diplomats at the United Nations for an easing up on prisoners. Kissinger admitted that Popper had not been informed about his negotiations, which made me wonder how much Popper's predecessor, Davis, had known of what the United States had been doing in Chile.

Only toward the end of our conversation did I tell Kissinger of the filmed interview with Cline, confirming that the operations against Allende had taken place and pinning the blame for them on Nixon and Kissinger. When I quoted Cline as saying he had opposed the CIA program, the secretary of state expressed surprise. "Did Ray say that?" he asked mildly. "That isn't my recollection of his role. I'll have to look it up."

On the following Monday, I went to Kissinger's scheduled news conference at the State Department in order to get his filmed reply to my question on Chile. (He had declined to give a filmed interview.) Smoothly, as though to deny any personal role in covert activities, he said that the CIA needed to be brought under better control. Hardly back at my office, I received a call from Kissinger's executive assistant, Lawrence Eagleburger.*"Would you be able to come back to the Department and see me?" he asked in a mock German accent. "Heinrich has instructed me to show you some interesting captured documents." What Eagleburger showed me were three top-secret papers, written in 1970 and 1973, listing various recommendations for opposing Allende — bribing members of Parliament to vote against his election, subsidizing opposition parties, and working with the Chilean military. Appended comments of State Department officials supported or criticized various courses of action. Each of the docu-

---

*Named ambassador to Yugoslavia by President Carter in 1977.

ments, however, bore handwritten remarks by Cline, generally supporting strong action and scoffing at the doubters. Regarding those concerned about the morality of bribing Chilean parliamentarians, for example, Cline wrote, "In the world of *Realpolitik*, sensitivities are not so tender and people are more concerned with who wins power rather than morality."

Cline had clearly miscalculated if he had thought he could attack Kissinger without having the book — and the secret files — thrown at him.*

A requested appointment with William E. Colby, director of the CIA, came through — with a warning that it would be for background only since the director never gave on-the-record interviews. The last time I had visited the CIA had been at lunch with Director Allen Dulles in 1958 in the agency's old building near the State Department. I had known CIA officers in my foreign travels; some of them had been not only sources, but friends. It was in a more skeptical role that I now made my first visit to the woods-shrouded CIA compound at Langley in suburban Virginia. Down the road past the guard post, with its blinking red warning lights, there stood a typical functional federal building, with a few distinctive touches. One was a statue of Nathan Hale, the founding spy. Another was the honor roll in the lobby of the CIA dead, with almost every other line blank for covert agents anonymous even after death. There was also, since I had arranged to film my "stand-up" in front of the building, a conspicuous sign in the lobby, "CBS FILMING," serving as a signal to all hands to stay out of camera range. Outside the building, I found myself facing an acre of emptiness — a frozen vista.

Having filmed my narration, I was taken up to Colby's office on the seventh floor in an elevator that opened to a security man's key and led almost directly into his suite — cream-walled, businesslike

---

*A staff report of the Senate Intelligence Committee in December 1975 revealed that the CIA had conducted a "two-track" program in Chile. "Track 1" covered efforts to oppose Allende's election by political and economic methods. "Track 2," ordered directly by President Nixon and known only to the White House and the CIA, involved the CIA in playing a direct role in organizing a military coup. In 1977, Cline told me that it was Track 2 that he had opposed, but because the information was still secret at the time of the interview, he had been unable to be specific. He said that this had enabled Kissinger to make him look deceptive by showing me his comments on Track 1.

and unostentatious. Everything about Colby struck me as a little less than expected — slighter of build, softer of voice, lower in key. He gave a pat little talk about how covert activities had sprung from the cold war, tapered off with détente, but were still necessary as a capability. I interrupted to say that I could not see him doing himself any harm by saying these things on film. He shrugged. "Okay." A moment later we were on our way down in the elevator past stunned CIA officers for the first filmed interview with the director of Central Intelligence.

The interview gave some sense of how the agency was absorbing the damage of the revelations about the operation in Chile. "So, as a professional," I concluded, "you pick up the pieces and go on?" "It's part of the hazard of the profession," he replied, playing perfectly the laconic role of the intelligence professional.

We assembled a two-part "enterpriser" on the CIA and its covert operations; they ran on the Cronkite show on October 17 and 18 to warm approval by the CBS producers.

Two months later Sy Hersh broke a new story. It disclosed that during the 1960s the CIA had maintained files and conducted surveillance over antiwar protestors and left-wing groups. I read the piece at breakfast and called Hersh to congratulate him. He said he had been working on it for two years. A few minutes later I had a call from my office saying that I should immediately pursue the surveillance story.

Our coverage was, at first, the cliché of predictable reactions — those in Congress who should have known stating indignantly that they had not known, the CIA saying it wouldn't say anything, the White House announcing that President Ford had called for a report. Within two days, however, the story took an unpredictable turn. On the morning of December 24, the word spread from the CIA that James Angleton, chief of counterintelligence, had resigned. The improper surveillance program had been under his jurisdiction — the implication seemed obvious.

Routed out of bed by a call from my office, I looked in the telephone book for Angleton, whom I had never heard of before, and drove to his home in North Arlington, Virginia. Cameras were already staked out on his lawn, but no one had tried to ascertain if he was home. My ring was answered by a groggy-looking, stoop-shouldered man in pajamas, who pointed at the Washington *Post* on his doorstep, on which I was standing, and said, "I certainly didn't expect you, Mr. Schorr, to trample on the press!" Encouraged by the recognition and the good humor, I asked if I could come in. "Well, I've been up all night," he said, "and my family is away, but I can offer you apple juice or Sanka."

Whatever the home of a chief counterspy is supposed to look like, this one resembled the home of a somewhat disorderly professor. Strewn about were books in many languages, mementos of Italy and Israel, worn rugs, pictures of his wife and two children. He agreed to talk to me, but not before the camera because he would be in mortal danger if recognized. For the next four hours — interrupted by telephone conversations in English, French, Italian and a "Shalom" for someone at the Israeli Embassy — he rambled discursively about a worldwide Communist conspiracy, managed by the Soviet KGB, which had lulled the West into believing in fictitious splits in the Communist camp. "The Nixon-Kissinger détente bothers me deeply," he said. Each time I asked him about improper CIA activities in the United States, he went off on further elaboration of his cold war theories. When I tried to bring him back to a question put fifteen minutes earlier, he said, "I am not known as a linear thinker, Mr. Schorr. You will have to let me approach your question my way."

Angleton painted the Palestinian Arab nationalists as pawns of a Communist conspiracy. He made a great point of having recognized, in a photograph, the escort of Yasser Arafat on a visit to Lenin's tomb in Moscow as an important KGB officer. Strewn through his recital were hints that Angleton's trouble with his agency had stemmed not from any CIA activity in this country, but from an internal conflict over the Middle East. For twenty-two years, as a sideline to his counterintelligence work, Angleton had taken personal charge of the "Israeli account."*He had plucked that "ac-

*Intelligence personnel, who like to call their agency "the Company" and its agents abroad "assets," also refer to cooperating intelligence services as "accounts" — as part of the jocular notion that they are all engaged in business.

count" from the pro-Arab Middle East Division, but lately had observed a growing pro-Arab drift in his agency, for which he blamed Kissinger. On Kissinger's request, Colby had canceled a trip to disputed East Jerusalem, during a visit to Israel, in order to avoid offending the Arabs. Angleton had rebuked Colby for yielding to Kissinger and thus offending the Israelis. It was then that Colby had called in Angleton, taken away the "Israeli account," and told him that it was time to prepare for "new leadership" in the counterintelligence office.

Colby had also casually mentioned that Angleton would be implicated in an impending Hersh exposé of the domestic surveillance activities. In fact, though the program had nominally come under Angleton's authority, it had been handled by his deputy, Richard Ober, reporting directly to Helms. Angleton, who had witnessed enough agency intrigues to understand when he had become the object of one, was ready to retire quietly — staying on the payroll for a time as a "consultant" in line with the usual CIA practice of easing the pain of ejection and minimizing hazardous resentments. The leak of his resignation two days after the *Times* story had made him appear the culprit of the spying on Americans. The episode sounded like material for a John Le Carré novel about the faithful spy thrown to the wolves to spare the headquarters embarrassment.

Angleton voiced no open complaint about his treatment, but he defended Helms who, he said, had only started keeping files on Americans because of presidential instructions. "Helms was deeply victimized," said Angleton. "He was set up as a scapegoat for Nixon."

It was now noon, and Angleton, still in pajamas, excused himself to dress, saying he had to go to the office. He repeated that he could never allow himself to be photographed, and I cautioned that he could hardly avoid being glimpsed by the cameras still waiting on his lawn. He shrugged, donned his diplomat-style black coat and fedora, walked out the front door and slowly across the lawn, then stopped directly in front of the three network cameras as though hypnotized. In some haste I picked up our microphone lying on the ground. Four hours of Angleton views were in my mind, but not on film.

"Why did you resign?" I asked.

"I think the time comes to all men when they no longer serve their countries."

"As determined by whom?"

"By themselves and their superiors."

Another reporter asked, "Did you jump or were you pushed?"

"I wasn't pushed out the window," said Angleton cryptically, recalling heaven-knew-what covert operation somewhere back in his thirty years as a secret agent. And then the nonlinear thinker, his cover and career blown, stumbled into his blue Mercedes, looking back with a dazed smile as his car left the driveway.

•   •

The disclosure that America's foreign intelligence agency had brought home its bag of espionage tricks to practice against American dissenters caused a public stir in a way that a covert operation against a distant South American regime had not. It twinged the Watergate-raw "invasion of liberties" nerve that the Ford administration had been trying to assuage. Most jarring to President Ford, who was on a skiing holiday in Vail, Colorado, was that he had not known about the CIA improprieties. He demanded of the agency an immediate explanation. Colby needed only to put a covering letter on a report of the CIA's own inspector general, which had been withheld from the White House for more than two years. Six pages long, with voluminous annexes, it was ready two days later, on Christmas eve. It contained nothing about Angleton, who was being fingered for the press that morning as though he were the central figure.

Colby wrote, "Dear Mr. President: This report is in response to your comments on the *New York Times* article of December 22nd alleging CIA involvement in a 'massive' domestic intelligence effort . . ." The burden of the CIA's red-faced defense was that it had not been "massive."

Colby gave the report to Secretary Kissinger, who was flying out to Vail, and also told Kissinger of some other activities that the agency had never before confided to the secretary or to the White

House. In Vail, President Ford announced that there was no *current* CIA spying in the United States and that he would soon decide what to do about the past improprieties. He was giving unusual public emphasis to a matter that the White House would normally have been expected to soft-pedal. Hardly back in Washington, the President announced on January 4, 1975, that a "blue ribbon" commission, headed by Vice President Nelson Rockefeller, would conduct a sweeping inquiry into CIA domestic operations in violation of its charter. The administration seemed anxious to seize the initiative, perhaps to head off a potentially more troublesome congressional investigation — a standard defensive tactic. President Nixon had also talked to John Ehrlichman, on March 27, 1973, about the idea of a presidential commission as a way of averting a Senate investigation of Watergate. The difference was that President Ford, unlike Nixon, seemed worried not about exposure of deeds in his own administration, but activities long buried.

The CIA had long lived comfortably with congressional oversight committees so complacent as to leave doubt about which meaning of "oversight" was intended. In the hope that congressional curiosity would remain within these safe confines, a series of hearings was quickly arranged before the intelligence subcommittees of the Senate and House armed services committees, which had legislative responsibility, and the subcommittees of the Senate and House appropriations committees, which were supposed to keep track of the CIA spending that had never appeared in any public budget. Chairman John McClellan emerged on January 15 from a hearing of his Senate Appropriations subcommittee, pronouncing himself "satisfied." Chairman John Stennis next day came out of a hearing of his Armed Services subcommittee saying he saw no need for any special investigation.

By prearrangement, McClellan released to the waiting press the testimony that Colby had read to the subcommittee — the first public statement on how America's international spying had come home to roost. With great emphasis on denying that surveillance had been "massive," Colby conceded most of the specific allegations — that the CIA had kept files on ten thousand Americans, had opened mail to and from the Soviet Union, had wiretapped twenty-one Americans while checking on security leaks, and had broken into the homes of some of its own employees and ex-employees.

Colby was one of two CIA figures on whom my professional life would focus in the ensuing year. He was in the position of clean-up man, the officer who had come back to Langley from Vietnam to uncover headquarters irregularities not of his own making, for which he had to give an accounting. At the center of what Colby was accounting for was his predecessor, Richard Helms. In contrast with the soft-spoken, bespectacled Colby, Helms was any casting director's model for a spymaster — tall, athletic, quick-witted and sardonic. Not being a member of the journalistic coterie whom Helms occasionally briefed at discreet social gatherings, I had only seen him once. Seventeen months earlier, in August 1973, he had testified before the Senate Watergate Committee, suavely explaining how he had resisted President Nixon's efforts to misuse the CIA in the Watergate cover-up. He had managed to convey the impression that, for his rectitude, he had been ousted by Nixon and exiled to the embassy in Iran. Reporters had wondered if he had been spared total dismissal only because of White House fears of what might lurk in his dossiers.

Helms' position had begun to look more ambiguous as subsequent disclosures indicated how he had tried to steer the FBI's investigation of Watergate away from his agency and had ordered his subordinates to keep quiet about the assistance given to E. Howard Hunt. Throughout the Nixon debacle, however, Helms had hunkered down in Teheran and kept out of the crossfire — even when his name figured in the climactic "smoking gun" tape that sealed Nixon's fate. Talking six days after the Watergate break-in of enlisting the CIA in the cover-up, Nixon had seemed to believe that Helms was under obligation to join the conspiracy. "Well," he had told Haldeman, "we protected Helms from one helluva lot things." Haldeman had replied, "That's what Ehrlichman says." That intriguing reference had gone unnoticed when the transcript was disclosed during the cataclysm of August that led to Nixon's resignation. Four months later, during the Watergate cover-up trial, I had run into Haldeman, lunching with his son in a delicatessen near the Federal Courthouse, and asked what Helms had been "protected from." Haldeman said he did not know. "I was just trying to hold my own in the conversation with the President, and I never did know what Ehrlichman knew about Helms."*

Back now in Washington to appear before the Rockefeller commission and congressional committees, Helms was clearly someone to be sought out for television. It took two days simply to discover where he was living — in a rented house in the northwest corner of Washington. His wife, Cynthia, sounded gracious as she promised that he would return my call. Predictably, he did not call me, and was "out" when I tried him at various odd hours.

Reluctantly, I agreed with assignment editors on a stake-out. At eight o'clock on the morning of January 10, 1975, I was outside Helms' house with a camera crew, its equipment stored in the trunk until I could arrange with Helms for an interview — a method I preferred to the surprise onslaught. In front of the house a State Department car waited, motor idling, at the wheel a foreign service officer to escort the ambassador. I rang the doorbell, and a uniformed maid said the ambassador had not yet come downstairs. A moment later the State Department officer, now aware of my presence, entered the house, immediately came out again, and drove around the

*In September 1971, Ehrlichman, seeking anti-Kennedy material for the 1972 campaign, obtained files from Helms on the Bay of Pigs invasion, the Cuban missile crisis, and Vietnam. A file on the coup against South Vietnam President Ngo Dinh Diem was considered by Helms to be so sensitive that he would only surrender it directly to President Nixon, saying, "There is only one President at a time. I only work for you." It was apparently knowledge of Helms' involvement in some of these events that Nixon believed he could use to force CIA cooperation. For example, he told Haldeman to make the point about Watergate that "the President believes that it is going to open the whole Bay of Pigs thing up again," an allusion that Helms was presumably supposed to understand.

In March 1976, in a written interrogation, the Senate Intelligence Committee asked the ex-President what he had meant about protecting Helms. Nixon replied that he had only been referring to the support given Helms when the CIA was fighting in the courts to block the publication of a damaging book by a disaffected former employee. The Senate committee was skeptical that routine assistance in a national security matter could have been regarded as placing Helms so much in Nixon's debt as to enlist him in an obstruction of justice conspiracy.

Ehrlichman's 1976 novel, *The Company,* caused intensified speculation. It had a Nixon-like President preparing to make political use of the complicity of a Helms-like director of the CIA in an assassination. The CIA director then forced the President to destroy the incriminating documents by threatening to expose a Watergate-like wiretap conspiracy. It ended with the CIA director demanding and obtaining an ambassadorship. Ehrlichman says, wryly, "Much of my novel isn't true."

corner into the alley behind the house, picking up Helms at the back door and swiftly driving off. The master spy had eluded me, but I wondered why he found evasive tactics necessary when it would have been so much easier for him to come out the front door and say, "No comment."

Three days later, as the Rockefeller Commission began its closed hearings, I saw the elusive Helms again. In the White House annex known as the Executive Office Building (which, in the days of smaller government, had housed the State, War and Navy departments), press and cameras waited in the corridor outside the office of the Vice President, watching the goings and comings. The first day's witnesses were Secretary of Defense James Schlesinger, who had succeeded Helms as CIA director in 1973; the incumbent, Colby, who had succeeded Schlesinger; and finally, Helms. My journal noted, "Helms, starting to look more and more like a defendant, comes running downstairs without a word."

Helms' first statement came three days later when he appeared, side by side with Colby, in closed session before Senator Stennis' subcommittee. There was clearly tension between Colby, cast in the role of accommodating confessor of CIA sins, and Helms, defender of the CIA faith. Unlike Colby, Helms admitted no questionable activities. His statement, released later by Senator Stennis, charged "distortion" and "irresponsible attack" by the news media. The CIA, he said, had become involved in surveillance of Americans only out of concern about "extreme radicalism" and "in response to the express concern of the President." That made Presidents Johnson and Nixon look responsible without quite claiming they had issued any orders.

While Senator Stennis addressed the cameras in the corridor, I saw Helms slip out of the hearing room and head rapidly for the elevator. A mobile CBS camera crew was standing by, ready for the latest evasive maneuver. We pursued Helms through the garage of the Senate Office Building and caught up with him striding briskly up First Street toward Constitution Avenue. I walked alongside him, holding a microphone, while an athletic cameraman walked backward, a few paces ahead of us, trying to control a shoulder-mounted camera. It was not much of an interview, but it was Helms' first. He said he did not feel like a defendant, had not done anything illegal and hoped that investigation would reveal that he had done his job well.

Further trouble awaited Helms a week later as he appeared before the Senate Foreign Relations Committee for his fourth round of testimony in nine days. Some of his testimony in his ambassadorial confirmation hearings two years earlier now looked shaky. He had denied passing money to Allende's opponents in Chile. He had denied any domestic spying. He had denied any pre-Watergate involvement with Howard Hunt. Now he blamed misunderstood questions for previous contradictions, saying that he "had no intention of lying" about the money given to anti-Allende groups in Chile. The Foreign Relations Committee asked the Department of Justice to look into the possibility of perjury.

The conflict over the testimony was part of a greater drama — personal and institutional — in which Helms was involved. In his six and a half years as CIA director, and two decades before them in covert operations, he had been accustomed to operating in undisturbed secrecy, answering only to sympathetic members of carefully selected subcommittees to whom, in his words, he could go "privately and say, please, will you pull back on that, we are getting into a very sensitive area." His appointment as ambassador had exposed him to questioning in a less clubby atmosphere. When he came before the Senate Foreign Relations Committee in February 1973, his very first exchange with Chairman William Fulbright underlined the strangeness of the occasion. Fulbright asked where he had worked for the past ten or fifteen years, and Helms replied, "I was working for the Central Intelligence Agency, Mr. Chairman." Fulbright noted, "I am glad to have it come out at last. This has all been classified." Helms had to face questions about much trickier matters — covert operations and Watergate connections — that he had never dreamed he would have to discuss on the record. Nor could he anticipate that in the aftermath of Watergate, information would soon be filtering out to expose his deceptions.

Other exposures — once inconceivable — threatened Helms. In

May 1973, after his departure from the CIA, his successor, Director Schlesinger, had become worried whether other improprieties like the CIA's assistance to Howard Hunt would emerge to embarrass the agency. In a "Memorandum For All CIA Employees," Schlesinger said, "Anyone who has such information should call my secretary (extension 6363) and say that he wishes to talk to me about 'activities outside CIA's charter.' " The result was a thick report with 693 items of questionable activity, some dating back a quarter century. In various versions the report was titled "Flap Potential Report" and "The Family Jewels." In August 1973, Colby, who meanwhile had succeeded Schlesinger, issued a series of directives, cutting back on "Operation CHAOS" — the domestic surveillance program — and other activities that might cause the agency trouble if exposed. No word of "The Family Jewels" was given to President Nixon — who might have used it for pressure against the CIA — nor was President Ford told about it until some of it came to his attention through the *New York Times.*

The report that Kissinger had brought to Vail told the President about "Operation CHAOS," about wiretapping, mail opening, experiments with behavior-influencing drugs and break-ins on the homes of CIA employees and ex-employees. Kissinger advised President Ford that, troublesome as the incidents at home had been, considerably more disturbing things had happened abroad. As soon as he was back in Washington, the President called in Colby for an unpublicized briefing. It was the next day that he announced the presidential blue ribbon panel, with an executive order that restricted the investigation to "activities conducted within the United States."

On January 16, the President had a White House luncheon for Publisher Arthur O. Sulzberger and editors of the *New York Times,* reciprocating a lunch they had given for him in New York. Toward the end of the conversation, the subject of the Rockefeller commission came up. One editor, noting the predominantly conservative and defense-oriented membership of the commission, asked what credibility it would have. President Ford explained that he needed trustworthy citizens who would not stray from the narrow confines of their mission because they might come upon matters that could damage the national interest and blacken the reputation of every President since Truman.

"Like what?" asked the irrepressible *Times* managing editor, A. M. Rosenthal.

"Like assassinations!" President Ford shot back, quickly adding, "That's off the record!"

The *Times* executives went into a huddle in their Washington office and agreed, after a spirited argument, to keep the President's confidence. The Washington bureau chief, E. Clifton Daniel, Jr., disqualified himself from taking a position on the ground that he was the son-in-law of a President (Truman).

Word of the luncheon began to circulate a few weeks later. I heard that, in a discussion of the Rockefeller commission, President Ford had mentioned a problem concerning "assassinations." Because of the commission's mandate to investigate activities at home, I surmised that he had referred to assassinations in the United States. For two weeks, with the help of others in CBS News, I looked for clues to unsolved murders where the CIA's hand might have been involved. We checked with the New York police about missing Communist block diplomats who might have been intelligence agents. Several hours were spent on an unexplained automobile accident in Central Park in which two members of the Soviet delegation to the United Nations had been killed some years back. A great many interesting theories emerged, but no facts.

I was about to give up when, on February 27, a long-standing request for a background discussion with Colby came through. For a half-hour we talked of CIA and Watergate and other matters. Finally, I said, as casually as I could, that I had heard President Ford had a problem about the CIA and assassinations. Colby fell silent.

"Has the CIA ever killed anybody in this country?" I asked directly.

His reply was quick and even: "Not in this country."

"Not in this country!" I stared at Colby as it sank in on me that I had been on the wrong track, but had now been put unintentionally on the right one.

THE KREMLIN SHOW. Nikita Khrushchev's television debut—the interview that President Eisenhower criticized. In his office in May 1957, the Soviet chief, flanked by his interpreter, Victor Sukhadrev, faces a CBS "Face the Nation" panel including Stuart Novins, moderator; B. J. Cutler, Moscow correspondent of the New York *Herald Tribune*; and Daniel Schorr, CBS bureau chief, who made the arrangements for the history-making interview that brought the top Communist leader for the first time into "America's living rooms."

RED SQUARE REPORTER. Broadcasting from Moscow in the mid-1950s. "CBS seemed not at all displeased when I was periodically cut off the air... for defying censorship, and finally excluded from Russia altogether."

DIVIDED CITY. In Germany with CBS in the 1960s. Left, a "stand-up" in beleaguered Berlin during the building of the Berlin Wall. Below, interviewing Mayor Willy Brandt in 1962.

OUT OF THE FRYING PAN. On the floor of the riot-besieged 1968 Democratic convention in Chicago. A few days later, Schorr was suddenly ordered to fly to Prague, which was being besieged by Soviet tanks. "Chicken!" joshed Art Buchwald.

TELEVISION "STAKE-OUT." President Nixon's Secretary of HEW, Robert Finch, leaves Walter Reed Army Hospital in May 1970 after suffering a collapse amid internal departmental conflicts over the invasion of Cambodia. A few weeks later Finch was dropped from the Cabinet and was replaced by Elliot Richardson.

GOVERNMENT-TELEVISION SUMMITRY. Chairman William S. Paley leads a CBS delegation at an unannounced meeting with President Nixon, one of three such sessions with the major networks in March 1971. The head of CBS News is absent as Paley is joined by (l. to r.) Robert D. Wood, president of the CBS Television Network; Richard W. Jencks, president of the CBS Broadcast Group; Frank Stanton, president of CBS, Inc.; and John A. Schneider, executive vice president. Also present were the President's chief of staff, H. R. Haldeman; his special counsel, Charles Colson, who claims credit for arranging the meetings; and Herbert G. Klein and Ronald Ziegler, communications and press assistants.

NIXON FAIRNESS DOCTRINE: IF IT'S NOT PRO-ADMINISTRATION IT'S NOT FAIR

©1971 HERBLOCK

From Herblock's State of the Union (Simon and Schuster, 1972).

FBI "JOB" INVESTIGATION. Herblock was among the early skeptics when the White House claimed, in November 1971, that the FBI had only been checking on Schorr because he was under consideration for government appointment. It was one of the many cover-ups that unraveled along with Watergate, ending up as one count in the proposed articles of impeachment against President Nixon.

THE NEWS AND THE NOOSE. After a long campaign of White House pressure, CBS suddenly abolished "instant analysis" of President Nixon's television statements in June 1973, then reinstated it five months later as a result of widespread criticism. A cartoonist comments wryly on the position of CBS analysts—like Dan Rather, Schorr, and Eric Sevareid—told by their nervous bosses to go back to analysis as usual.

INSTANT ANALYSIS

Eldon Pletche, The New Orleans Times-Picayune

-PLETCHER-

Janice Ducasse. Courtesy of *Public Telecommunications Review*.

SHOULDER TO SHOULDER. Network correspondents—Sam Donaldson of ABC, Schorr of CBS, and Douglas Kiker of NBC—are confined to a tiny area outside the Senate Caucus Room to address their separate cameras during recesses in the 1973 Watergate hearings. During such an appearance, Schorr rushed on the air with the first list of the "top twenty" Nixon enemies, provided by John Dean, and discovered his own name among them.

United Press International.

ACCUSATION OF THE ACCUSED. Former Director Richard Helms, under investigation in April 1975 by a presidential commission in connection with CIA assassination conspiracies, turns on Schorr, who first broke the story, and accuses him of being unfair to the agency. In the corridor, outside camera range, Helms went further, calling him "Killer Schorr" and more obscene epithets.

Below, a cartoonist's interpretation of the Helms-Schorr contretemps.

MR. HELMS, AS FORMER CIA DIRECTOR, COULD YOU TELL US WHETHER THERE HAD EVER BEEN ANY DISCUSSIONS OF PLOTS TO ASSASSINATE FOREIGN LEADERS?

TATTLE-TALE, TATTLE-TALE, HANGIN' ON A PIGGY'S TAIL! NYYAA-NYAAHHH!!

Dennis Brack, from BLACK STAR.

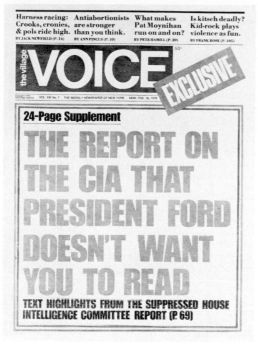

the village VOICE

EXCLUSIVE

VOL. XXI No. 7   THE WEEKLY NEWSPAPER OF NEW YORK   MON. FEB. 16, 1976   50¢

24-Page Supplement

THE REPORT ON THE CIA THAT PRESIDENT FORD DOESN'T WANT YOU TO READ

TEXT HIGHLIGHTS FROM THE SUPPRESSED HOUSE INTELLIGENCE COMMITTEE REPORT (P. 69)

THE LAST STRAW. Publication of the suppressed report of the House Intelligence Committee in *The Village Voice* in February 1976 climaxed the internecine war in the government over national security vs. disclosure, leading the House of Representatives to launch an investigation of Schorr's role and the source of the leak.

PRESIDENTIAL TARGET. At President Ford's press conference on February 17, "I sat in the last row while the President denounced the leaking of the Pike report. . ." It was the last time Schorr was at the White House for CBS.

"ANOTHER CONFRONTATION" was the way the front page of the Washington *Star* described a picture of Schorr in conversation with the new CIA director, George Bush, arriving on February 18 for testimony before a Senate committee. Though it was a completely friendly talk, the interpretation reflected the harsh spotlight on the CBS correspondent. That afternoon CBS took him off the air.

" The 'C' means 'Courage', which brings us to the 'B.S.!'"

Bill Mauldin makes a succinct comment on Schorr's suspension.

MAIL CALL. CBS suspension and congressional investigation start to reverse the tide of adverse comment. In their "mailroom," normally the dining room, Schorr and his wife, Lisbeth, are cheered as they sample the hundreds of letters and telegrams, noting that "the pile marked 'Pro' gradually climbed up to and then moved higher than the 'Anti' heap."

Below, an example of the hate mail on the "Anti" pile: an anonymous ill-wisher clipped this cartoon from an unidentified newspaper and sent it to Schorr after scrawling a vituperative anti-Semitic message beneath it.

CAUGHT

Tony Auth, *The Philadelphia Inquirer.*

THE GUSHER. "The idea of the massive machinery of Congressional investigation being geared up to track down one of the many Capitol leaks became the stuff for mocking cartoons…" Tony Auth's is a notable example.

The impending hearing, with its overtones of "witch hunt," also inspired these incisive cartoons:

Right: Tom Engelhardt in the St. Louis *Post-Dispatch*
Below: Tony Auth in the Philadelphia *Inquirer.*

'We Can Make Things Hot For You'

Engelhardt in the St. Louis *Post-Dispatch.*

'The charge against you, Mr. Schorr, is assault with intent to commit truth.'

Tony Auth, *The Philadelphia Inquirer.*

LAWYER-CLIENT RELATIONSHIP. Schorr meets with Joseph A. Califano, Jr., to work out legal strategy to cope with the House Ethics Committee investigation. "I could not have hoped for a better counsel... He seemed to respect me as a journalist almost as much as I respected him as a lawyer."

REPORTERS RALLY. Summoned by subpoena to appear before the House Ethics Committee and name his source, Schorr is supported by a nationwide petition campaign of news unions, climaxed by a press conference in the House Office Building on the eve of the hearing. Randy Furst of the Minneapolis *Star*, initiator of the campaign, checks messages from supporters while CBS News Correspondent Dan Rather listens to columnist Mary McGrory defending Schorr. Others who spoke were (below, left) Carl Bernstein of the Washington *Post,* I. F. "Izzy" Stone, and (right) Seymour Hersh of the *New York Times.*

PRELUDE TO CONFRONTATION. Schorr, with his wife and lawyer, wait on September 15, 1976, in the crowded hearing room for the First Amendment collision he had tried to forestall. Finally, the last of more than four hundred witnesses in the seven-month, $400,000 House search for a reporter's source, he is sworn in to testify about his role.

"Mr. Chairman and members of the committee...to betray a confidential source would mean to dry up many future sources for many reporters..."

"...your willful refusal will be deemed by this committee to constitute a failure to answer a question pertinent to the subject under inquiry, and will subject you to prosecution and punishment by a fine or imprisonment or both..."
(Chairman John J. Flynt, Jr., D., Ga.)

"...and...to betray a source would for me be to betray myself, my career and my life. And to say that I refuse to do it isn't quite saying it right. I cannot do it."

"...I support you a hundred percent — or if the vogue is a thousand percent, or whatever it is — in your refusal to disclose your source."
(Charles E. Bennett, D., Fla., member of the Ethics Committee)

DANIEL IN THE HOUSE ETHICS. COMMITTEE

EPILOGUE. After the Ethics Committee's retreat,
the view from the East and West coasts.

"...AND THAT'S THE WAY IT IS..."

"I leave CBS with sadness, but without rancor."

"Who?" I asked, still trying to sound casual, but, I fear, not succeeding very well.

"I can't talk about it," said Colby.

"Hammarskjöld?" A shot in the dark. The United Nations secretary general had been killed in an airplane crash in Africa in 1961.

"No, of course not!"

"Lumumba?" I was searching rapidly through musty attics of memory. The left-wing leader in the former Belgian Congo had been killed in 1961, supposedly by his Katanga rivals.

"I can't go down any list with you, sorry!"*

Without confirming anything about the past, Colby nevertheless wanted me to know that assassination was not currently a method being used by the CIA. It had been banned since 1973, after the post-Watergate internal investigation in the agency. He did not deny that the information uncovered in that investigation had been kept from President Nixon and — until it had been demanded two months before — from President Ford.

I returned to my office, my head spinning with names of dead foreign leaders. The imaginative political editor of CBS News, Martin Plissner, joined me in a brainstorming session. We recalled that former President Johnson had once talked about the United States as operating "a damned Murder, Incorporated, in the Caribbean." That brought up names like Che Guevara of Cuba, Rafael Trujillo of the Dominican Republic, and "Papa Doc" Duvalier of Haiti. With a gleam in his eye, Plissner mused, "How do we know it wasn't someone generally believed to have died of natural causes? Stalin? De Gaulle?" We realized that speculation was heading toward sheer foolishness, and gave up, leaving me to stew through the evening about an assassination story without a corpus delecti.

It suddenly struck me the next day that I had failed to perceive what my story really was. While lacking the names of victims (I still assumed there were some), I nevertheless knew a great deal — that

*Lumumba turned out to be close to the mark. A report of the Senate Intelligence Committee in November 1975 disclosed that the CIA had been plotting to poison Patrice Lumumba, but he was killed by others before arrangements could be completed.

the CIA had been involved with assassination of foreign leaders, had recently banned future plots, had not advised the White House, that President Ford, belatedly informed, was now trying to shield the information from public knowledge, and that this, in fact, might partially explain why a presidential commission had been appointed with such fanfare to focus public attention on the less sensitive issue of domestic CIA improprieties.

I sat down at the typewriter, and my script almost wrote itself. "President Ford has reportedly warned associates that if current investigations go too far they could uncover several assassinations of foreign officials involving the CIA . . ."

The script was subjected to considerable scrutiny by CBS News editors, producers and executives in both Washington and New York, but no one questioned that, however explosive, it had to be broadcast. I taped it for the Cronkite show and was given an unusually long two minutes for a "tell" story.

The official comment from the White House that night was, "There will be no comment." It was ironic that President Ford, worried about a leak, had become the source of the leak, even while expressing his worry. Two weeks later the President met with Vice President Rockefeller and asked him to add the subject of assassination plots to his commission's mandate. It involved a feat of contortionism since the mandate had been written specifically to exclude that subject.

On a rainy Sunday night in mid-March, I met Rockefeller at National Airport, as he arrived on his private plane from a weekend at his New York home in Pocantico Hills. The interview underlined the awkwardness of his situation. After talking to the President, he said, there could be matters connected with assassinations presenting "a possibility of deviation from the domestic code, in which case we would have the responsibility." What that meant, it subsequently developed, was that the commission was investigating those assassination plots that had involved significant activity and recruiting in the United States — the plot against the Dominican dictator Rafael Trujillo and especially the long series of conspiracies against Cuba's Fidel Castro. The anti-Castro plotting had gone on for years and was in progress in 1963 when President Kennedy was assassinated. Indeed, President Johnson, after having been briefed by Helms in 1964, had become convinced that the Kennedy assassination represented Castro's revenge for attempts on his life. So he had told his domestic staff chief, Joseph A. Califano, who now recalled it to me as a speculation worthy of renewed attention.

Adding another two months to its three-month term, the Rockefeller commission started a new series of hearings. Once again Helms was called from Teheran, this time to be interrogated on the subject he clearly regarded as his biggest secret of all. For two days he was questioned by the staff, and, on April 28, went before the full commission for four hours. Though, in a sense, my broadcast about assassination plots may have helped to spark the investigation that had brought Helms back, I was not thinking of it in personal terms as I waited in the corridor, with three or four other reporters, for him to emerge from the Vice President's office and to invite him to be interviewed before cameras staked out in the press room across the hall.

As I offered my hand in greeting, with a jocular, "Welcome back," Helms' face, ashen from strain and fatigue, turned livid. "You son-of-a-bitch!" he raged. "You killer! You cocksucker! 'Killer Schorr' — that's what they ought to call you!" Continuing his string of curses, he strode toward the press room, apparently already intent on making his first voluntary appearance before television cameras. I was flabbergasted by the personal attack and by his apparently uncontrolled behavior, uncharacteristic for an intelligence professional with the reputation of being the coolest in the business.*

A few minutes later, as I stood rather nervously at his side, Helms faced the cameras and gave a tempered version of his denunciation:

---

*Helms' outburst baffled many who had worked with him. Two years later Colby told me, "I never understood it. It was so totally out of character." Lyman Kirkpatrick, a former deputy director, said that not even during the Bay of Pigs crisis did Helms raise his voice or call anyone by an angry epithet. Thomas Powers, a biographer of Helms, wrote in *Rolling Stone* that "something in Helms broke" because the long-suppressed secret of CIA assassination plots, "concerning which he knew so much and would say so little," had been finally forced out into the open. There may, however, have been a certain element of premeditation. His wife told friends that, at breakfast before leaving Teheran, he had said he was going to denounce me in public when he got to Washington.

"I must say, Mr. Schorr, I didn't like what you had to say on some of your broadcasts on this subject. And I don't think it was fair, and I don't think it was right. As far as I know, the CIA was never responsible for assassinating any foreign leader."

"Were there discussions about possible assassinations?" another reporter asked, and Helms began to lose his temper again: "I don't know whether I stopped beating my wife, or when you stopped beating your wife — talk about discussions in government, there are always discussions about practically everything under the sun."

"Of assassinations?"

"Of everything under the sun."

"But you never answered my question," the reporter persisted.

"Well, I'm not trying to answer your question," said the former CIA chief, and strode out of the room.

I pursued him down the corridor, curious about his outburst. He would not pause until I said, "Mr. Helms, there are things you just don't know," a remark that turned out to be as irresistible to a CIA officer as to a reporter. I explained to him that it had been President Ford's luncheon indiscretion that had raised the assassination issue. Calmer now, he apologized for his corridor attack, which he hoped (in vain) had not been overheard, and said he had long admired my reporting, but that my "assassination" broadcast had simply been too much for him. We shook hands and talked of someday filming a long interview to put things in perspective — when he was free of all the investigations. Our quarrel was over. For the public it was about to start — on the news wires and the television evening news. The reconciliation never did catch up with the legend of a great feud. A week later Secretary Kissinger emerged from a session with the Rockefeller commission, calling out to the assembled reporters, "Where's Schorr? I have a new name for him."

The "feud" had one salutary effect — it attracted volunteer informants hostile to Helms and the CIA. The next morning, a retired air force colonel, L. Fletcher Prouty, telephoned to say he was so angry about Helms' conduct that he was ready to disclose a secret he had kept until now. As air force liaison officer with the CIA (a fact the CIA confirmed), he had provided a small plane in 1960 to fly two

Cuban exiles from Eglin Air Force Base, Florida, to the outskirts of Havana to try to kill Castro with a rifle equipped with a telescopic lens. In our video-taped interview, later broadcast on the Cronkite show, Prouty said that overseeing the operation was the assistant deputy director for plans — Richard Helms. This did not specifically belie Helms' carefully phrased defense that the CIA had not actually killed any foreign leader, but it suggested, at least, his knowledge of assassination planning.

This seemed to tie in with the reaction of Senator Frank Church, heading a Senate committee that was clearing the ground for its own investigation of the assassination issue. Church came out of Vice President Rockefeller's office on May 7, after a meeting on the investigation, with this cryptic remark, "When Helms says that the CIA never killed any foreign leader, that statement is correct, but not necessarily complete."

Church continued throwing out tease lines for the television cameras as though to maintain suspense about assassinations. On May 22, he called Colby's testimony "candid, but chilling," and, after the CIA director had completed three days behind closed doors, Church emerged to say, "It is simply intolerable that an agency of the United States government may engage in murder." It appeared that when the presidential commission completed its report on assassination conspiracies, it might have a critical Senate committee looking over its shoulder. Suddenly, President Ford ordered Vice President Rockefeller to drop the assassination issue and let the Senate committee handle that investigation. The official explanation was that there was not enough time to do it right. It was also clear that the plots involved vague and hotly disputed links to previous Presidents of both parties, making them a politically sensitive subject for a presidential report. At the outset, President Ford had expressed fear that the "assassination" mess could blacken the reputation of every President since Truman. It could also be a minefield for any President who had to judge his predecessors.

"Can I conclude," I asked Rockefeller when I caught up with him on Capitol Hill, "that you have decided not to steal the Senate's thunder, but instead to pass the thunder to the Senate?"

"A very reasonable conclusion!" said Rockefeller, laughing appreciatively.

I attended President Ford's news conference in the White House rose garden on June 9. My journal noted, "He seems very fidgety about the assassination business." The files, he announced, would be turned over to Senator Church's committee, but "under procedures that will serve the national interest," apparently meaning that the administration expected to retain some control.

The Rockefeller commission report — delayed by an intramural squabble about whether it should be released under vice-presidential or presidential auspices — was put out by President Ford's press office the next day. Although its domestic investigation seemed now overshadowed by the grim glamour of foreign plots, it was far from a whitewash. It documented the charges of domestic surveillance that had called it into being, describing "Operation CHAOS" as a program of checking on the foreign contacts of American dissidents that had started during the Johnson administration and expanded, under Nixon, until it had collected 13,000 files and maintained a computerized index of 300,000 persons and organizations. The program had gone beyond surveillance to penetration of dissident organizations. Some forty agents had been infiltrated into New Left groups that were planning to go abroad. CIA agents had been slipped in among the organizers of the 1971 May Day demonstrations against the Vietnam war. The CIA had investigated five newsmen and nine other American citizens.

The blue-covered report told of the twenty-one-year program of mail intercepts, principally between the New York post office and the Soviet Union — 2,300,000 items checked in one year and 8700 opened.*It revealed, for the first time, the program of testing LSD and other mind-altering drugs on uninformed subjects, one of whom — an Army Department employee — had committed suicide. His

*I was represented in those statistics, as I discovered in 1977 when I obtained portions of my CIA file through a Freedom of Information request. Eleven letters to me were inspected in 1956 and 1957 when I was stationed in Moscow. Several of them were from CBS. The CIA provided pictures of the envelopes, but said copies of the contents had been destroyed. One letter, from Max M. Kampelman, a Washington lawyer and friend, was noted as being "innocuous." Neither Max nor I can remember what the letter was about.

name — Frank R. Olson — would later emerge, and his family's suit would become a cause célèbre.

The commission did not find the CIA embroiled in Watergate, but concluded that the agency had complied with "improper" White House requests before Watergate, and afterward had destroyed possibly relevant files and given an "incomplete or delayed" response to the FBI and Justice Department. Soft, but meaningful language!

The report had a few cryptic lines about random eavesdropping on Americans in the course of testing new monitoring equipment. That was all that remained of a chapter on the Big Brother technology of the space age, most of which had been deleted from the public report at the last minute on White House instructions. The suppressed portion, I was told, described the new tools for picking up international and domestic communications carried by microwave, the electronic spying on telephone and teletype traffic of those named on White House "watch lists" and the computer-aided retrieval of messages triggered by a programmed name or subject.

"The Rockefeller report is just the tip of the iceberg," proclaimed that fertile phrasemaker Frank Church, reflecting the zest on Capitol Hill for picking up where the Executive Branch had left off. The "son of Watergate," like the parent Ervin investigation, held promise of rich political dividends.

The breach in the wall of secrecy that Congress now vowed to widen had already caused deep wounds inside the intelligence community. Many orthodox intelligence professionals were up in arms Colby's belief that salvation lay in cooperation with investigations ran up against ingrained convictions that an intelligence secret was forever and its disclosure close to treason. The struggle had become personified in the Colby-Helms conflict. Colby had provided most of the information that belied and incriminated Helms. He had referred some matters involving Helms to the Justice Department for criminal investigation.

We learned that Vice President Rockefeller had urged President Ford to discharge Colby as too forthcoming — with his commission, among others. The same plea, in more emotional terms, was made by Secretary Kissinger, so deeply involved with Helms that he could end up sharing his fate. The President, with more sensitivity to congressional feeling, decided that it would be dangerous to fire Colby until the investigations had run their course.

What lay ahead was the most traumatic secret of all — the assassination plots, which the White House had found too difficult to handle. That "assassination" had become a subject by itself was partly an accident of history; in practice, it was part of the larger issue of clandestine operations. An agency created in 1947 to find out for the President what was happening had developed into an agency trying to make things happen. Assassination — "executive action," or "termination with prejudice," or any of the euphemisms that please the bureaucrats — was simply the most extreme form of covert operation designed to influence the course of events in a foreign country.

When the nation came to understand the CIA's flirtation with murder, it would then understand a great deal about where the spymasters — and their political masters — went wrong.

VIII

THE ASSASSINS

EVERYTHING ABOUT assassination seems un-American. The word assassin comes from "hashish." The first assassins, almost a thousand years ago, were the *"hashshāshīn,"* the "hashish-users," a fanatical Moslem sect in Persia who considered murder of their enemies a sacred duty. Violence may be, in the words of the black militant H. Rap Brown, "as American as cherry pie," but for most Americans political assassination was an Old World phenomenon of bomb-throwing Bolsheviks and Balkan fanatics. Even though four Presidents fell to assassins' bullets and others were targets of assassination, the staff of President Johnson's National Commission on Violence concluded in 1969 that the general pattern was not one of conspiracy, but of "freelance assassins in varying states of mental instability." The wave of assassinations that cut down, in less than a decade, President Kennedy, Senator Robert F. Kennedy, Martin Luther King, Jr., Medgar Evers and Malcolm X troubled Americans deeply, making them wonder if this alien aberration was becoming a feature of American life.

Now, in the summer of 1975, there was the nagging suspicion that for *some* Americans, in some shadowy recess of government, the idea of assassination had long been a way of life. Because of this, Senator Church's committee, pushing on with the investigation from which President Ford had recoiled, found itself enveloped in tension. The CIA felt threatened by an assault on its deadliest secrets. The White House saw America's reputation in the world endangered. Senators found themselves walking a tightrope across an abyss of dark deeds plotted under two Democratic and two Republican Presidents. And, if all this were not neuralgic enough, they would end up with the nightmarish question of whether assassination cast upon the Cuban waters might somehow have returned to Dallas.

Under Presidents Eisenhower, Kennedy, Johnson and Nixon the CIA had been involved, in varying degrees, in plots and coups against eight foreign leaders:

In 1960, against Lumumba. He had threatened to bring Soviet troops into the Congo. Plans had been made, poisons shipped, access to Lumumba sought. But he was killed by others before the CIA plans could be realized.

In 1961, against the Dominican dictator Trujillo. His brutality had inspired fear of another Castro-style revolution. He was killed by Dominican dissidents, who had received American arms, though it was unclear whether these were the guns used.

In 1963, against Ngo Dinh Diem. His repressive actions had led to fear of an uprising in Vietnam. He was killed in a generals' coup, supported by the CIA, but without evidence that the United States wanted him dead.

In 1970, against General René Schneider, the Chilean army chief of staff. He had stood in the way of a CIA-supported military coup against Allende. The CIA backed a plan to kidnap Schneider, but apparently did not foresee that he would be killed when he resisted abduction. By the time of the coup against Allende in 1973, the CIA claimed it had "separated" itself from the military plotters.

Evidence indicated that some thought had been given, at various times, to the assassination of President François Duvalier of Haiti and President Sukarno of Indonesia, both of whom died in the early seventies of apparently natural causes.

The chief target was Fidel Castro of Cuba — the closest to America's shores, and the closest to America's trauma. He became the subject of much of the goings and comings of an unbelievable array of witnesses before Senator Church's committee, which had moved, for the purpose, into the securest hearing room on Capitol Hill — the windowless penthouse of the Joint Committee on Atomic Energy. Some of the activities surrounding the closed hearings are drawn from my journal:

June 13: Helms is back from Iran and before the Senate committee. To avoid reporters, he goes up the side stairs to the closely guarded hearing room. Senator Mansfield suggests on the Senate floor that Helms should stop shuttling back and forth from Teheran and stay here until his problems are settled.

June 18: Former Presidents have become involved in a game of political football. Despite President Ford's admonition against "Monday morning quarterbacking" about presidential responsibility for assassination plots, Rockefeller has said on NBC's "Meet the Press" that there was "White House knowledge and/or approval of all major undertakings." Senator Goldwater has said he wouldn't be surprised if President Kennedy knew all about plots against Castro. Senator Church: "I will have no part in pointing a finger of guilt toward any former President, none of whom are alive today." (He has forgotten, of course, that Nixon lives.)

June 20: Sam Giancana of the Chicago Mafia was killed last night. He was to have been a witness before the Senate committee to be asked about his part in the CIA plots against Castro. His one-time lieutenant, John Rosselli, subpoenaed for next Tuesday, is already in Washington, hiding out. Rosselli's lawyer quotes him as saying he doesn't think Giancana's murder was connected with his prospective Senate testimony. Vice Chairman John Tower, presiding over today's hearing, says, "The committee, of course, notes with interest that Mr. Giancana was done away with." Colby, after testifying, says the CIA certainly had nothing to do with Giancana's murder.

Trying to find John Rosselli, we call all the Washington hotels. There's a John Rosselli registered at the Watergate. The telephone in his room is answered by a man who says, "Mr. Rosselli is out playing golf," assuring me that this Mr. Rosselli is a businessman from Florida who knows nothing about the CIA or crime. Maybe!

June 24: This is the morning Rosselli is supposed to testify. At 7:45 A.M. I try the Watergate again. Same voice, but this time he answers to his name. Says he's waiting to hear from his lawyers about when he goes before the Senate Committee. I offer to supply the information because it's on the committee calendar. He says, "Let my lawyers do it. I pay them enough." Adamant about no interview, no picture.

The committee cooperates by slipping Rosselli,.with Capitol Police escort, up the backstairs, and later out through an unannounced exit. By having several camera crews and with walkie-talkie communications, we manage to catch him getting into his car, so there are pictures for the Evening News. Later, Senator Church indicates that Rosselli has told a vivid, but incomplete story about trying to kill Castro. Missing are the names of gangland associates, which he refuses to give, and the identities of those who set the whole thing in motion, which he does not know.

June 26: In a briefing outside the hearing room, Senator Church says there will be a report, but no open hearings on assassination plots because the committee doesn't want to "hold this sordid story before the world." Vice Chairman Tower adds puckishly, "I might say further that the matter of assassinations might be viewed in a broader context of other options that might have been available within the proscriptions of certain policy guidelines." When I say I'm not sure I understand him, Tower says, "Well, perhaps that's good."

July 18: Senator Church, at one of his regular posthearing briefings, says, "The agency [the CIA] may have been behaving like a rogue elephant on a rampage." Church, now obviously nurturing presidential dreams, would find life more comfortable if he could exonerate the Kennedys and pin all the assassination plots on Helms and his cloak-and-dagger band.

July 20: On CBS's "Face the Nation," Senator Richard Schweiker, a Republican on the Intelligence committee, disputes Church on the "rogue elephant" theory. "I think it's only fair to say there was no direct evidence that exonerates Presidents from assassination attempts . . . It's hard for me to conceive that someone higher up didn't know."

July 22: Lawrence Houston, retired CIA general counsel, while on Capitol Hill for testimony, agrees to be interviewed on film. He says that in 1962 he briefed Attorney General Robert Kennedy about the CIA-Mafia plots to kill Castro and that Kennedy's only reaction was that "if we were going to get involved with the Mafia again, please come to him first because our involvement with the Mafia might impede his drive against the Mafia in general crime-busting." Houston implies Kennedy didn't object to the assassination plans as such.

July 30: Senator George McGovern, back from Cuba, holds a news conference to release a Castro book recounting twenty-four plots against him, all allegedly CIA-inspired, the last of them in 1971 when Castro visited Chile. Confessions of would-be killers are quoted, mostly Cubans. The weapons pictured range from dynamite to a gun hidden in a television camera. McGovern notes that many of these plots were hatched after President Kennedy's pledge, in return for Bay of Pigs prisoners, to avoid future violence against Cuba. McGovern says that either the CIA acted on its own or President Kennedy broke his promise.

Soon afterward, in another room of the Senate Office Building, Robert Maheu, who has just completed testifying, holds a news conference. The former Howard Hughes lieutenant, one-time FBI agent, has told the Senate committee of his role in the anti-Castro plots. Before the press his elaborate gestures and long-windedness remind me of W. C. Fields playing a con man. Maheu's story boils down to this:

On the CIA payroll since 1954, he was asked, in 1960, as part of the planning for the Bay of Pigs invasion, to contact Rosselli to help remove Castro. He holed up in the Miami Beach Fontainebleau Hotel with Rosselli and Giancana, and there they planned how to poison Castro in Havana. It all sounds so silly that one wonders what kind of nitwits ran the clandestine operations. For his services, Maheu says he got $500 a month, but claims that his real motive was patriotism.

An interesting sidelight: Maheu says that in 1966, when Howard Hughes employed him in Las Vegas, his employer ordered him to set up a big covert operation for the CIA. Hughes "wanted this kind of protection from the government in case he ever became involved in any serious problem with any agency of the government." Maheu does not explain whether Hughes wanted the government vulnerable to blackmail or just in his debt.

September 22: The investigation of the plots to assassinate Castro has developed strange and tenuous links to the assassination of President Kennedy. The Church committee has evidence that the FBI destroyed a letter from Lee Harvey Oswald threatening to blow up the FBI office in Dallas if the bureau didn't leave his wife alone.

Also, the National Archives has declassified an FBI report on the Soviet defector, Lieutenant Colonel Yuri Nosenko of the KGB. He had handled the Oswald case in Moscow and defected to the United States in Geneva ten weeks after the Kennedy assassination. Nosenko told the FBI that the KGB considered Oswald mentally abnormal, possibly an American agent, and never tried to recruit him. When Oswald turned up in the Soviet Embassy in Mexico City in September 1963, trying to get a visa to return to Russia, the KGB vetoed it. Nosenko also said that after the Kennedy assassination, Khrushchev ordered a crash KGB investigation to learn if Oswald had returned to the United States in 1962 with any Soviet instructions, and was relieved to get a negative answer. John McCone, who testified before the Warren Commission as CIA director in 1964, never mentioned Nosenko. McCone happens to be in Washington today and tells me in an interview that the CIA didn't trust Nosenko at first because his coincidental defection looked so suspicious, but now the agency accepts the story as true. Nosenko was held incommunicado for three years at the CIA's Camp Peary, Virginia. The Rockefeller report, without giving his name, cited his case as a gross example of mistreatment of a defector.

Another document just released by the Archives is the top-secret 1964 memorandum for the Warren Commission reviewing conspiracy theories. In it William T. Coleman, Jr., and W. David Slawson, staff lawyers for the commission, traced Oswald's pro-Castro activities in New Orleans and said, "Simple retaliation is a motive which must be thoroughly considered" in the light of Castro's record. They suggested "additional investigation" along these lines, not even knowing of the plots against Castro. Coleman, now secretary of transportation, tells me on the phone that he was satisfied, in the end, that Oswald was not part of a conspiracy. Slawson, now at the University of Southern California, says he would have liked to have seen more investigation of possible influences on Oswald.

Senator Church says he is appointing a subcommittee, with Senators Schweiker and Gary Hart, to conduct a special investigation of what the CIA and FBI told the Warren Commission — and what they failed to tell. By an ironic coincidence, Senator Edward Kennedy appears before the Church committee today to testify that he is "morally certain" that neither of his brothers had any role in the plots against Castro.

October 28: Senator Church states that the White House is opposing the release of the completed report on assassination plots — even though President Ford last June asked the committee to conduct the inquiry.

November 2: Colby is fired by President Ford, along with Defense Secretary Schlesinger. Under fire from Rockefeller and Kissinger for candor that contributed to the troubles of Helms, Colby had clearly been on the skids, but his removal had not been expected until the congressional investigations were finished.*

November 3: The Church committee meets to consider a letter from President Ford demanding that its assassination report be held secret on the ground that it would "result in serious harm to the national interest and may endanger individuals." The committee votes unanimously to release the report, but, as a concession to Senators Tower and Goldwater, agrees first to give it to the Senate in secret session. Senator Church, denouncing the administration, says, "Concealment is the order of the day," and he has no doubt that Colby was fired for being too forthcoming.

Colby is called before the committee, and instead of walking briskly past our stake-out as he usually does, pauses for a brief on-camera interview. I ask if he thinks he has been too candid about disclosing his agency's past sins. "No," he says, "I don't think so. I think it was best to get rid of the past and start a transition to a

---

*Colby, Schlesinger's successor as CIA director, visited him that afternoon in his Virginia home, he later told me, and Schlesinger remarked, "Well, Bill, it looks as though Dick Helms outlasted both of us."

future structure of intelligence under the Constitution." Colby has drawn the line more clearly than ever before between his reformist philosophy and Kissinger-Helms secretiveness. Later, Senator Church calls Kissinger the moving force in the shake-up, adding, "He is the prime minister, the President taking care of the ceremonial functions."

November 4: As Colby is clearing off his desk, he gets a call from the White House. The President wants to see him tomorrow and will ask him to stay on for a couple of months. It seems that Ford acted too hastily in firing Colby, not thinking that the new nominee, George Bush, ambassador in Peking, cannot come back in the midst of arranging a presidential visit to China. Colby says okay — if it's understood that he remains in full charge.

November 19: In the spherical-roofed auditorium at CIA headquarters in Langley, Colby calls one of his rare news conferences. The assassination report is due to go to the Senate tomorrow morning and then be publicly released. Colby demands the deletion of the names of those who worked for the CIA, saying, "Exposure of our people to hostile and irrational retaliation is not within the tradition of our country." This must be to set the stage for some kind of last-minute maneuver in the Senate to block the report.

November 20: The names — which strangely include Giancana, Rosselli and Maheu — are indeed the springboard for a three-hour procedural debate in secret session of the Senate. The underlying issue is: Who decides what is secret? Robert Griffin, the minority whip, argues that confidential material received from the President cannot be released without presidential permission. The Senate overrides him.

In the Senate Caucus Room — Ervin "Watergate country" — the Intelligence committee assembles for a news conference, without the dissenting Tower, Goldwater and Baker, to display its first fruit — the first official report on America's cloaked daggers. There is some speechmaking. "We regard assassination plots as aberrations," says Senator Church. "The United States must not adopt the tactics of the enemy." Senator Mondale says, "We're not good at assassinations, and thank God!" As the news conference ends, I stand up before my camera in the back of the room to ad lib what will be the close of my report for the Cronkite show. I think back to my confrontation with Helms.

"It turned out as Helms said," I conclude, "that no foreign leader was directly killed by the CIA. But it wasn't for want of trying."

• •

Nothing says more about what was wrong with the CIA — the James Bond role-playing, the loss of touch with reality, the intellectual incestuousness of professionals shielded by their secrecy from any accountability — than the grand obsession with Fidel Castro. "We were hysterical about Castro at the time of the Bay of Pigs and thereafter," testified former Defense Secretary Robert McNamara. Between 1960 and 1965 the clandestine services nurtured eight separate plots to kill him, with various mixtures of absurdity and ingenuity.*

They started, in March 1960, wanting not to kill Castro, but just his public image. In the next six months, as planning for the Bay or Pigs invasion proceeded, they discussed spraying Castro's broadcasting studio in Havana with a mood-altering chemical; arranging to get him to smoke a cigar soaked with a disorienting drug before delivering a speech; dusting his shoes with thallium salts, which was supposed to make his beard fall out and thus cause him to lose face, so to speak, with his worshiping citizens. Speaking of worshiping, my favorite plot — nonlethal — was what someone in the CIA called "elimination by illumination." It was dreamed up by General Edward Lansdale, Robert Kennedy's coordinator for the hidden war against Castro. Never put into execution, the plan was to spread the word in Cuba of the imminent Second Coming of Christ, with the corollary message that Castro, the anti-Christ, would have to go. At the appointed time, American submarines would surface off the coast, sending up star shells, which would presumably inspire the Cubans to rise up against Castro.

*The CIA disclaimed credit for the twenty-four plots that Castro had told Senator McGovern about. In nine of those cases, the agency admitted "operational relationships" with some of the individuals, "but not for the purpose of assassination."

More serious — though hardly less absurd — were the various plots on the life of Castro unearthed by the Senate Intelligence Committee.

The Accident Plot. In July 1960, the Havana station chief of the CIA was startled to receive a message saying, "Possible removal top three leaders is receiving serious consideration at HQs," starting with Fidel Castro's brother, Raul. A Cuban agent was to be offered $10,000 for "arranging an accident." The agent, also promised a college education for his children in case of his own death, agreed to take a "calculated risk," limited to possibilities that might pass as accidental. The agent returned from meeting Raul Castro, reporting he had not been able to arrange the accident.

Poison Cigars. In October 1960, experts in CIA's Technical Services Division completed work on treating a box of Castro's favorite cigars with a toxin so potent that "a person would die after putting one in his mouth." In February 1961, the cigars were delivered to a contact in Havana. The files do not make clear whether any attempt was made to pass the cigars to Castro.

Mafia, Phase One. In September 1960, Robert Maheu, whose private detective agency was on CIA retainer, was asked to contact John Rosselli, involved with the gambling syndicate, and enlist his aid in an assassination plot. Rosselli agreed to go to Florida and recruit Cubans for the enterprise. To assist him, Rosselli brought in Momo Salvatore "Sam" Giancana, the Chicago-based gangster, and Santos Trafficante, the Cosa Nostra chief in Cuba, who made frequent trips between Miami and Havana. (A comedy of errors sidelight was the CIA wiretap put on the telephone of Giancana's girlfriend, Phyllis McGuire, in Las Vegas, because of his concern about her fidelity — a wiretap discovered by the FBI, which then had to be dissuaded from prosecuting.) A scheme evolved to have one of Trafficante's agents put a poison pill in Castro's drink. One batch of pills was rejected because they would not dissolve in water. A second batch was tested on monkeys and found effective. In March 1961, Rosselli reported that the pills had been delivered to an official close to Castro, his cooperation purchased by kickbacks from the gambling interests. The Cuban official reported, however, that he had lost his position before he could poison Castro's drink, and he turned back the pills with regrets. Another effort was made to administer the lethal pill through a contact in a restaurant frequented by Castro, but Castro stopped frequenting the restaurant.

Mafia, Phase Two. In the shake-up after the Bay of Pigs fiasco, a veteran clandestine operator, Bill Harvey, was assigned to develop an "executive action capability" — the disabling of foreign leaders, with assassination as a "last resort." In April 1962, Harvey reactivated the Rosselli operation, trying to get the same Cuban who had failed so ignobly before to try again with four new poison pills for Castro, pills that "would work anywhere and at any time with anything." The pills got to Cuba — along with guns and radios that the Cuban had asked for. A three-man team was slipped into Cuba to help "penetrate" Castro's bodyguard. The CIA had put a price of $150,000 on Castro's head. When nothing had happened by February 1963, Harvey called the whole thing off — forgetting to withdraw the reward offer. The reward for Rosselli, who boasted of never having taken a nickel for his patriotic contribution, was that he was able to call on the CIA for help whenever he was in trouble with the law — which was often, since he was a convicted extortionist being pursued by the Immigration and Naturalization Service as an illegal alien. He had still not been deported when, like Giancana, he was murdered. In August 1976, his body was found in an oil drum floating in the bay near Miami.*

Seashell and Diving Suit. By early 1963, the CIA's assassination planners were called "Task Force W," led now by a legendary secret agent, Desmond Fitzgerald. They worked on the idea of creating an exotic seashell, rigged to explode, which would be deposited in an area where Castro usually went skin diving. When that proved impractical, the Technical Services people came up with a diving suit, dusted inside with a fungus that would produce a chronic skin dis-

---

*In the *New York Times* of February 25, 1977, Nicholas Gage reported that Rosselli had been killed by members of the underworld as a direct result of his testimony before the Senate Intelligence Committee, "his murder approved by the commission of bosses that sets policy for the twenty-six Mafia families in this country." According to Gage's sources, Giancana, on the other hand, was not killed because of his planned testimony, but "because he tried to reassert his authority in Chicago after a ten-year absence."

ease, its breathing tube contaminated with tuberculosis germs. The idea was that an unwitting James Donovan, who was going to Cuba for President Kennedy to negotiate the release of Bay of Pigs prisoners, would present the diving suit to Castro as a gift. Donovan was so unwitting that, on his own initiative, he presented Castro with a different diving suit.

The Inside Man. Starting in 1961, the CIA had been developing its most prized "asset" — a disgruntled official still close to Castro. By the end of the summer of 1963, having given up on the American underworld, the agency turned to him for an "inside job" of assassination.

His code name was AM/LASH. (His closest associate was, of course, AM/WHIP.) The real name of AM/LASH is Rolando Cubela Secades, a physician and army major (Cuba's highest rank), who had led the Castro guerrillas in the Escambray Mountains. After the overthrow of the Batista dictatorship, Cubela served briefly as deputy minister of interior, then left the government to head the Federation of University Students. As soon as he got his medical degree in 1962, he was named director of a large hospital. Castro apparently regarded him as too unstable, extremist and violence-prone to remain a member of the ruling revolutionary directorate. Major Cubela was also sent on frequent missions abroad — such as an international conference of students in Paris. This made it easy for the disaffected revolutionary to establish contact with the CIA.

In periodic discussions with his CIA "case officer," a plan began to evolve for the assassination of Castro. Dr. Cubela wanted American support in the form of weapons and an invasion. The clandestine negotiations, in obscure places in Paris, Madrid and elsewhere, went on until the summer of 1962, then lapsed for a year.

On Saturday, September 7, 1963, AM/LASH met again with his CIA contact. Afterward, the "case officer" reported to headquarters that, with U.S. support, AM/LASH was ready to organize Castro's overthrow.

That night a strange thing happened. Fidel Castro, who rarely went to foreign embassies, showed up unexpectedly at the Brazilian National Day reception at the Brazilian Embassy and made an off-the-cuff speech accusing the CIA and President Kennedy of plotting against him. Castro was quoted as saying, "Let Kennedy and his brother Robert take care of themselves since they, too, can be the victims of an attempt which will cause their death."

During the reception, Castro gave an interview to Daniel Harker, correspondent for the Associated Press, accusing the United States of "aiding terrorist plans to eliminate Cuban leaders" and threatening to retaliate. The interview was published in American papers on Monday, September 9, striking most readers as typical Latin Communist rhetoric about imaginary plots. In Washington, a medium-level interagency "Cuban Coordinating Committee" met to analyze the implications of Castro's threat. None of those present knew of the real basis for Castro's charge about American plans to "eliminate Cuban leaders," with the possible exception of the delegate from the CIA. The committee compiled a memorandum concluding that a "likely" possibility was an attempt to kidnap or assassinate an American official somewhere in Latin America. It considered "attacks against U.S. officials" within the United States "unlikely."

The CIA planning with AM/LASH went on undeterred by Castro's warning. His CIA contact told him that his proposal for a coup, starting with Castro's assassination, was under consideration at the "highest levels." Major Cubela asked for a meeting with Robert Kennedy to get personal assurance of American support. Instead, Desmond Fitzgerald, the head of the Cuban operation, arranged to meet with him in Paris on October 29 as Attorney General Kennedy's "personal representative." Fitzgerald recklessly ignored warnings from CIA security experts that this direct contact by a ranking American intelligence official was risky. A counterintelligence officer thought the whole operation was "nonsense" and "counter-productive" and that AM/LASH's "bona fides were subject to question."

Accompanied by the Spanish-speaking CIA "case officer," Fitzgerald, introduced under an alias, told Major Cubela that the U.S. would provide support only after a successful coup. The major asked for an assassination weapon — preferably a high-powered rifle with telescopic sight. He also wanted a more sophisticated weapon that might give him a chance to kill Castro at close range without getting caught. CIA technicians went to work fashioning a ballpoint pen concealing a hypodermic needle "so fine that the victim would not notice its insertion." It took a little longer than expected to make that exotic weapon and Major Cubela, planning to leave Paris for Havana on November 20, was asked to wait for a meeting on November 22.

At the November 22 meeting Fitzgerald called attention to a speech President Kennedy had made four days earlier, which the CIA official said he had helped to draft. He said the President had called the Castro government "a small band of conspirators," which, once removed, would assure American support for progressive goals. That, he told Cubela, was the signal of the President's support for a coup. It was a gross distortion of a speech in which Kennedy had actually extended a hand of friendship to Castro on condition the Cuban regime cease subversive efforts in other West Hemisphere countries.

Cubela was given the poison pen and told that he could fill it with a commercial poison, "Black Leaf 40." An air drop of high-powered rifles with telescopic sights at a prearranged place in Cuba was promised.

A chillingly laconic CIA memorandum records, "Fitzgerald left the meeting to discover that President Kennedy had been assassinated. Because of this fact, plans with AM/LASH changed . . ."

• •

In Dallas, President Kennedy lay dead from an assassin's bullet. In Paris, a high CIA operative purporting to represent the President's brother (there is no evidence that Robert Kennedy knew) was meeting with a prospective assassin of Fidel Castro. In Havana, at the same moment, Castro was meeting with a French journalist, Jean Daniel, bearing a message from President Kennedy of his wish to explore ways of improving relations. No Hollywood scenario could match the irony — and the madness — of this triangle.

How could such things be? Had President Kennedy been pursuing a "two-track" policy of offering Castro friendship while plotting his murder? Or were the cloak and dagger people, in Senator Church's words, off like a "rogue elephant" on a singular private rampage? The mountains of testimony and documents indicate that these things could be because the CIA — proceeding on what it claimed as previous "general authorization" — kept its incessant plotting secret, ostensibly to spare the White House embarrassment. The Kennedy administration — for ten months exploring the idea of accommodation with Castro — had kept that initiative confined to a few trusted individuals, none of them in the CIA.

For CIA professionals, deceiving the U.S government was almost as natural as deceiving the U.S. public. The customary tactic was to tell higher authority of the operation in the past, not the one in progress. In May 1962, Robert Kennedy was briefed on Phase One of the Mafia plot, but not Phase Two — despite his demand to be told next time. In 1966, Helms told Secretary of State Dean Rusk in a memorandum that "the agency was not involved with AM/LASH in a plot to assassinate Fidel Castro." That, Helms admitted under Senate questioning ten years later, was "inaccurate." Despite the Kennedy assassination, contact with AM/LASH for the assassination of Castro was resumed a year later — and continued until June 1965, when it was ended only because it was finally judged to be compromised: the FBI had found out about it independently.*Yet when President Johnson demanded a report in 1967, Helms told him only about AM/LASH during the Kennedy administration, but not about the revived plotting during his own administration. This was despite the fact that Major Cubela confessed his role as a CIA agent at his public trial in Havana in March 1966, asking a death sentence ("To the wall! To be executed is what I want!") and being sentenced

*Although 1965 marked the end of anti-Castro plots as far as recorded in Senate reports, new charges were made by Castro in October 1976. Before a rally in Havana's Revolutionary Square, he blamed the CIA for an explosion on a Cubana Airlines plane in Barbados that had killed seventy-three persons, and asserted that the CIA had also renewed attempts on his life in retaliation for Cuban involvement in the war in Angola. Castro read what he described as the text of a message to a CIA agent in Havana asking for the itinerary of his proposed travels outside Cuba. The message, he said, was obtained through a double agent recruited ten years before by the CIA who had kept the Cuban government "fully informed." He added that he was willing to end the usefulness of this agent because of the "value of revealing the conduct and activities of the CIA." Secretary Kissinger stated that "no one in contact with the American government" had anything to do with the sabotage of the plane, but the U.S. government had no comment on the alleged message to Havana.

to thirty years' imprisonment after Castro had opposed execution.*

Had the CIA been acting on its own volition, and then deliberately deceiving one President after another about its murderous activities? In extensive interrogation before the Senate Intelligence Committee behind closed doors, Richard Helms sought to explain and justify.

There was, he said, "intense" pressure by the Kennedy administration to overthrow Castro. "I believe it was the policy at the time to try to get rid of Castro and if killing him was one of the things to be done in this connection, that was within what was expected . . . Any of us would have found it very difficult to discuss assassinations with the President of the U.S. I believe we all had the feeling that we're hired to keep these things out of the Oval Office . . . No member of the Kennedy administration . . . ever told me that assassination was proscribed or ever referred to [it] in that fashion . . . Nobody ever said that [assassination] was ruled out . . . Nobody wants to embarrass the President of the United States by discussing assassination of foreign leaders in his presence."

Every surviving intimate has testified that President Kennedy wanted no assassination, but somewhere amid all the winks and nods and euphemisms about "getting rid of" and "eliminating," something had gone off the rails. McNamara acknowledged a dilemma when he testified before the Senate committee. On the one hand, he said, "I know of no major action taken by the CIA during the time that I was in government that was not properly authorized by senior officials." On the other hand, every senior official he knew was opposed to assassination. So, he concluded, "I find it almost inconceivable that the assassination attempts were carried on during the Kennedy administration without the senior members knowing it, and I understand the contradiction that this carries with respect to the facts."

All the talk did not change the fact that President Kennedy, in whose name the CIA had tried to kill Premier Castro, was dead —

*In fairness it must be said that Communist "show trials" were not taken seriously in those days. A *New York Times* editorial on March 7, 1966, said, "Premier Castro blames the United States Central Intelligence Agency, but that is a stock charge."

at the hands of an avowed admirer of Castro named Lee Harvey Oswald.

• •

One investigation breeds another. The exposure of the plots to assassinate Castro raised new questions about the assassination of President Kennedy. Was there a connection? Why had the Warren Commission not been told about the anti-Castro plots? That became the subject of the final report of the Senate Intelligence Committee — actually filed by Senators Richard Schweiker and Gary Hart in June 1976, after the committee had disbanded. It unveiled a strange and sinister cover-up.

CIA Director John McCone, appearing before the Warren Commission in June 1964, accompanied by his deputy, Helms, was asked by Congressman Gerald Ford, a member of the commission, if he had "full authority" to disclose any information in the CIA files. "That is right," said McCone, including "all information of every nature in our files or in the minds of employees."

Questioned about any possible conspiracy, foreign or domestic, Russian or Cuban, McCone's answer was that an investigation had turned up "no evidence to support such an assumption." Helms went so far as to assure Ford that "we haven't stopped our inquiries" and that anything subsequently learned would be forwarded to the commission.

REP. FORD: In other words, the case isn't closed.
HELMS: It is not closed as far as we are concerned . . . I would assume the case will never be closed.

That turned out to be true in ways that Helms may not have anticipated. In July 1975, he was before the Senate Intelligence Committee behind closed doors, being questioned by Senator Robert Morgan of North Carolina.

MORGAN: You had been part of an assassination plot against Castro?
HELMS: I was aware that there had been efforts made to get rid of him by these means.

MORGAN: . . . You were charged with furnishing the Warren Commission information from the CIA, information that you
thought relevant?

HELMS: No, sir. I was instructed to reply to inquiries from the
Warren Commission for information from the Agency. I
was not asked to initiate any particular thing.

MORGAN: In other words, if you weren't asked for it, you didn't
give it.

HELMS: That's right, sir.

It was worse than that. The CIA *had* been asked and had evaded
giving the information. Still worse, there was evidence that it actively
planned to prevent its "Cuban connection" from coming out.

A possible "Cuban connection" should have been a natural line of
inquiry for the Warren Commission. After all, Oswald had been
arrested in New Orleans in August 1963 for making a scene while
distributing leaflets for the pro-Castro Fair Play for Cuba Committee. On a New Orleans radio program, he had extolled Cuba and
defended Castro. He had used the alias of "A. J. Hidell" because it
rhymed with Fidel, his wife, Marina, testified. Less than two months
before the assassination, in late September, Oswald had visited the
Cuban consulate in Mexico City and tried to get a visa. Staff lawyers
Coleman and Slawson had emphasized in their report that "the
Cuban government might have been involved" in the Kennedy assassination because it "had ample reason to dislike and distrust the
government of the United States and the late President in particular." There were, however, powerful forces in government with dis-
parate motives for playing down the Cuban connection.

The Johnson administration had an immediate concern about al-
laying American panic over a possible conspiracy. Deputy Attorney
General Nicholas Katzenbach wrote Presidential Assistant Bill
Moyers on November 25, three days after the assassination, "Speculation about Oswald's motivation should be cut off, and we should
have some basis for rebutting the thought that this was a Communist
conspiracy . . ."

The CIA — up to its neck in anti-Castro plotting — had a special
interest in steering the investigation away from the Cuban angle.

The morning after the Dallas assassination a cable went to the AM/LASH case officer with orders to "break contact." The same day, Deputy Director Helms, while telling his subordinates that there would be full cooperation with the investigation of the Kennedy assassination, put the coordination of information from the CIA into the hands of a desk officer from Counterintelligence who knew nothing of the anti-Castro plots. This officer told the Senate Intelligence committee, thirteen years later, that had he known about the poison pen being slipped to AM/LASH "that would have become an absolutely vital factor in analyzing the events surrounding the Kennedy assassination." The AM/LASH case officer filed his report on the Paris meeting on November 24 and was ordered by Fitzgerald, he later testified, to delete reference to the delivery of the poison pen. The case officer was then quickly reassigned to a faraway post.

On November 26, Helms cabled the CIA stations in Europe asking for "any scrap" of information that might bear on the Kennedy assassination. Promptly, one European station cabled back that it had information from "a specified sensitive and reliable source" (electronic eavesdropping) indicating, as the sanitized Senate report put it, tht "AM/LASH was indiscreet in his conversations." Translated, Major Cubela had talked so freely about the plan to kill Castro that word had been picked up in overheard conversations. The cable was quickly filed away; no mention of it was made to the CIA officer coordinating information on the Kennedy assassination. The CIA "coordinator," cut off from any significant information touching on Cuba, was also not permitted to know what the FBI had found out. He completed a short report late in December for President Johnson, barren of any word of relevant CIA activities.

After the creation of the Warren Commission, Counterintelligence Chief James Angleton took over the CIA's part of the investigation in January 1964. To make the cover-up accident-proof, he sought to insure that the FBI did not tell the commission anything the CIA was trying to hide. FBI documents reveal that Angleton contacted William Sullivan of the FBI, saying that "it would be well for both McCone and Hoover to be aware that the commission might ask the same questions wondering whether they would get different replies from the heads of the two agencies." Angleton gave examples of what questions might be asked and how they should be answered:

(1)   Q. Was Oswald ever an agent of the CIA?
      A. No.
(2)   Q. Does the CIA have any evidence showing that a conspiracy existed to assassinate President Kennedy?
      A. No.

Angleton chose his team from his own counterintelligence staff, which was preoccupied with the Soviet Union and the KGB. There was no one from Fitzgerald's task force on Cuba. Exhaustively, the Angleton group analyzed Oswald's activities in the Soviet Union, and assiduously it stayed away from every Oswald link with Cuba. Indeed, as the Senate report noted with astonishment, AM/LASH, who still had access to high officials in Havana, "was never asked about the assassination of President Kennedy in meetings with the CIA in 1964 and 1965." It could only be assumed the CIA was afraid of what Cubela's answer might be. Angleton, who believed that all Communist activities basically started with the KGB, would have loved to find a Russian conspiracy. Unfortunately for that search, Lieutenant Colonel Yuri Nosenko of the KGB, who had defected early in 1964, only offered information to counter such a theory. The report of his interrogation was filed with a mass of material at the end of the Warren investigation, but never mentioned in the hearings. Angleton, to this day, believes Nosenko was a plant, although the CIA — after three years of dealings with Nosenko as their prisoner — had long ago concluded that Nosenko told the truth.

The Warren Commission did not push the CIA for information about Oswald's Cuban associations, this despite the fact — or perhaps because of the fact — that one of its members was former CIA Director Allen Dulles, who knew about the early plots against Castro. Of thirty-four requests for information from the Warren Commission to the CIA, fifteen dealt with the Soviet Union, one with Cuba. That one asked about Jack Ruby's alleged visit to Cuba in 1959. In the Warren Commission, former Senator John Sherman

Cooper told the Senate committee, no word was ever said about CIA anti-Castro plots. "The subject never came up . . ."

CIA officials, such as Helms, who knew about AM/LASH, insisted in 1975 that there had been no reason to see any connection with the Kennedy assassination. But in 1965, when the CIA finally gave up on AM/LASH, fearing that the operation had become too widely known and might blow up in its face, the counterintelligence officer of the task force on Cuba wrote this assessment for the CIA:

> The AM/LASH circle is wide and each new friend of whom we learn seems to have knowledge of plan. I believe the problem is a more serious and more basic one. Fidel reportedly knew that this group was plotting against him and once enlisted its support. Hence, we cannot rule out the possibility of provocation.

By then the Warren Commission — to whom Helms had indicated that the case would remain open — had gone out of business.

"All the Government agencies have fully discharged their responsibility to cooperate," said this high board of inquiry, as it concluded:

> . . . no evidence that Oswald was involved with any person or group in a conspiracy to assassinate the President . . .
>
> . . . no evidence to show that Oswald was employed, persuaded, or encouraged by any foreign government to assassinate President Kennedy . . .

• •

The Warren Commission's confidence in 1964 that government agencies "fully discharged their responsibility to cooperate" sounded in 1976 like a melancholy travesty as the final report of the Senate Intelligence Committee concluded that "for different reasons, both the CIA and the FBI failed in, or avoided carrying out, certain of their responsibilities in this matter." The FBI mainly covered up the extent of its contacts with Oswald; the CIA worked assiduously to steer the Warren Commission away from any knowledge of its own activities in Cuba.

Would anything be different if the Warren Commission had not been so manipulated?

The commission might have probed the "Castro retaliation" theory and run up against lack of evidence of Cuban involvement. It might have investigated the alternate theory of the commission staff — that Oswald could have been programmed by anti-Castro exiles to simulate a pro-Castro assassination — and also run up against a blank wall. What the commission might have discovered was not evidence of a conspiracy, but a clear indication of what set Oswald off. It could probably have wound up its historic mission less baffled about his possible motive, less mystified about when the assassination idea formed in his disordered mind.

Had the commission not been so completely sidetracked from every Cuban lead, it might have found what this reporter was able to find — buried in the commission's own files or later dug up in congressional investigations and from other sources.

Where the "Castro revenge" theory had run aground was on the lack of evidence that Oswald had any contact with anyone who knew about the CIA's secret plotting against the Cuban leader. But Oswald did not need to have such contact to reach the conclusion that Castro, his hero, was being threatened and that he, in turn, could become a hero in Cuba by responding to the threat.

Oswald, his wife, Marina, testified, was an avid newspaper reader. On September 9, 1963, Castro's Associated Press interview was printed on the top of page 7 of the New Orleans *Times-Picayune.* It started this way:

> HAVANA (AP) — Prime Minister Fidel Castro said Saturday night "United States leaders" would be in danger if they helped in any attempt to do away with leaders of Cuba.
>
> Bitterly denouncing what he called recent U.S.-prompted raids on Cuban territory, Castro said, "We are prepared to fight them and answer in kind. United States leaders should think that if they are aiding terrorist plans to eliminate Cuban leaders, they themselves will not be safe."

The interview was not mentioned in the Warren Commission's report. It was not simply an oversight. A staff member, Wesley J. Liebeler, had written a memorandum urging that attention be paid to it, but General Counsel J. Lee Rankin ruled against its inclusion on the ground that there was no evidence that Oswald had seen it. Liebeler shot off another memo saying that Rankin seemed to be applying a different standard with regard to some Dallas leaflets that Oswald had almost certainly never seen, and he charged that the exclusion of the Castro interview had "obvious political overtones."

The CIA's liaison officer with the Warren Commission, Raymond Rocca, said — eleven years later — that he thought the Castro interview was pretty important. In May 1975 Rocca wrote a memorandum to the Rockefeller Commission expressing the personal view that the Castro threat "represented a more-than-ordinary attempt to get a message on the record in the United States"* and that it "must be considered of great significance in the light of the pathological evolution of Oswald's passive-aggressive make-up." When Rocca wrote this, he still did not know about his agency's anti-Castro plotting, which would be revealed only a few months later.

The Castro accusation of "plans to eliminate Cuban leaders" and his warning to "United States leaders" came at a time when Oswald was in New Orleans in a state of agitation and frustration. In July, he had lost his job in a coffee machinery plant. In August, he had been arrested in a scuffle while distributing pro-Castro leaflets, and had engaged in angry debate on the radio, asserting that "Cuba is the only real revolutionary country in the world today."

After the publication of the Castro interview, events in Oswald's life began to move decisively. On September 17, he cashed his unemployment check at a Winn Dixie store. On September 23, he sent his wife and child to Irving, Texas, to live with their friend Ruth Paine. Oswald stayed behind in New Orleans, ostensibly to look for work.

Instead, in great secrecy, he left by bus for Mexico City, arriving on September 27 and going almost directly to the Cuban consulate to ask for an immediate visa, announcing himself as a "friend of Cuba." He signed an application for a transit visa, saying he was on

*In a June 1977 interview with Barbara Walters on ABC, Castro said he was reluctant to make charges against the late John and Robert Kennedy, but did say, "I think it is absolutely impossible that the CIA adopts decisions of such importance and such intransigence on its own. It seems to me absolutely impossible that they could have carried out...these kinds of plans...for almost ten years without the express or explicit authorization of the top authorities of the country."

his way to the Soviet Union, but Marina Oswald later testified that Cuba had been his real destination.

Silvia Duran, a Mexican clerk in the Cuban consulate, arrested on the day after the Kennedy assassination, told the Mexican police that Oswald, upon being refused permission to enter Cuba until he could obtain a Soviet visa, got into an argument with Consul Eusebio Asque. The consul finally ordered Oswald to leave the office, telling him that he would never give him a visa because "a person like him, instead of aiding the Cuban Revolution, was really doing it harm."

The CIA had attempted to prevent the arrest of Señora Duran, but by the time its station in Mexico City got the message from Washington, it was too late. Asked why the CIA tried to interfere, Thomas Karamessines, who had been Helms' deputy in covert operations, was quoted, in April 1976 testimony before the Senate committee, as having "speculated that the CIA feared the Cubans were responsible [for the Kennedy assassination] and that Duran might reveal this during an interrogation." In other words, if the Cubans had, in fact, been involved in the Kennedy assassination, the CIA would have preferred to see that information suppressed rather than risk disclosure of the agency's plotting against Castro.

Señora Duran's statement — which the Warren Commission had to get directly from the Mexican police — did not implicate the Cubans in any way. The consular clerk, who later complained of having been mishandled by the police, did not say in her statement what had made her boss so angry with Oswald as to throw him out of the consulate and accuse him of wanting to harm Cuba. There was clearly something missing in her account. Coleman and Slawson, the commission staff lawyers in charge of investigating conspiracy theories, wanted to go to Mexico City and interview her, but Chief Justice Earl Warren vetoed the idea — as everything connected with Cuba seemed to be mysteriously vetoed.

Nonetheless, unsolicited, the commission got further word on what had happened at the Cuban consulate. On June 17, 1964, J. Edgar Hoover sent, by special courier, a top-secret letter to Counsel Rankin. It said that "through a confidential source which has furnished reliable information in the past, we have been advised of some statements made by Fidel Castro, Cuban Prime Minister, concerning the assassination of President Kennedy."

The paragraph containing what Castro said was deleted from the letter as released in 1976. It stated, I have since learned, that Oswald, on his visit to the consulate, had talked of assassinating President Kennedy. The consul had taken this as a deliberate provocation. The Cuban ambassador in Mexico City had reported the incident to Havana. It had not been taken seriously at the time, but after the Kennedy assassination, Castro had come to suspect that the effort to get Oswald into Cuba was part of a right-wing conspiracy. Oswald would return from Cuba, then assassinate the President, and it would look as though Castro had been responsible.

Like so many Cuban clues, the Hoover memo was not acted upon. Slawson does not recall even having seen it.

What the FBI learned through secret means in 1964 was told by Castro publicly in more detail three years later. In an interview in July 1967 with a British journalist, Comer Clark, Castro said that Oswald had come to the Cuban consulate twice, each time for about fifteen minutes. "The first time — I was told — he wanted to work for us. He was asked to explain, but he wouldn't. He wouldn't go into details. The second time he said he wanted to 'free Cuba from American imperialism.' Then he said something like, 'Someone ought to shoot that President Kennedy.' Then Oswald said — and this was exactly how it was reported to me — 'Maybe I'll try to do it.' "

Castro said that he had not thought of warning the United States government because Oswald had been considered a "wild man" and not taken seriously. "We didn't have any relations with the American government anyway," his interview continued. "If I'd taken it seriously I might have informed the United Nations or some other official agency like that. But who would have believed me? People would have said that Oswald was just mad, or that I'd gone mad . . . Then, too, after such a plot had been found out, we would be blamed — for something we had nothing to do with. It could have been used as an excuse for another invasion try."

When Castro said the assassination was "something we had nothing to do with," he may not have been quite accurate. It was likely that Castro had had an effect on Oswald that he did not realize or preferred not to speculate about. Former President Johnson, a year before his death, told columnist Marianne Means of his conviction that Oswald acted "either under the influence or the orders of Castro." The "influence" may have been as simple as reading Castro's public denunciation of attempts on him and the warning of possible retaliation.

The possibility that Oswald acted on his own, inspired by Castro's statement, cannot today be proved, but it has the elements of the fortuitous and the lunatic that sometimes govern history. The "conspiracy," then, would have been a conspiracy of interlocking events — the incessant CIA plots to kill Castro, touching off a Castro warning, touching off something in the fevered mind of Lee Harvey Oswald.

It would be comforting to know that Oswald acted on his own — not as part of some dark left-wing or right-wing plot to strike down a President. It is less comforting to realize that the chain of events may have started with the reckless plotting of the CIA against Castro, perhaps in pursuit of what it thought to be Kennedy's aim. An arrow launched into the air to kill a foreign leader may well have fallen back to kill our own.

IX

THE LEAK AGE

WATERGATE HAD BROUGHT the "leak" into its own. The anonymous source acquired a new degree of respectability. Because anonymous sources had been mainly "good guys" blowing the whistle on the misdeeds of "bad guys," status was conferred on the whole process. The specter of the leak also became a new kind of ombudsman. The risk that secrecy would be "blown" became a factor to be considered in the early planning stage of any bureaucratic project or in the later stage of a brewing scandal. It was less a matter of post-Watergate morality than post-Watergate caution. "How will we look if this leaks?" was a question that probably aborted many a gestating plot. After Watergate, the drought of cover-up had produced the deluge of disclosure.

The leak was not new to Washington — it was as old as the secret, which is, roughly, as old as the government. But it was an institution in a process of evolution. For one thing, it had evolved grammatically — from a noun into a verb. Once a leak, as the word implies, had been an accidental seepage — a loose-tongued remark picked up by a sharp-eared reporter, a lost document, a chauffeur's unwary anecdote about his boss. The government turned the leak into a verb — something consciously done to enhance an official, float a trial balloon, promote a viewpoint or torpedo a contrary viewpoint. The air force "leaked" classified information about what was wrong with the army's missiles; at appropriations time the whole Pentagon leaked classified studies of Soviet armed might; a "senior official" traveling on Secretary Kissinger's shuttle-diplomacy plane developed leaking into an art form. Kissinger both leaked and condemned leaks. Leaking could vary from a telephoned tip to a breakfast backgrounder. Formalized clandestine meetings on "deep background" became known to reporters as "leaking sessions."

Alas, the growth of the high-level authorized leak detracted from the assiduous work of dedicated journalists using their own initiative to develop stories, mainly at the working level of government. The public got the impression of journalists as simply passive recipients of manipulated information sprinkled on them by the self-interested and complacently absorbed into their news columns and broadcasts. A little band of Seymour Hershes and Woodward-Bernsteins knew that the story that read so comprehensively, so smoothly that it seemed to have been copied intact from a bestowed document, often was the product of weeks of painful digging, prying and assembling from many reluctant sources, some of them even unwitting sources. An American Embassy officer in a European capital once called me to ask in astonishment where I had gotten a story broadcast in the United States and quoted in a cable from the State Department, apparently unaware that he himself had provided me with the decisive clue. Contrary to public impression, more stories are gotten than given — at least the big ones that journalists like to remember.

In the Nixon White House, the leak was the subject of a twofold obsession. The unauthorized leak would cause President Nixon — and hence his lieutenants — to fly into fury, launching investigations, ordering wiretaps, seeking court injunctions against publication. Nixon once had to be dissuaded by Haldeman — on feasibility grounds — from administering lie-detector tests to thousands of government employees in the search for a leak. At the same time, leaking was a cottage industry in the White House. Dozens of memoranda of the Watergate period routinely advised the planting of specific stories with friendly columnists like Victor Lasky and Evans and Novak. In a nasty twist to the leaking industry, subcontractors were commissioned to supply material to be leaked. The White House "Plumbers," so designated because they were supposed to plug leaks, also had the mission of filling the reservoir for other leaks. The cables linking President Kennedy to the assassination of Ngo Dinh Diem that Charles Colson wanted Howard Hunt to forge were to be leaked to *Life* magazine. (*Life* had also been the recipient of the Justice Department leak about Justice Abe Fortas' retainer from a financial wheeler-dealer that drove him from the Supreme Court.) If Hunt and Anthony Ulasewicz, a private eye for the White House, had learned anything damaging about Senator Kennedy and Chappaquiddick, the information would have been leaked. The whole operation against Daniel Ellsberg — to "pin him to the wall," in Colson's phrase — was to get information about his sexual and emotional life to be used as a counterleak. By smearing him, it would deny him public acclaim for an act of conscience in leaking the Pentagon Papers. It is possible that Watergate itself was the initial stage of a leak project — seeking material from Lawrence O'Brien's files and phone conversations that could be disseminated to his and the Democrats' disadvantage.

The expanding influence of the news media contributed to the expansion of leaks. If senators — and even Presidents — routinely allowed their speeches to be quoted before being made, it was because, increasingly, the news media were the real audience. If congressional committees devoted almost as much of their secret sessions to scenarios of how to publicize their work as they gave to doing the work, it was because they considered their product largely futile if it didn't get on the evening news. In an era where perception seemed to overshadow reality, where image was the decisive political force, it was almost inevitable that the walls of discretion and restraint would be cracked by the manifold temptations to create and to alter public impressions.

Watergate added another element to the game — often war — of leaks. It brought "national security" into disrepute by making it synonymous with cover-up. The Nixon administration had cried "wolf" too often and too mendaciously, and the invocation of national interest no longer rang true. Too often had Nixon stamped "secret" on his own guilty secrets and proclaimed "national security" when only his security had been involved. The Nixon administration had cried "national security" to stop the publication of the Pentagon Papers, but had been unable to convince a federal judge that even one of the thousands of pages entailed a security risk. Nixon's lawyers had used the same argument as a reason to withhold the White House tapes. Nixon had told the Justice Department to stay away from the Liddy-Hunt break-in on Ellsberg's psychiatrist because "that's national security." A tacit consensus between America's citizens and their elected leader had rested on a pillar of confidence that the President could be believed when he uttered the phrases "national interest" and "national security." That pillar had crumbled.

A generation of public servants who had seen "secret" stamped on everything from cost overruns to undeclared wars had begun to wonder if conscientious leaking was a duty and unquestioning obedience a cop-out. To many, Ellsberg, who violated his pledge and leaked the Pentagon Papers as a protest against the Vietnam war, was a folk hero — despite Colson's efforts to rectify that situation. "Deep Throat," the sobriquet for Bob Woodward's source on Watergate, symbolized a new breed of American hero — the daring anonymous inside scourge of evil in government. As the "secret" became discredited, the "leak" became a pervasive way of life — to the dismay of that part of government, the intelligence community, to which secrecy was the very breath of life.

• •

Against this background, congressional investigations of the intelligence agencies became simply another phase of the disclosure deluge. The Senate and House investigators, to the extent that they were ferreting out information from secret files and providing it to the public, represented, to the distraught intelligence community, one massive leak. It was usually not too difficult for reporters to unlock additional information that the committees were not prepared — or not *yet* prepared — to release. The press — Seymour Hersh in the forefront — had stimulated Congress to expose the errant ways of the intelligence agencies and could settle back and watch while Congress wrestled with the administration for its secret documents. To some extent investigative journalism in this post-Watergate period became probing by proxy.

To supplement the search for primary information one could cover a public hearing, to which the administration had been figuratively dragged, kicking and screaming. The first public hearing of the Senate Intelligence Committee, on September 16, 1975, exposed, over strenuous administration protests, how CIA scientists had squirreled away deadly poisons — shellfish toxin and cobra venom — in the face of orders from President Nixon, in compliance with an international treaty, to destroy the poisons. Once efforts to block the hearing had failed, the story was comprehensively told. Colby testified that it had taken ten years and $3,000,000 to develop the poisons, but the only time that shellfish toxin had been actually employed was when it was concealed in the silver dollar that Francis Gary Powers, the U–2 pilot, carried with him — but never used — on his ill-fated 1960 flight over the Soviet Union. Colby let senators pose with a dart gun devised to administer the poisons, but carefully avoided being photographed with the weapon himself. Angleton testified that it was not customary for secret agencies to have to abide by publicly proclaimed policies of the President.

Details of the twenty-year mail-snooping program — going far beyond what the Rockefeller Commission had disclosed — were also revealed in public hearings. Among those whose mail had been opened and photographed while they were visiting the Soviet Union were Dr. Martin Luther King, Dr. Arthur Burns, Senator Edward Kennedy and Senator Frank Church. In the mail opened was a letter from Church to his mother-in-law while he was in Moscow in 1971. Howard Osborn, former chief of security for the CIA, confirmed that the mail opening was only halted in 1973 because of fears inspired by Watergate. Frederick Schwarz, the committee's counsel, asked, "So we can say, 'Thank God for Watergate!' on occasion, can we?" Osborn replied, "I'm not gonna say that. *You* said it."

One of the deepest secrets — the National Security Agency, with its massive capability for electronic eavesdropping — was unveiled at a hearing of the Senate committee on October 29. The White House had tried to block the hearing, and Attorney General Edward Levi had pleaded with Senator Church not to hold it. The existence of this agency, nominally under the Pentagon, had hardly been known.

Now its head, Lieutenant General Lew Allen, Jr., looking for all the world like a meek professor in uniform, was obliged to testify that between 1967 and 1973, his agency had monitored telephone calls and other communications of some 1700 Americans on a "watch list" provided by the CIA, a list loosely described as having been compiled for protecting the President, watching for drug smuggling and checking on antiwar dissidents.

Another big secret of communications eavesdropping was exposed by Congresswoman Bella Abzug, heading a House subcommittee on privacy. As she prepared to open her hearing, Attorney General Levi again made a dramatic visit, pleading with her not to do it. She brushed him aside, walked into the hearing room, big hat flapping furiously, banged the gavel and proceeded to read a statement at a rapid clip as though fearing she would not complete it before someone gagged her. ". . . The Federal Bureau of Investigation and the National Security Agency," she read, "have regularly intercepted and copied personal telegrams and cables for the last thirty years without court order . . ."

Later I obtained unreleased details from the subcommittee staff. An FBI agent, Joe Craig, would daily visit Western Union and borrow cablegrams for copying. At Western Union International, the NSA maintained its own copying machines to photograph all foreign embassy cables. The FBI obtained the numbers of the channels, or frequencies, used by foreign missions so that the NSA could plug into them directly. Agent Craig visited ITT World Communications about 11:00 A.M. daily to pick up cables from a selected list of about fifty countries, Communist and non-Communist. The most recent additions to the list had been Israel and Mexico.

Not every exposure originated with Congress, but congressional sources were usually available to add details. One big story started early in 1975 with documents stolen from a Howard Hughes warehouse in Los Angeles and offered for sale. The Los Angeles *Times* learned the contents of one intriguing document and — although the newspaper was induced by the CIA to move the story, between editions, from the front page to an inside page — it led to the disclosure of the mystery of the *Glomar Explorer*. Crammed with sophisticated electronic gear and specialized machinery for exploring the sea bed, it had been represented as part of a Hughes project for ocean mining of minerals. Hughes was only a cover for the CIA, which had built the ship specifically to try to recover a Soviet nuclear submarine sunk in the Pacific Ocean off Hawaii.

Reporters' questions to the CIA in Washington produced an astonishing response — a visit by Colby to the office of each inquiring news organization. He provided a briefing on the *Glomar Explorer* and explained that it would be helpful if the story could be withheld because only part of the Soviet submarine had been recovered, and it was hoped to send the *Explorer* back during the ensuing summer to try to complete the job. I found the Colby briefing so mystifying that I decided to wait a day before determining what to do about it. Within hours, however, columnist Jack Anderson broke the story on his evening radio program, and the rest of us followed — I on CBS Radio, by telephone from my home, at eleven o'clock at night. Eventually, congressional sources came up with information on the dimensions of the project — an expenditure of more than $300 million — and the fact that a request for a supplemental appropriation had been withdrawn, meaning that the mission was being terminated because of all the publicity.

•   •

The issue of leaks versus national security reached a climax with the House Intelligence Committee. The history of this investigation was a saga of its battle to get secret information and the process of osmosis by which that information seeped out to the press and public. The Senate committee went in for backstage quarrels and on-stage accommodation with the administration; the more combative House panel more often went in for on-stage quarrel and center-stage confrontation. In its early stages, the House committee, rent with internal conflict, had been trying to justify its existence, and, in its later stages, was playing catch-up with the Senate, scrambling for short cuts to sensation. The House committee, consequently, seemed on a constant collision course with the administration over secrecy and leaks. It eventually resulted in a head-on collision, whose shattering effects I observed — and felt. This account, based on journal notes, reflects the stormy, and leaky, voyage of the House Intelligence Committee:

June 5, 1975 — Fitful stirring in the House committee (which has been trying since February to get organized). An open session is called, goes into closed session, then spends an hour debating whether to fire Chairman Lucien Nedzi. A majority opposes him because he headed the oversight committee on the CIA which did nothing in 1973 when it was briefed by Colby about assassinations and all the rest . . .

June 12 — The House committee is getting to look like a Mack Sennett comedy. In a big display of activity, and without much preparation, it calls a public hearing with Colby as witness. Great going and coming of members while Colby sits at the witness table. It develops that Chairman Nedzi, angry at being overridden on the composition of a subcommittee, has resigned and has gotten Republicans to boycott the hearings. This means that legally it can't be held.

June 16 — The House votes, by an overwhelming 290 to 64, not to accept Nedzi's resignation. A big personal victory for Nedzi, but leaving him to head an investigation he would rather scrap.

July 9 — A move in the House Rules Committee to abolish the Intelligence Committee. The committee staff reacts defensively with leaks intended to show it must be kept alive to fulfill an important mission. One committee member says he's been told in a staff briefing that the CIA penetrated the news media. Another says that for years the CIA penetrated the White House and government agencies, and that this stopped only after the 1973 inspector general's report. The CIA says, "Any agency personnel on duty at the White House were detailed there with the knowledge of the White House."

July 10 — Nedzi, presumably with CIA permission, reads on camera for me the page of the inspector general's report that apparently is the basis for the White House "infiltration" report. It indicates that there was a practice of detailing CIA employees to the White House and various government agencies — perhaps a way of providing personnel their budgets wouldn't have to justify. It isn't the same as infiltrating an unwitting White House, though the I.G. report mentions CIA officers in "intimate components of the office of the President." Colby issued orders in 1973 that the "CIA will not develop operations to penetrate another government agency, even with the approval of its leadership."

July 11 — When Richard Helms excoriated me publicly for reporting assassination plots, Fletcher Prouty, former air force liaison with the CIA, came forward to disclose one foray against Castro that he had helped arrange for Helms. Now Prouty has called me again to volunteer a story about the CIA and the White House. In a live interview on the CBS Morning News (he is also on the NBC "Today" show, filmed last night) Prouty says that Alexander Butterfield, former Nixon assistant, had two CIA connections. First, says Prouty, Butterfield, as an officer in the air force, had "CIA clearance" — access to intelligence documents. Second, when Butterfield served in the White House, he was known to Prouty as the "CIA's contact." Prouty says that in 1971, needing help on a problem concerning prisoners in Vietnam — some of whom were CIA personnel — he had gone to see Howard Hunt and Robert Bennett in Bennett's Washington publicity firm of Robert R. Mullen and Company, a CIA front. Prouty says that Hunt referred him to Butterfield as "our contact in the White House."

Butterfield is unavailable; his wife says the story is "ridiculous." The CIA says that Butterfield, while in the air force, did have CIA clearance because of his job, but never served the agency in any capacity. What makes the story so mind-boggling is that it revives the unanswered questions about why Butterfield exposed the Nixon tapes. After appearing on CBS, Prouty is interviewed by the House Intelligence Committee staff.

July 15 — Butterfield, on CBS's "60 Minutes," has categorically denied any CIA connection. Prouty has insisted, "He was known as the CIA's contact. Certainly, Howard Hunt seemed to know him that way." Hunt, interviewed today in prison at Eglin Air Force Base, Florida, says, "At no time did I ever mention Alex Butterfield, who, in fact, I didn't know." Robert Bennett, now a vice president of Howard Hughes' Summa Corporation in Los Angeles, also says he had not heard of Butterfield at the time. This leaves Prouty's story denied by everyone involved. Which, of course, might also happen if it were true. But neither congressional committee seems inclined to credit it.*

July 31 — The House committee has been through death and resurrection — abolished and reconstituted with a new chairman, Otis Pike of Long Island. In its belated first public hearing, the chairman vows that his committee "shall find out" where the intelligence dollar goes despite budget secrecy. The first witness, Comptroller General Elmer Staats, who is the financial watchdog of Congress, testifies that his office tried for twenty

---

*The Prouty interview provided me with a painful lesson in the perils of live television. Although his allegations received considerable attention in other broadcasts and newspapers, I found myself criticized for having harmed Butterfield. For example, *Time* magazine, accusing me of failure to check in advance, quoted me as saying, "You can't check the validity of everything," cutting out the rest of my sentence, ". . . during a live interview." Having done all we could to reach Butterfield before the interview, having broadcast the denials and comments of everyone involved, I cannot, to this day, see how it would have been possible to ignore the account of a former officer who appeared to have serious credentials.

years, and in 1962 gave up trying to check what the CIA does with its money.

September 11 — The House committee releases at a hearing some of the secret CIA intelligence estimates before the 1973 Yom Kippur war. No administration witness will testify. The analyses seem to have been abysmally off the track. A day before the outbreak of the war, the estimate said, "They [the Egyptians and Syrians] do not appear to be heading for a military offensive against Israel." Even after the assault had started, the CIA said, ". . . no hard evidence of major coordinated Egyptian-Syrian offensive."

September 12 — Big explosion! The committee released something the CIA forbade. In open session, Assistant Attorney General Rex Lee reads a statement saying President Ford wants all his secret papers back and won't provide any more unless the committee agrees not to release anything in the future without his permission. Chairman Pike thunders, "The Executive branch is telling this committee of the House that it may not continue to operate!"

This afternoon Colby holds an unprecedented news conference in Langley to say the issue comes down to four words contained in the material the committee issued yesterday. He won't identify the four words, saying this in itself would violate the rules for protecting intelligence sources and methods. However, other CIA sources identify the four words. They appear in an intelligence summary of the Defense Intelligence Agency for October 6, 1973. Why they are considered sensitive is not readily apparent. The paragraph reads:

> EGYPT — The [deleted] large-scale mobilization exercise may be an effort to soothe internal problems as much as to improve military capabilities. Mobilization of some personnel, increased readiness of isolated units, and greater communication security are all assessed as part of the exercise routine . . . there are still no military or political indicators of Egyptian intentions or preparations to resume hostilities with Israel.

The four words are "and greater communication security."*

Pike has, for the first time, clearly enunciated the doctrine that Congress

---

*What was apparently involved was the means by which American intelligence could monitor tactical communications closely enough to know when Egyptian tanks had started maintaining radio silence. For that purpose, a nearby monitoring post was needed. The location of that post was probably disclosed a year and a half later when King Hussein of Jordan, explaining the millions of dollars of CIA payments that the Washington *Post* had disclosed, said that the assistance "was designed only to enhance our intelligence and security capabilities," serving the "identity of interests between our two countries."

has as much right to control secrets as the President has. The CIA has adroitly drawn the battle line on a technical matter of sources of electronic intelligence which it says it can't even talk about.

September 26 — In a summit conference in the Oval Office, President Ford, accompanied by Kissinger and Colby, meets leaders of the House and its Intelligence Committee. They agree on a "compromise" — that a dispute between the committee and the CIA about whether something should remain secret will be referred to the President, who must certify that it would be against the national interest to disclose it. Interviewing Congressman Pike, I observe that he appears to have yielded on the central issue that the President, not Congress, has the final control of the secret stamp. He does not disagree, but says that, with a divided committee, it was the best he could do. On this issue of who decides on secrecy, Pike has marched farther up the hill than anyone in Congress before — but has marched down again.

September 29 — Apart from the issue of what the House committee can disclose publicly, another issue has arisen of what it can receive in secret. The committee wants, as part of its review of intelligence failures, to see the estimates made before the 1968 Tet offensive. Its request is turned down by Kissinger and Colby. In the formal preliminary to recommending a citation for contempt of Congress, the committee votes, ten to three, to declare the documents "necessary" for its work.

October 1 — Colby sends over most of the papers on the Tet offensive.

October 31 — Kissinger, before the Pike committee, refuses to discuss covert operations in public session, and the press is shooed out of the room. First, however, the committee adopts a resolution of Jim Johnson, a young Republican maverick from Colorado, proposing to release — subject to the presidential veto — reports on certain unspecified covert operations. I am struck by the phrasing of the resolution: "The American people have a right to know when their government commits their resources and name in an armed conflict or a paramilitary operation in another nation." Johnson later tells me he cannot say what "conflict" and "operation" because that is precisely the issue in dispute.

November 1 — Though it's Saturday, I am intrigued enough by the mysterious Johnson resolution to spend some time on the telephone trying to find out what sort of covert operations he was referring to. After a day of work I have one of the operations pieced together, and I report it on the CBS Saturday News.

President Nixon, visiting Teheran in 1972, promised the Shah to provide arms for Barzani's Kurdish rebels in Iraq. The Shah apparently wanted to keep Iraq off balance for bargaining purposes of his own. Over State Department opposition, Nixon had Kissinger order the agency to conduct the operation, then sent his friend John Connally to Teheran to deliver the good news to the Shah; Soviet arms were obtained from Israel's captured supplies, and delivered through Iran to the Kurds. When the Shah got the agreement he wanted with Iraq, he pulled the rug (Persian and American) from under the Kurds, allowing their insurgency to be crushed.*

November 4 — At a hearing of the House committee, Chairman Pike motions to me and says sardonically, "Mr. Dan Schorr, who shares membership on this committee from time to time, had a very interesting story on television last Saturday night . . . It is possible that we do have a leak on this committee. It is also possible that somebody else who wants to make it appear that we have a leak on this committee did, in fact, provide the source or was the source . . . I can only say that it bothers me greatly and I am sure that it bothers most, if not all, of the members of the committee."

After further committee discussion, Pike asks me, "Mr. Schorr, I don't suppose you want to reveal your source or method at this particular time?" I reply, "No, thank you." David Treen, Louisiana Republican, moves to have me called before the committee in closed session. Pike says, "My guess is that Mr. Schorr is one of those reporters who would rather go to jail than reveal his source, and I think that would be a relatively meaningless operation, unless, of course, you want to put Mr. Schorr in jail." The committee finally votes to shelve Treen's motion, and I find myself sweating.

December 12 — At issue for the past month have been seven subpoenas for documents, most of them aimed at Kissinger. This time, the committee has gone as far as sending to the House a resolution to cite Kissinger for contempt, and it is awaiting action. Today, a compromise is reached that gives the committee only a part of the documents it demanded. The impetus for confrontation appears to be ebbing. The administration's resistance to investigation appears to be solidifying.

December 18 — Colby, in a closed session, opposes the issuance of the three reports on covert operations that the committee wants to release. They have to do with the arming of the Kurds, intervention in Angola and CIA involvement in an election in a West European country that I have not yet identified.

December 19 — A tie vote in the Pike committee has the effect of killing the report on the Kurds. The other two reports will go to President Ford, under the terms of the September agreement, in the form of a request that

*The Saturday-night broadcast played a marginal role when President Ford next morning discharged Schlesinger and Colby. Coming out of the Oval Office, Colby met Schlesinger going in. Schlesinger asked what was going on. Not wanting to be the one to break the bad news, Colby evasively answered that one of the things on the President's mind was "Dan Schorr's report last night on the arming of the Kurds."

he overrule Colby's objections. The election, I learn, was in Italy. In 1972, the CIA, with President Nixon's approval, funneled about $10 million to parties and candidates supported by the United States.

December 30 — The body of Richard Welch, the CIA's station chief in Athens, killed in an ambush near his home, is flown into Andrews Air Force Base. I cover the arrival, live on the CBS Morning News. The air force cargo plane circles fifteen minutes before landing promptly at 7:00 A.M., when the Morning News starts. Welch was on a list of CIA agents published in an antiestablishment quarterly called *Counter-Spy*. Colby has spoken of a "paranoiac attack on . . . Americans serving their country." Interviewed during our coverage of the arrival, David Phillips, a friend of Welch's and president of an association of retired intelligence officers, says that American agents are in less danger today from the KGB than from "moral primitives" who "condemn by label." My commentary says, "Welch, in death, may have started the rollback of investigations that President Ford, Secretary Kissinger and the whole CIA seemed unable to accomplish."

January 6, 1976 — President Ford and Secretary Kissinger attend the chapel service for Welch. The press is barred — on request of the family, we are told, because the press is somehow held to blame for his death.* Shivering outside in the cold, I also note an absence of members of the Congress — especially the investigating committees. Burial is in the Arlington National Cemetery with full military honors, and the coffin is carried on the same horse-drawn caisson that carried the body of President Kennedy. The folded flag is given by Colby to the widow. This is the CIA's first secret agent to become a public national hero.

January 7 — Despite the rising commotion about leaks, a new one occurs — this time from another committee. Colby has told a House international relations subcommittee — one of those that must be briefed on covert operations under a year-old law — of plans to intervene in the next Italian election with $6 million for anti-Communist parties. The subsidy was urged by Ambassador John Volpe, supported by Kissinger and its necessity certified by President Ford, as required by the recent law.

January 8 — White House aides are telling congressional committees, writing oversight legislation for the future, that if they hope to get secret intelligence information, they will have to cut down the number of commit-

---

*Only when the Senate Intelligence Committee's final report appeared three months later did it become known that Welch had failed to comply with the recommendation of the CIA that he change his residence because his house had been "previously identified as belonging to the former station chief." The chief of the CIA's "cover staff" testified that by the time a CIA officer becomes chief of station "there is not a great deal of cover left." Walter Mondale, who was a member of the Senate committee, told me that he had resisted strenuous efforts by CIA Director George Bush to delete from the report the fact that internal security laxity may have been as much responsible as anything for the murder of Welch.

tees that have access and set stiff penalties for leaks, possibly including expulsion from Congress.

Colby, in a swan song filmed interview, which CBS plans to broadcast as a special, says, "I just don't believe that it's possible for us to conduct secret operations by sharing them with large numbers in Congress . . . Congress has to take the position that it represents the American public and isn't just the conduit for every secret."

January 16 — The Pike committee gets a letter from President Ford vetoing the release of its reports on covert operations in Angola and Italy. The letter itself is stamped "Secret." A frustrated Congressman Pike tells me that he will try to get some of the suppressed information into the committee's final report. I don't quite understand how he can get away with that, having lost the battle for the committee's right to declassify last September.

January 20 — Behind closed doors, the Pike committee studies a draft of its final report. It's about 340 pages, I'm told. It includes accounts of Angola, Italy and the Kurds, though not by name. The report estimates intelligence costs at $10 billion annually, and says the country isn't getting its money's worth.*It cites intelligence failures in foreseeing the 1968 Soviet invasion of Czechoslovakia, the 1973 Middle East war, the revolution in Portugal, the coup in Cyprus and the atom bomb explosion in India. Despite the fact that the CIA is still fighting to "sanitize" this report — or maybe *because* of that fact — it is amazingly easy to learn details of the draft, even small details. There is one bizarre footnote in the report about a pornographic film made for the CIA by Robert Maheu of the Howard Hughes organization. It was supposed to show Indonesian President Sukarno (not named in the report) having sexual relations in Moscow. The purpose was "black propaganda" — to represent the reenacted film as made by the KGB, thus inciting Sukarno to wrath against the Russians. The title of the film was *Happy Days.* At the rate the draft report is leaking, there won't be much news left when it is released.

January 21 — The committee tentatively approves the draft report, eight to four, and Chairman Pike comes out of the meeting, stating, "To say that this committee can't write a report and file a report without clearing it with the Executive Branch is just preposterous." The ranking Republican, Robert McClory, warns, however, that "it would be a violation of our agreement with the White House and with the intelligence agencies if we were to use

---

*The total amount spent for intelligence, never officially disclosed, depends on what one chooses to include under that general heading. The *New York Times* reported that in March 1977 the Carter administration requested $6.2 billion for intelligence for the fiscal year 1978 and that the figure for the year reviewed by the House report was about $6 billion.

the materials which were submitted to us under an agreement of confidentiality." The CIA gets one last chance to argue for changes and deletions. It files eighty pages of specific objections, with a letter calling the report "biased, pejorative and factually erroneous . . . all the flavor of the *National Enquirer.*" Ironically, the CIA's secret letter is leaked to me. Pike says he is not impressed with most of the objections.

January 23 — The Pike committee, having accepted some of the changes the CIA wanted, but having rejected about 150 others, votes final approval of its report, nine to four. It goes to the Government Printing Office, scheduled for public release by January 31 when the committee's mandate ends.

January 25 — I now have a copy of the Pike report! So much of it has already been touched upon in news reports that the immediate problem is to find a fresh story for broadcast tonight. A long footnote contains a hitherto unreported CIA memorandum indicating that in February 1973 Senator Henry M. Jackson gave the agency "extremely helpful" advice on how to handle a threatened investigation by Senator Church's Subcommittee on Multinational Corporations, which would have laid bare the cooperation of the CIA and ITT in opposing Allende in Chile. I manage to locate Senator Church (at an Israeli bond luncheon) and Senator Jackson (preparing to fly to Florida to campaign in the primary) for filmed interviews. The story leads the inaugural broadcast of the CBS Sunday News. The memorandum is exhibited on television, leaving no doubt that we have the report in our possession.

January 26 — The *New York Times* appears with a big story by John Crewdson summarizing the whole Pike report under a three-column front-page headline. I am called at 5:00 A.M. to come to the studio and give the highlights on the CBS Morning News at seven — showing a copy of the report. Throughout the day I give longer excerpts on radio.

In the afternoon, Colby, due to be succeeded by Bush tomorrow, calls his third and last news conference at Langley. It is a bitter protest against the substance and the leaking of the Pike report. He denounces the "bursting of the dam protecting many of our secret operations and activities." Though the contents are generally known, Colby says, "This report should not be issued!" Clearly some move is afoot to try to block it, though with final approval by the committee, it is hard to see how that could happen.

January 28 — Dale Milford, a conservative Texas Democrat on the Pike committee, who has been trying to figure out a way to block the Pike report, suggests that I watch the Rules Committee today. It is considering a routine resolution that would enable the Intelligence Committee to file its report on Friday, when the House will be in recess. The resolution suddenly becomes no longer routine when Milford's Texas friend, John Young, offers an amendment that would keep the report secret until it has security clearance from President Ford. The Rules Committee adopts the amendment, nine to seven. The House will vote tomorrow. On the Cronkite show this evening, I once again display the report and say, "If the House backs up the Rules Committee, it means that this report, already obtained by CBS News and others, will be filed with the Clerk of the House as a confidential document . . . It's the first good news the administration has had in a long time on the subject of leaks and secrecy."

January 29 — It is evening before the House votes, 246 to 124, to accept the Rules Committee proposal. The resolution requires all copies of the Pike report to be locked up by the Clerk of the House. Meeting the majority leader, Thomas "Tip" O'Neill, Jr., at an Israeli reception, I ask him to explain the surprising development. He says his colleagues told him that "this is an election year, and they're getting a lot of flak about leaks, and they're going to vote their American Legion posts."

February 3 — The Pike committee is still meeting, its life extended only to complete its legislative recommendations. Milford, now seeking a way to get the Pike report sanitized and published, moves to have it sent to the White House for the necessary editing. Holding that the committee no longer has power to do anything about the report, Pike rules him out of order. It looks as though the House has snarled itself in its own red tape and left itself with no way to publish its report in any form.

February 5 — Secretary Kissinger, testifying before a Senate committee on future congressional oversight of intelligence, says that foreign policy won't work unless congressional leaks are plugged. Of the Pike committee he says, "I think they have used classified information in a reckless way, and the version of covert operations they have leaked to the press has the cumulative effect of being totally untrue and damaging to the nation."

February 10 — The Pike committee adopts its legislative recommendations and disbands in an atmosphere of general defeat, confusion and frustration. Congressman Pike, finding no uplifting words to conclude these eight months, closes by saying, "Let's adjourn to another room where we can perhaps celebrate in a more fitting manner." On the way out, a staff member remarks to me wryly, "You've been showing our report on television. Why don't you publish it and take us all out of our misery?"

•   •

Starting on January 28, when the House Rules Committee moved so unexpectedly to bottle up a report already bearing the "final" approval of the Pike committee, I had an increasing sense of being thrust into a situation no previous experience had prepared me for. It was underlined by the paradox of appearing live on the Cronkite show, displaying a document while announcing its suppression. I had created a challenge to myself. I was figuratively standing before the American public, holding up a symbol of a clash between disclosure and secrecy. For me — and, I believed, for CBS — it suggested that, however the House viewed its duty, we should stay on a journalistic course of reporting what we knew, releasing the information we had.

Aware of possible risks, I had no doubt where journalistic duty lay. The House, responsive to what it perceived as constituent opinion — a concern about national security, a reaction against too much disclosure — had made a political decision to hold back a committee report that most of its members had not read. As a reporter, I marched to a different constitutional drummer. If Congress could be manipulated into deciding to suppress information, I could not help to implement that decision. For me to "file and forget" a document already in my possession would, as I saw it, have made me the ultimate suppressor. *Not* to publish was to me the unacceptable decision; to try to arrange publication was the natural duty of a reporter.

What I wanted, more than anything else, was to make dissemination an organizational enterprise. A breakfast meeting of Washington staff members with CBS News executives from New York next morning at the Hotel Shoreham seemed a heaven-sent opportunity. I began buttonholing executives as we all stood around exchanging greetings. One suggestion to John Sharnik, vice president in charge of documentaries, was that we do a quick half-hour television special, perhaps entitled, "The Suppressed Report." Sharnik was dubious about getting the necessary air time from network executive John Schneider. My interview with William Colby had been recently on the air, and the whole "CIA business" seemed a drug on the television market.

Turning to Salant, I explained the possibility that the House might be on the verge of suppressing its own report, presenting us with both an opportunity and a challenge. CBS, I proposed, should take the initiative in publishing the report in book form as a First Amendment demonstration. Salant shook his head in what I took to be rejection of the idea, and turned to speak to someone else.*

Bill Small, CBS news director, came up to me to outline a story idea that I should work on for the Cronkite show. It would be on "the politics of leaking," explaining who leaked intelligence material like the Pike report, and why. I replied that it would be an interesting story, but another reporter should be assigned to it because I could hardly theorize about my sources. Abruptly, Small said, "Fuck you, Schorr!" and moved away.

To Sanford Socolow, easygoing young Washington bureau chief, I renewed my suggestion of a book. "Sensational idea!" he said and promised to consult Joseph P. Bellon, a CBS executive in New York who specializes in promoting book projects based on CBS source material. It was Bellon who had arranged for publication of my previous book, *Don't Get Sick in America,* derived from a "CBS Reports" documentary. Socolow said he would get an answer as quickly as possible.

To get some idea of the work that would be involved, I dug out previous paperbacks based on important public documents — the *New York Times* edition of the Pentagon Papers, the White House transcripts in both the *Times* and Washington *Post* editions, the Dell edition of the Senate Watergate report, for which I had written the introduction. The Pike report would need not only an introduction, but extensive annotation. For my introduction to the Watergate report, I had been paid by the publisher. In this case, because of the demonstrative nature of the enterprise, personal remuneration was unthinkable; I began to think about some public cause to which I could assign any payment offered me.

My colleague, Frederick P. Graham, the CBS legal affairs correspondent, was a trustee of the Reporters' Committee for Freedom of the Press. I was involved with the group in a court suit over the telephone company's right to provide the police and FBI with report-

*In a postmortem in 1977, Salant said his mind must have been elsewhere and that he had simply not heard me, which he himself found strange since he had been alerted at dinner the previous evening by Congresswoman Barbara Jordan to the possibility that the House might vote to lock up its report.

ers' toll records. The committee was organizing a fund-raising drive to provide legal defense in First Amendment cases. I asked Graham whether the Reporters' Committee would be interested in receiving, as a contribution, any fee that I might be due — from CBS, or from an outside publisher, if it came to that. After polling the executive committee, Graham reported to me the unanimous decision that the organization would be happy to receive the assignment of any such money.

On Monday, February 2, back from a weekend speaking engagement in Texas, I decided to make sure, before proceeding with the book project, that there was no further broadcast interest in the Pike report. Asked by various producers to outline what might still warrant attention, I distributed a memorandum headed, "House Report Nuggets That Could Still Be Mined," summarizing five possibilities while making clear that we had already covered the main highlights. The "60 Minutes" unit showed a flicker of interest, which was soon extinguished.

On Tuesday, when it became clear that the Pike report was bottled up beyond early hope of extrication, I made some calls to learn the status of Socolow's efforts for a CBS-sponsored book. Bellon had expressed himself as intrigued with the idea, but had been told by Small to do nothing without a go-ahead from Salant. I telephoned Salant, urging him to reconsider his negative attitude, emphasizing the prestige that CBS News could gain by a demonstration of commitment to the First Amendment. Salant, still sounding not much taken with the idea, said he would explore it with the CBS book publishing division. (CBS owns a group of publishing houses, including Holt, Rinehart & Winston and a paperback firm, Popular Library.) As an afterthought, a quarter hour later, I called Salant again.

"Just to make sure there is no misunderstanding," I said, "I am offering first refusal to a CBS subsidiary because it would be nice to keep this in the family. I am not asking your permission to publish the report. That is a matter of personal professional conscience."

Salant, indicating he was late for a meeting, said, "I understand."

Another matter, partly related, added to my sense of growing isolation. I had also asked Salant how it was that Paley was having a luncheon for George Bush, the new CIA director, to which I had not been invited to join Walter Cronkite, Mike Wallace and Eric Sevareid. I said that, as the CBS correspondent assigned to cover the CIA, my effectiveness would surely suffer from my absence at an introductory meeting with the new director. Salant said he would see what he could do, but I had not heard from him by the time the luncheon was held the next day.

Another day passed without word of any CBS decision on a book. Socolow did arrange to have photocopies made of the Pike report to be shipped to news executives attending a CBS management conference in Florida, but Salant later advised the Washington bureau to have them sent to New York instead. From the Florida resort I heard only reports of Salant's irritation about my "pressure" over the Pike report. Socolow, at one point, told me on the phone that "Salant is crawling up the walls."

It was getting home to me that I was being unrealistic in expecting a company constantly worried about the good will of Congress to sponsor an act that would be represented as defiance of the will of the House of Representatives. I had been too involved with my symbolic assertion of First Amendment obligations to realize that from the moment a premature leak had turned into a prohibited leak, a new and unprecedented situation had been created. CBS executives had been backing away from the Pike report as though it were the plague — and from me and my proposals for documentaries and publishing projects as though I were a plague carrier. Furthermore, who knew what had gone on between Paley and Bush at the luncheon from which I had been excluded, or what pressures CBS was being subjected to? If CBS was not, at this point, part of the answer to suppression of CIA secrets, was CBS perhaps part of the problem?

Without waiting for formal word that CBS had decided against publication — which might have been accompanied by orders to me to cease and desist — I decided to go it alone. My conviction remained that the Pike report belonged to the public, that the secrecy backlash had to be resisted, that if Congress could be manipulated into suppression, journalists should not be. I said nothing of my plans to my superiors, hoping that they would later appreciate having been left in a position of "plausible deniability" of responsibility for my actions.

I asked Fred Graham if the Reporters' Committee could assist me to find a publisher. He put me in telephone contact with a New York lawyer, Peter Tufo, whom he described as knowledgeable about publishing. Tufo and I discussed the general contents of the Pike report and which publishers he would approach. We agreed to limit the field to paperback houses, geared to speedy publication. I also suggested avoiding Quadrangle Books, owned by the *New York Times.* Believing that the *Times* also had a copy of the suppressed document, I assumed that it might also be considering publication. In retrospect, I realize that, in response to some reflex, a competitive element had entered my thinking — I wanted to beat the *Times* Goliath single-handed.

A telephone call suddenly changed the premises on which I was acting. William Safire, preparing to write a column for the *Times* about the arming of the Kurds, asked if he could read that section of the Pike report. "Glad to help," I said, "but why don't you get it from your own paper?"

"I asked," replied Safire, "but they say they don't have a copy."

It took me a few minutes to absorb the idea that the *Times,* which had stated in print that the report had been made available to the paper, did not possess it. John Crewdson, it developed, had been allowed to read the report and take extensive notes, but had not been able to retain it. It dawned on me, as I told my wife that night, "I may just have the only copy of this goddamn document in the whole free world!"

I seemed to have the report exclusively — perhaps too exclusively for comfort. Several leaks would have made it difficult to ascertain my original source; a single leak was another matter. To add a layer of protection for my source, it seemed advisable to conceal my role, leaving some uncertainty about which copy of the report was being published. That would mean dropping my original plan to come out boldly with a by-lined introduction and statement of purpose. In retrospect the plan for anonymous publication was a spectacularly bad one. It would require conspiratorial silence on the part of the Reporters' Committee, which had agreed to cooperate on the assumption of overt publication. It would invest a demonstrative act of disclosure with an ironic and confusing mantle of secrecy. It would sharpen the paradox of the reporter's insistence on the public's right to know everything — except the reporter's sources and methods.

On Thursday evening, February 6, Tufo called me at home. His "bad news" was that he had made little progress with paperback publishers. They were afraid of spilling some national security secret that would bring them adverse publicity or trouble with the law; they would only be interested on condition of joint sponsorship with a respectable newspaper. I said that, unable to obtain CBS sponsorship, it was inconceivable for me to go into partnership with another organization. Tufo's "good news" was that he did have one offer to publish the text and make a contribution to the Reporters' Committee: it came not from a book publisher, but from Clay Felker, the head of *New York* magazine and the *Village Voice.**

"Oh, Christ, not that!" I said. My thinking had gone entirely in the direction of a book, with the connotation of general availability under neutral auspices, rather than a periodical, with more exploitative implications. Furthermore, I remarked to Tufo, I had no warm regard for Felker's publications because both of them had printed unflattering profiles of me.

"Is there no other possibility?" I temporized.

"Not that I can see, not in the near future," Tufo replied.

"Does Felker want it for *New York* or the *Voice?*"

"He won't say. He has also mentioned a third possibility — printing it separately."

I told Tufo I was unhappy, undecided and would like to think about it.

---

*Tufo did not tell me that he was director and legal adviser of the parent corporation of Felker's publications, but has been quoted as saying that this did not affect his negotiations to find a publisher. Tufo subsequently represented Carter Burden, a major stockholder, in the sale of both publications to Rupert Murdoch, the Australian publisher. Tufo is also the chairman of the New York Board of Corrections, which oversees New York jails. As of this writing, I have yet to meet the young lawyer who played such a key part in my life.

"You don't have much time," he replied. "Felker says his offer expires tomorrow."

Early Friday morning I called Tufo and accepted the proposal as a last resort, but said that I no longer wished to write an introduction or to do any of the work of preparing it for publication. I asked that my identity as the origin of the document be held in confidence. When Tufo began discussing the financial arrangement, I interrupted to say that this was entirely between him and the Reporters' Committee, and I didn't want to know anything about it. Because I had an early assignment on Capitol Hill (Attorney General Edward Levi testifying on future control of intelligence operations), I said that I would leave the report at home to be picked up by any messenger Felker would send.

"Just have him say he's from New York to get the package Mr. Schorr left," I suggested.

My wife — bless her! — thought to take the report out of its gray CBS interoffice envelope and put it in the requisite plain brown wrapper before leaving for her appointments.

•   •

I felt I was nearing the end of some long road. As a result of my inability to bring home to my own news organization what I perceived as an obligation to resist the suppression of information, I found myself now involved in a quasi-clandestine operation. The rebuff over Paley's lunch for Bush assumed larger proportions in my mind as a symbol of alienation — CBS socializing with the CIA inside while it kept its own CIA reporter outside.

Over the weekend I wrote Salant that I did not believe I had my employers' confidence; I avoided saying that they no longer had mine either. "In an atmosphere I find depressing," I wrote, "I have about run out of motivation." My proposal was a meeting to "consider together a definite resolution of what appears to have become, in CBS, 'the Schorr problem.'" I am not sure precisely what outcome I expected. The alternatives that flitted through my mind were resignation, a terminal leave of absence — or a miraculous clearing of the air and a new start. Salant's response was to invite me to lunch in

New York with him and Small the next Friday, February 13.

The following Tuesday, an eddy of CBS-CIA dealings swept again across my path. The Washington *Post* reported that at the luncheon with CBS Bush had found support for his idea of "burying the past" and not trying to expose journalists who had worked for the CIA. For CBS News, Salant denied any such position and demanded, on the contrary, that the list of journalists who had served the intelligence agency be released "as a matter of simple justice to the vast majority of American journalists who have never engaged in such practices." The luncheon I had been excluded from I now had to report, by secondhand sources, for the Cronkite show.

As I worked on my script, an astonishing "new angle" dropped into my lap, casting Salant's position in a curious light. Barry Lando, a Washington producer for "60 Minutes," dropped in late in the afternoon and offered me some information, outdated for him because it was about to break in the *New York Times*. Sig Mickelson, former president of CBS News, was prepared to state that two former CBS stringers had worked for the CIA. On the telephone, Mickelson, now president of Radio Free Europe, told me he had learned from CIA Director Allen Dulles in 1956 that Frank Kearns, stringer in Cairo, was actually in the agency's employ.* So was Austin Goodrich, one-time stringer in Stockholm, about whom Mickelson said he had learned, of all places, in Paley's office. In October 1954, just back from his introductory tour of European bureaus as head of CBS News, Mickelson said he was called in by Paley and introduced to two CIA officials. They wanted to know why he had not met with Goodrich while in Stockholm, which would have been useful for Goodrich's cover. Mickelson, who knew nothing of the arrangement, said Paley seemed fully conversant with it as he listened to the exchange.

I called Salant about the story and said I was working under pressure to get it on the air before it appeared in the *Times*.

"So," said Salant, "what do you want from me?"

*Kearns subsequently resigned from the CIA and was appointed a CBS News staff correspondent, risking his life many times in the Middle East and Cyprus battles.

"I need Paley's reaction, and I don't have the guts to ask him for it."

"What makes you think that *I* have?" asked Salant, jokingly.

A few minutes later Small called to say tersely that Paley's reaction was that Mickelson's statement was "totally untrue."

Some studio technicians had dubbed me "one-take Schorr" because of my facility in recording scripts on the first try. This time, working minutes before air time to tape my story for the Cronkite show, it took me four "takes." Each time I reached the name of Paley, I would start to stammer.

Hardly off the air, I was asked by the CBS Morning News producer, Charles Thompson, to arrange a live interview with Mickelson for the following morning. Mickelson agreed to come to the studio at 6:30 A.M. That night the early edition of the *Times* appeared with the story of the two CBS stringers as related by Mickelson, but, curiously, omitting mention of Paley. Near midnight Thompson called in distress to say that he had been ordered by "higher authority" to cancel the Mickelson interview for the Morning News. He proposed that I broadcast instead a recapitulation of the story from the studio. That plan was also canceled during the night by an order from Socolow. It was the first time in my entire CBS experience that executives had intervened to veto a program producer's request for a correspondent's report.

Mickelson was asked to come to the studio at 10:00 A.M. for a taped interview — to be reviewed by executives before any decision was made whether to broadcast it. Under the circumstances, I refused to conduct the interview. Bruce Morton, who substituted for me, asked Mickelson if he stuck to his guns about the meeting in Paley's office in the face of the chairman's denial. Mickelson said emphatically that he did, and added that he had often been given credit for his good memory.

"What made you decide to go public with this?" Morton asked.

"I went public because I was asked the question," replied Mickelson, "and I have a very difficult time trying to avoid telling the truth and trying to be evasive."

"But you chose to keep silent on this for some almost twenty years?"

"Nobody ever asked me," said Mickelson, unshaken.

The interview was transcribed and the text sent to CBS executives, including Paley. No part of it was ever broadcast. The CIA-Paley connection had got on the air when it looked like a good idea for CBS to tell its own story before the *Times* did. From the moment of the *Times'* inexplicable grant of immunity to Paley, the story became nonnews on CBS.

Further episodes in my adventures with the CIA and CBS now began crowding rapidly on top of each other — the next one a few minutes after I had finished watching on a monitor the Mickelson interview for the CBS files.

•   •

For five days since Friday, when the Pike report had been picked up in my absence by Felker's messenger, I had talked to no one about it and had no idea when or precisely where it would appear. Now a Washington *Post* reporter, Laurence Stern, called to say that the *Village Voice* was out with a twenty-four-page supplement, the blazing headline covering the whole front page, "THE REPORT ON THE CIA THAT PRESIDENT FORD DOESN'T WANT YOU TO READ." Stern asked me to confirm what he said he already knew from a friend on the Reporters' Committee — that I was the origin. I engaged in a series of on-the-record disclaimers and sophistic evasions ("the *Village Voice* is the last organ I would deal with") combined with off-the-record appeals for fraternal understanding that I could not be as candid as I would like because I was trying to protect a source. His reaction made clear that as a burgeoning subject of news, I could not count on any professional dispensation and that my cover would soon be blown.

Copies of the *Village Voice,* air-dispatched by the CBS News assignment desk in New York as a subject for my exploration, arrived on my desk about lunchtime. I brought one into Socolow's office and dropped it on his desk. The subheadline read, "The Pike Papers: An Introduction by Aaron Latham." Socolow pointed to that, looked up and said, "Are you thinking what I'm thinking?" Latham, Washington correspondent for *New York* magazine, was a friend (later husband) of Lesley Stahl, a CBS News correspondent. Some evenings he was in the newsroom, waiting for her to finish work. It was a situation that CBS News executives, generally wary of prying visitors, had never enjoyed because they considered the Felker publications (with some justice, I thought) as hostile to CBS. I realized that Socolow, totally unsuspecting of my role, was fashioning a hypothesis, compounded of the coincidence of a Latham byline, Latham's evenings in the newsroom and the Xerox machine in the middle of the newsroom where the Pike report had been copied for CBS executives. My response to Socolow was an elaborate shrug. By morning it would be clear enough, in the pages of the Washington *Post,* who the *Voice*'s source had been. Before saying anything myself, I wanted to work out a general plan for shedding my ill-conceived anonymity, a plan that would take into account any possible legal jeopardy.

Next morning the *Post,* scooped on the Pike report itself, enjoyed with front-page relish its tangential scoop on how the report had gotten to the *Village Voice.* In his story, Stern posed the question of whether the whole matter of a suppressed report on the CIA represented "a substantive scoop or a journalistic morality play," making clear his preference for the latter. The Ford administration seemed more than happy to shift the issue from *what* had gotten out to *how* it had gotten out. The White House announced that the President was offering Speaker Carl Albert the services of the FBI and other executive agencies to help track down the leak. Secretary Kissinger, with one of his most magnificent displays of outrage, told a news conference that in the leaked Pike report "we are facing a new version of McCarthyism."

I telephoned my friend Joe Califano for advice on the problem of disclosing my role — to my employers, to begin with. He counseled full disclosure, but warned that CBS executives and I might be forced to testify in some future investigation, with a chilling effect on freedom of the press, unless we took care to protect my communication to CBS. The best way, he said, was to make the disclosure in the presence of a CBS lawyer, acting in the role of my counsel, which would establish a privileged lawyer-client relationship.

I immediately invited Socolow to join me in a meeting that afternoon with Joseph DeFranco, the CBS Washington attorney. I explained the reason for the unusual arrangement, which must have made it clear what I was going to disclose, and, to make it clearer, advised him to dismiss from his mind any theory he might be entertaining. When we arrived at the lawyer's office, DeFranco, on second thought, decided that he should be alone with me to maintain the integrity of the lawyer-client relationship, leaving a furious Socolow waiting outside. I told DeFranco the entire story, and he immediately briefed Salant in New York by telephone.

Next day, Friday, the thirteenth, I drafted a public statement. It disclosed my role in providing the report to Felker and said, "I felt myself confronted with an inescapable decision of journalistic conscience. It was whether, as possibly the sole possessor of the document outside the government, to cooperate in what might be the total suppression of a report originally meant for public distribution . . . I decided that, with much of the contents of the report already known, I could not be the one responsible for suppressing the report. That decision was entirely mine."

The statement expressed regret that the Reporters' Committee had not been able to maintain the confidentiality of the arrangement, adding, "I am fully aware of the irony of my complaining about leaks."

Before releasing the statement, I sent it to Salant and Small to prepare them for responding to inquiries. It was the day I had been scheduled to have lunch with them in New York to discuss my possible departure from CBS, but that had been postponed by Salant, who said that, under the circumstances, my arrival at CBS News headquarters in New York might stimulate rumors of dramatic events. Lunchtime found me in Socolow's office, speaking on the phone with Salant and Small in New York. Salant, suffering from a bad cold, left most of the talking to Small.

They had read my statement, said Small, and would respond to queries by saying that they had no comment in view of possible.

federal investigations. They would also state that I would have full support from CBS against any effort to compel me to reveal my source. Under CBS policy precluding a correspondent from covering a story in which he had become personally involved, I would not cover the specific controversy surrounding the Pike report, but would continue on other aspects of my intelligence assignment.

That, said Small, was how the situation would remain until all threat of investigation had ended. After we were out of the woods, he said, we could discuss my own problems with CBS. "If any," added Salant, reassuringly.

With that clarity of vision which is the hallmark of a news analyst, I felt hopeful that the "Pike affair" would soon blow over. It was, of course, only the beginning.

X

THE OTHER SIDE
OF THE BARRICADE

ON THAT FRIDAY, the thirteenth, Roger Wilkins, member of the editorial board of the *New York Times* and veteran civil rights activist, finished an editorial for the Sunday edition, turned it in to A. H. Raskin, the acting editor, and went home for the weekend, to be "shocked, embarrassed and chagrined" when he opened the paper on Sunday morning. The authorship of an editorial is a secret at the *Times* comparable to the identity of a secret agent at the CIA, but Wilkins later broke his own cover to recount what he called "the worst experience I have had at the *Times.*"

Wilkins had proposed an editorial criticizing President Ford's proposed use of the FBI to track down the leak of the Pike report. Raskin had suggested that he be not too negative about the FBI and that he also get in something critical of the way "that goddamned Schorr" had made his deal with "the goddamned *Village Voice.*" Then, said Wilkins, Raskin scrapped all of the long editorial except the critical paragraph written at his request, which he proceeded to expand and point up. It was printed without further consultation with the writer. Raskin, interviewed a year later, did not dispute the essential facts, and explained that it had been his judgment that a brief single-issue editorial was more effective than a long, rambling one and that he considered the most important immediate issue to be the ability of the press to police itself. Raskin did not wish to discuss an incident that had apparently resulted in a feud with Wilkins, but said, "I am willing to accept the responsibility."

Coming a few days after the appearance of the *Village Voice,* it was the first significant editorial comment on the subject. Its caption was "Selling Secrets," and in vehement language it spoke of "making the report available for cash sale . . . commercial traffic in such documents . . . the attempt to launder the transaction by devoting the proceeds to high constitutional purposes . . ."

Several friends, including A. M. Rosenthal, managing editor of the *Times,* telephoned to say they considered the editorial unfair. In dismay, I sat down and wrote a letter to the *Times,* which was published the following Sunday. Noting that the *Times* profits from its dissemination of news from government sources — and the additional publication of books such as the Pentagon Papers — I took the editors to task: "What you are really accusing me of is *not* selling secrets in the customary, or *Times* way . . . Is it not really unbecoming, if not downright hypocritical, for a paper that has so successfully profited from secrets to apply a term like 'laundering' to one who is trying to avoid a profit and divert it to a cause he believes in?"

I soon learned from bitter observation what a bellwether the *Times* is for editorial opinion around the country. The Chicago *Tribune* soon followed with "peddling . . . to the highest bidder," the Buffalo *Evening News* with "inexcusable merchandising," and it played in the Peoria *Journal-Star* as "Was Daniel Schorr an accomplice to a crime?"

Among those who read the *Times* editorial with great interest was Congressman Samuel S. Stratton of Amsterdam, New York, who was already planning action against me and wondering how much opposition to expect. The nine-term conservative Democrat, a former navy intelligence officer and a former television news commentator, was one of the staunchest upholders of secrecy in the House Armed Services Committee. A year earlier, he had initiated charges against Congressman Michael Harrington of Massachusetts for alleged disclosure of secret information about CIA operations in Chile. While on a skiing trip the day before the *Times* editorial appeared, Stratton later told me, he did "a slow burn" at the idea that I had published the Pike report "precisely because" the House of Representatives had voted not to release it. Returning to Amsterdam on that Saturday, he announced that when the House reconvened on

Tuesday, he would move to have me forthwith cited by the entire body and punished for flouting its decision. His statement said that "this is not a case of freedom of the press," but "contempt of Congress."

My wife and I brooded over Sunday breakfast about the Stratton statement, threatening summary action in the House, and the *Times* editorial, threatening to leave me abandoned by the press. "I have to keep working," I said. "I have to stay on the air." Calling some administration sources — and relieved that they were still talking to me as a working reporter — I proceeded to develop a preview of what President Ford was planning to propose later in the week for future control of intelligence operations. The executive producer of the Sunday News at first turned me down, saying that it would be awkward for me to appear on the same program where Congressman Stratton would be seen attacking me. On my appeal, Small reaffirmed that I was still covering the intelligence beat and that my stories should be considered on their merits. In quick succession, I broadcast on the Sunday News, the later Sunday Night News, the Monday Morning News and on a host of radio programs.

Tuesday, I was still working, trying to act oblivious to the growing tension. The Justice Department information office was telling the press it would "determine if there is any reason to investigate for a possible violation of law," and at a legal conference in Philadelphia, President Ford's counsel, Philip Buchen, mentioned the possibility of a violation of the special statute prohibiting "unauthorized disclosure of signal intelligence." I was meanwhile at Langley, outside the gate of the CIA compound, waiting to interview Senators Walter D. Huddleston and Charles Mathias. They were conferring with Director George Bush about arrangements to get the records of journalists who had worked for the CIA — a subject of investigation by the Senate Intelligence Committee.

Tuesday evening, President Ford had scheduled a press conference at the White House. Socolow urged me not to attend, fearing that I might provoke a presidential attack on live television. I replied that, as long as I was covering my beat, I insisted on being present, but promised to ask no question of the President. Entering the East

Room, I met Bob Mead of the White House press office, a CBS news alumnus. "Sorry, you aren't allowed," he gibed. I sat in the last row while the President denounced the leaking of the Pike report and promised tighter measures to safeguard "critical intelligence secrets."

On Wednesday, I was still working at being the uninvolved reporter, but with diminishing success. Newsmen turned to stare when I rose at a White House briefing to question Attorney General Levi on the implications of administration proposals to tighten security against leaks. Interviewing Senator Church on his reaction to White House recommendations as he landed from Europe at Dulles International Airport, I had to take time out to answer *his* questions about *my* situation. A brief chat with George Bush, arriving at the Capitol for a closed-door session with the Senate Foreign Relations Committee, produced an Associated Press picture that dominated the front page of the evening Washington *Star*. The caption, recalling my quarrel with Richard Helms, spoke of "another confrontation" with a CIA chief. A puzzled Bush telephoned me to apologize if "my thoughtful expression looked to someone like anger" and caused me embarrassment. The Netherlands ambassador, who happened to have among his dinner guests that evening both the Bushes and the Schorrs, greeted us nervously, and was relieved to hear from Bush and myself that we were on good terms, whatever picture captions might be saying.

Although prepared to brave the outside spotlight, I was not ready for what happened that day within CBS. In the late afternoon, as I discussed with producers how we would assemble the day's heavy volume of film, video tape and information into a package for the Cronkite show, Socolow asked me to come into his office. To my plea of deadline pressure, he said the matter wouldn't wait. In his office Socolow told me he had just received a new order from Salant and Small: "They want you off the intelligence beat and on general assignment."

"I can understand that things are getting tough," I said, "and maybe I should take a few days off. I'm pretty worn down anyway. Let's talk about it when I've finished this piece for Cronkite."

"You don't understand," he said uncomfortably. "The decision is effective immediately."

As former associate producer of the Cronkite show, Socolow knew better than anyone what enormous problems, in purely mechanical terms, such a late-hour switch on a complicated story would create for the Evening News.

"Why can't we make this effective at seven P.M. instead of four P.M.?" I asked.

Socolow called Small to urge that I be permitted to complete my story. He returned to my office to say, "I'm sorry, and I don't understand it, but they say you're off the story as of this minute." Bob Schieffer took over the narration of the day's developments, and I went home. The rigid abruptness of the decision, leaving Cronkite show producers aghast at the wrench thrown into their machinery, made me wonder whether news executives were still in complete control or acting under mounting outside pressure.

I did not know at that time of the intervention of the CBS affiliates a day earlier, which came out two weeks later in the trade journal *Broadcasting.* On February 17, Salant had received messages from the organizations of CBS radio and television affiliates demanding that I be banished from the air. Thad M. Sandstrom, owner of Station WIBW in Topeka, Kansas, sent a teletype message conveying the unanimous recommendation of the radio affiliates' executive committee "that (1) Schorr be taken off the air immediately pending a full investigation by CBS News management, (2) CBS News management strongly consider dismissal of Correspondent Schorr." Sandstrom talked on the telephone to Charles Brakefield, the head of WREG-TV in Memphis, Tennessee, and chairman of the television affiliates, who then sent Salant a personal message to the same effect.

A year later Sandstrom told me amicably that he still did not understand who in CBS had leaked his confidential message, but he had no regrets about his action. It was motivated, he said, by "your willingness to turn the secret report over to a third party, that party a publication of a questionable nature, and in consideration of a contribution. I was, frankly, not aware at the time that you had already broadcast highlights of the report, but that happened before the House declared it secret, and would not have bothered me."

The stations' criticism of me was also voiced in editorials on the air. "Not freedom of the press, but abuse of that freedom," said WBT-TV in Charlotte, North Carolina, headed by Charles Crutchfield, my one-time admirer. "We don't think newsmen should be able to break reporting rules with a claim of individual conscience," said WSAU in Wassau, Wisconsin. "It could well have harmed the national interest, and Schorr's action shouldn't go unanswered," said WISN in Milwaukee. My favorite editorial, refreshing in its acknowledgment of self-interest, came from John M. Rivers, Sr., the courtly seventy-five-year-old head of WCSC, the leading station in Charleston, South Carolina, himself a former chairman of the CBS affiliates. "The real trouble for stations like WCSC," the broadcast said, "is the anger of Congress against the networks. Our problems now and in the future with CATV [cable television] and pay television stem from the mad in Congress at the television networks. Congress and the FCC apparently are about to give CATV and pay television what these operators want in the way of privileges . . . The damage will not be to the networks. The damage will be to small broadcast operators like WCSC. Hence, Mr. Schorr's mistake of judgment can have bad reactions to local broadcast stations . . . We wish Mr. Schorr had not helped publish the Pike report!"

For some local stations, the issue seemed to be less the nation's security than their own financial security. In 1972, the franchised lords of the TV channels had quaked before the dangers that network investigations of Watergate threatened to unloose on them from the White House. Now, as they saw it, one network reporter threatened to bring Congress down on them. Word of my removal from the air was quickly given to John Carmody, television reporter of the Washington *Post*. When he asked for the reason, a "senior network source" told him it was because of "the conviction of some of our conservative affiliates . . . that there are some reporters who wear their hearts on their left sleeves."

The network leak exposed what the news division goes to great pains to avoid — the public impression that affiliates can dictate its decisions. In 1974, when Dan Rather, anathema to conservative station owners, was taken off his White House beat after the Nixon resignation, CBS insisted that the affiliates' ire had played no part. When word leaked of the affiliates' demand for my scalp, Bill Small told the *New York Times* that internal CBS decisions were not influenced by such pressures, though "we take affiliate criticism quite seriously."

Speaking to me a year later, Sandstrom had no doubt of the affiliates' impact. He said, "CBS is very responsive to the suggestions and the criticisms of the affiliates. And if we're right, they'll usually do something about it. I'm not saying we were right in this case, but I think they're quite responsive — much more so than other networks."

•   •

On Thursday, February 19, a day after my removal from the air, the House met to consider the issue, not missing the point that it now had an undefended target for its counteroffensive against leaks. Once before the House had moved toward punitive action against a broadcaster — Frank Stanton in 1971 — but had been turned back by a massive lobbying effort. This time there was no organized resistance to be feared.

Rising to offer a resolution "involving the privileges of the House," Representative Stratton emphasized that members were hearing "from people back home that they do not want all of our secrets leaked in the newspapers and on television." Underlining my lack of press support, he noted that "the *New York Times,* which probably takes second place to no one in its concern for freedom of the press, has already excoriated Mr. Schorr." His original idea of immediate action by the House to punish me for contempt would not be feasible, he said, having discovered that this procedure would require "a virtual trial on the floor of the House of Representatives." Instead, looking toward "some kind of punitive action," he proposed an investigation by the Committee on Standards and Official Conduct — the so-called Ethics Committee, which, in its previous ten years, had never investigated anything. It was chosen after the assignment had been rejected by Peter Rodino, chairman of the Judiciary Committee, and Ray J. Madden, of the Rules Committee.

After a short debate, the House adopted the Stratton resolution by a vote of 269 to 115. I heard about it at home, listening on the radio. My wife learned of it while testifying before a House Commerce subcommittee on children's health. The hearing was suspended as a buzzer sounded three times, signaling a quorum call. When the members filed back into the hearing room, Congressman James H. Scheuer of New York told my wife, "They just voted to investigate Dan." Scheuer is an old friend, at whose home my wife and I originally met in 1966.

Within two hours of the House vote, Socolow telephoned to say that Salant wanted to see me in New York the following morning for unspecified reasons. When I asked whether I would need a lawyer, he said he would check, and called back to say, "That's up to you." When I said the appointment would then have to wait until my lawyer was available, Socolow called again and reported, "Salant says you won't need a lawyer to start with, and whether you will need one later will depend on what happens." Socolow said he was to accompany me to New York.

The House vote set my telephone ringing with incessant requests for comment from wire services, newspapers and distant radio stations, responding automatically to my status as a target of investigation. I found myself echoing the kind of comments I had recorded from my targets over the years about confidence in the constitutional process and expectation of being vindicated. Some calls were not from reporters, but anonymous — abusive and even menacing. CBS in New York passed on word of a call to the switchboard threatening to "waste that traitor." When my wife and I returned from dinner at the home of friends, the baby-sitter reported that she had been frightened by a stranger coming to the door, asking about me and refusing to leave a name. The police promised to patrol during the night, and they advised us to get an unlisted telephone number.

My wife and I were awake much of that Thursday night, listening for prowlers, talking about not having our children walk home from school anymore. In the morning I called Socolow saying that, though not wishing to sound alarmist, I didn't feel like starting my car, parked outside my house, and asked if he would pick me up on his way to the airport. On the plane to New York, he wondered, as I did, about the reason for the summons. We read together the latest newspaper attack — Charles B. Seib, press "ombudsman" of the Washington *Post,* writing about "The Secret Report Caper." He said, "Schorr should have recognized that the dollar sign is a danger sign in journalism . . . The cause of free journalism has been damaged."

Under fire from Congress, the press and local broadcasters around the country, I arrived in Salant's ground-floor office in the CBS News building on West 57th Street, wondering: what next?

Waiting with Salant were Small and Robert Chandler, Salant's assistant. Without preliminaries, and with no indication of the purpose of the meeting, Salant asked me to go over in greater detail than I had given CBS lawyer DeFranco the sequence of events involving the publication of the Pike report. Salant interrupted at one point to say that he had no recollection of a second phone call on February 3, the one in which I had served notice that, with or without CBS cooperation, I planned to publish the Pike report. He asked whether I viewed the Pike report as CBS or personal property. I replied that I had never thought of it in those terms, considering the uncopyrighted government report to be public property. He asked why I had acted without waiting for the CBS decision on publication. I replied that, having had no word from him, and having learned that he had changed his mind about having copies of the report sent to him in Florida, I had concluded that CBS was not interested. He confirmed that there had been a negative decision, which he had been saving to tell me at our canceled luncheon of the previous Friday. He asked why I had not told CBS that I was going ahead on my own. I replied that I had hoped, by so doing, to relieve CBS of any responsibility for my action.

After two hours of interrogation, Salant said, "If you will step outside, we will consider our decision." Then, changing his mind, "No, I don't want you wandering the halls. You stay here and *we* will step out."

Decision about what? I did not have long to wait. Within five minutes the four filed back into the room and gravely took their seats, looking for all the world like a jury.

From twenty years of association I knew that when Salant laboriously cleared his throat and looked down at his desk while speaking, he had something most unpleasant to say. He handed me three pieces of paper which he said he had drafted as possible outcomes of this meeting. Each started with, "After intensive consideration of the available facts and circumstances . . . and after discussion with Mr. Schorr . . ." There were alternate conclusions:

". . . I have concluded that there exist no grounds for any disciplinary action by CBS News against Mr. Schorr."

". . . I have asked for, received and accepted his resignation; we will, however, pay him for the amounts which would have become due him during the remainder of his contract."

". . . I have decided that while we will continue to pay him for the amounts due to him for the remainder of his contract, we do not intend to ask him to perform any further duties for CBS News."

The first, he said, was not applicable, and I could choose between the other two. Dazed with fatigue, I was slow to perceive that some sort of hearing had occurred and that I had been found guilty of some unspecified charge. I shuffled the three papers in my hand, not quite understanding what was expected of me. Gently, Chandler explained that the first was what would have happened if the decision had gone the other way. In effect, I had the choice of resigning immediately and continuing to be paid, or, if I refused to resign, just being paid out without being used.

I argued that to be publicly dismissed now would surely prejudice my position in the impending congressional investigation. Salant replied that he was sorry, but it had to be that way. I declined to say anything more without consulting my lawyer. Salant said I could have until next day, Saturday, but no longer. Then he excused himself, saying he was late for a speaking engagement at Yale University.

A week after being assured that internal problems, "if any," would wait until the threat of government investigation was over, I had been fired in a weird star-chamber proceeding. Though I had myself been thinking of resigning — on financial terms much less favorable than those now being imposed on me — that had been before the launching of a congressional investigation. What was shattering was the brutal disregard of my position as a target of Congress and possibly the Justice Department.

After lunch with my brother, Alvin, a social-work executive in New York, I flew back to Washington to tell the news to my family. Eight-year-old Jonathan asked whether it meant that he would no longer be going with me to the studio on Sundays for the sandwiches that followed "Face the Nation." It was somehow cheering to know that there would be no greater trauma for a child so accustomed from infancy to his father as a television figure that, at two, he had crawled behind the back of the television set to look for me when my face disappeared from the screen.

The house was strangely silent. My wife had prevailed on the telephone company, during my absence in New York, to change our telephone number with record speed. Later I would look back to this, the first unlisted number in my life, as a painfully symbolic milestone of conversion from reporter to cause célèbre, ending the accessibility that had always been so vital to me professionally. At that moment, however, I welcomed the isolation. What I had been hearing on the phone had been, for the most part, dispiriting when not menacing. The newspapers were bad enough.

Our friends, Judith and Milton Viorst, unable to reach us by phone, brought over a bottle of wine. They said they didn't want us to feel the way blacklisted writers felt in the McCarthy days — shunned and abandoned by fearful friends. Another neighbor, Richard Dudman of the St. Louis *Post-Dispatch,* left a note of personal support. His paper thought I was being made the object of a deliberate campaign of misrepresentation and was going to say so editorially. These hand-delivered messages, before other expressions of support began to reach me, were rare enough on that dismal weekend to be long remembered.

More concrete encouragement came when I called Joe Califano to tell him I had, in effect, been fired. He said he would not only advise me as a friend, but would undertake to represent me, adding that there was no need to worry about the bills if CBS did not see fit to pay them. I could not have hoped for a better counsel. As attorney for the Washington *Post,* Califano was emerging as a leading First Amendment lawyer. As a former assistant to President Johnson and counsel to the Democratic National Committee, he was sure-footed in dealing with government and Congress. As a partner of the legendary Edward Bennett Williams, he inspired awe in circles where I badly needed to have some awe inspired. Most of all, he seemed to respect me as a journalist almost as much as I respected him as a lawyer.

We agreed to meet at his office on Saturday morning and consider first how to deal with CBS's precipitate action — bound to whet the congressional appetite for a pursuit of me as soon as it became known. I arrived at Califano's office with an idea I had been working on since dawn. It was to appeal to CBS, in the common interest of defending the First Amendment, not to put itself in the position of prejudging me. I would publicly concur in my own suspension, if couched in terms that did not appear disciplinary. I had drafted a suggested statement that began, "In view of the adversary situation in which Daniel Schorr is placed in pending government investigations, he has agreed with CBS News that he will be relieved of all reporting duties for an indefinite period." Reached on the telephone by Califano, the mercurial Salant said that he had also been having unhappy second thoughts about his action, and personally welcomed our proposal, subject to consultation with his superiors.

Telephone negotiations between Califano in Washington and Salant and Small in New York stretched through the day and into the evening, while we fended off reporters inquiring about my fate. Late Saturday night the draft statement was tentatively agreed upon after one last change that Salant said he was obliged to insist upon. It deleted his own phrase, "if any," from the sentence which had read, "We shall postpone further CBS News action, if any, relating to Mr. Schorr until all proceedings have been resolved." The deletion made the camouflage somewhat thinner, but we were not disposed to argue.

On Monday, February 23, Califano and I flew to New York to

complete the arrangements. CBS corporate lawyers were on hand in Small's office. I was asked to sign an agreement that not only relieved me of all duties indefinitely, but also committed me to resign when CBS "in our sole discretion shall determine that there is no reasonable risk to you of there being governmental proceedings involving you . . ."

Califano and I looked at the document in astonishment. It was tantamount to an undated resignation, containing the conditions for final settlement of my contract. Small said that before CBS would agree to a statement about temporary suspension, it insisted on the arrangement for termination of my employment — although the latter made a mockery of the former. Unprepared for the nature of the discussion, I called in my business manager, Richard Leibner, who spent the next two hours discussing financial details of the settlement while Califano negotiated my release from contractual obligations, especially the famous clause once invoked to restrict my public speeches. Small, with CBS lawyers, handled details, occasionally referring a question to Salant, who frequently phoned superiors to get "clearance" on one point or another. Eager for the signed resignation, they were generally accommodating on financial concessions — for example, readily accepting Leibner's proposal that, after paying my salary for more than two years to come, they would then provide additional severance pay.

To Califano, undergoing his baptism in the font of "show business," the proceeding seemed utter madness. When we were alone, he pointed out that CBS was signing away a large amount of money, permitting me to seek other employment, closing off any chance of changing its mind — in return for nothing of substance, only a piece of paper that ratified the obvious. The proceeding seemed to us so irrational that we concluded it had resulted from the peremptory demand of someone at the top — presumably Paley — to see a piece of paper guaranteeing that Schorr was finished.

As we exchanged signatures, Salant seemed elated about a painful problem resolved. Small did not join in the euphoria. He sat at his desk and said, "This is a tragedy!"

Months later, the responsibility for the strange undated resignation would vanish into the mists of executive suites. Salant, a lawyer, would tell me that he had not immediately understood what the corporate lawyers had framed. Arthur Taylor, then the CBS chief operating officer, would tell me that he hit the roof when he learned about it subsequently. Paley, the chairman, would tell me that he had nothing to do with the negotiations, except to clear the financial settlement.

CBS and I were embarked now on an uncomfortable cover-up of my forced resignation. CBS sought to have it both ways by telling insiders that I was fired and outsiders that I was not. For my part I agreed to give public assent to the arrangement. Accompanying the CBS "relieved-of-all-reporting-duties" statement was my statement accepting the "reality" of being unable "to work as a reporter while personally involved in a controversy over reporters' rights," as though I had simply put aside my normal duties to deal with a First Amendment contest.

There was a delay in releasing the statements while Califano and I flew back to Washington. An hour before the release, Sandstrom, the radio affiliates' chairman who had demanded my discharge, was paged at the El Paso, Texas, airport (so he told me a year later) to be given advance word by Sam Cook Digges, president of CBS Radio, who "wanted to say to me personally that he had supported my action one hundred percent." Whatever the public was being told, as far as the affiliates were concerned I was through.

As I walked into my office in Washington — still *my* office, officially — the wire services had started running bulletins. They ignored the delicate "relieved of duties" language and said I had been "suspended." That somehow sounded harsher, and public reaction soon made it clear that not even our public statements had managed to conceal the prejudicial impression of disciplinary action.

Skeptical questions to CBS and me served to escalate our dissembling, justified in the name of our uneasy partnership in defending the freedom of the press. Deception, I discovered, often consists of convenient half-truths repeated often enough to become self-deception. When CBS News employees in New York sent Salant a petition in my support, saying, "Many of us have heard that CBS News may wait until the current matter involving Daniel Schorr is resolved and then fire him," Salant responded with a memorandum posted in bureaus throughout the country: "For the record, I would like to be sure that all of us in CBS News are aware of the facts concerning our position in the Dan Schorr matter. Dan has not been fired. He has been relieved . . ." Etcetera, etcetera. To Congresswoman Bella Abzug, Salant wrote that "we have taken no position and will take no position for the time being" on the release of the Pike report to the *Village Voice.* To Congressman Robert F. Drinan, Small wrote that problems relating to CBS policies "are being held in abeyance." To Studs Terkel, Salant wrote, "I have thought it wisest to say, or decide nothing." Even Paley, responding to a question at the annual CBS shareholders' meeting in Chicago, stated that I had been suspended pending the outcome of the congressional investigation. As these statements accumulated, Califano would look at them and ask, "How are they going to explain when it comes out that they fired you last February?"

• •

With "suspension," the tide of press and public opinion began to shift toward the "underdog." The first leading commentator to write in my support was Tom Wicker of the *New York Times.* His February 24 column was forthrightly titled "Defending Dan Schorr" and charged that CBS, in "suspending" me, had "succumbed to a campaign launched within the Ford Administration." In a more satiric vein, another *Times* columnist, Russell Baker, depicted a reporter refusing to accept an official's proffer of secret documents, saying to himself, "Doesn't he know I can be wiped out if I start reporting things the Government doesn't want people to know? I am scared . . . Scared that the CBS affiliates will phone my boss and ask him to fire me."

A CBS survey showed that mail which, "presuspension," had been "eight to one against Schorr, ten to one against CBS," was running "postsuspension" at a ratio of "seven to four in *favor* of Schorr, four to one against CBS." In my own "mailroom" — the converted dining room where my wife, with the assistance of friends, sorted a flood of letters and telegrams — the pile marked "Pro" gradually climbed up to and then moved higher than the "Anti" heap. I began to feel less depressed about some of the hate mail — the "Jew bastard" and "Benedict Arnold" and "Communist traitor" letters and postcards — lying at the bottom of the "Anti" pile.

By the middle of March things no longer looked as gloomy on Woodley Road as they had on that February weekend when our friends were being reminded of the McCarthy days. Appearing with me on a Washington television program, John Henry Faulk, subject of a recent CBS drama, "Fear on Trial," reenacting his blacklisting as a CBS radio personality during the Red scare of the 1950s, suggested that twenty years from now CBS would be presenting a drama about my case. I thanked him, but said my experience did not compare with his ordeal. "This is a different era," I told him. "People are no longer scared into silence. I'm under a lot of fire, but unlike you, I feel neither menaced nor abandoned."

In this era, the mounting of a House investigation, with the overtones of "witch hunt," appeared to generate more opposition than fear. As the Ethics Committee set about organizing itself, asking the House for $350,000 and getting $150,000, hiring retired FBI agents as investigators, opinion began to swing more decisively. A. H. Raskin weighed in with a second *Times* editorial, this one captioned, "Overkill on the Hill" — an overkill, I mused, that might have been averted if he had struck that note in his original editorial instead of "Selling Secrets." From "Panic in the House" in the St. Louis *Post-Dispatch* to "House in Disgrace" in the San Jose, California, *Mercury,* newspapers began to look aghast at what was being contemplated in Congress. The idea of the massive machinery of congressional investigation being geared up to track down one of the many Capitol leaks became the stuff for mocking cartoons and a springboard for satirists. "A lunatic course, once embarked on, must be pursued to the end — hang the expense and the reputation of the House," wrote Mary McGrory in the Washington *Star.*

It looked as though some of my blunders, which had led to confusion, misunderstanding and criticism of my action in publishing the Pike report, might yet be offset by the overreactions of others. As I

occasionally my patience came near the snapping point when asked, for what seemed like the millionth time, "Why did you sell the Pike report?" Reporters' questions seemed to blur into a pattern as though a printed list was preceding me from town to town. In their hands there sometimes appeared clippings from the same unflattering magazine profiles. A hundred times I was asked about my advertised abrasiveness (I have still not worked out a smooth answer), about my relations with CBS colleagues, about my "arrogance" in "defying" Congress and my own employer.

Fully aware of the irony of viewing the press for the first time from the other side of the barricade, I nevertheless shared the resentments of many who had been in the spotlight before me. "I'm fighting for the freedom of the press, and sometimes I also feel like fighting for freedom *from* the press," I told one news conference, undoubtedly helping to reinforce my abrasive image. While not prepared to join Nixon in complaining of being "kicked around" by the press or Agnew in charging a media conspiracy, I began to understand what politicians and public policy advocates meant when they accused the press of being negative and trivial, oriented more to gossip than to issues.

I found myself also echoing the sentiments of many critics of the press in the feeling that the news media were on a different wavelength from grass-roots people. It was clearly a subjective impression, but it struck me that everyday citizens were quick to grasp the larger implications of what I had become involved in while the press remained mired in parochialism and cliché responses. What also struck me was the slight impact of the press — how little it seemed to matter to a campus audience, for example, what a local editorial had said. During that period, I fell out of love with the press and into love with "the People."

Free of any obligation to work for CBS, waiting for the lagging Ethics Committee to organize its investigation, I was able to take advantage of a plethora of invitations for public appearances. In the year 1976 I made seventy-three speeches, most of them on campuses, crisscrossing the country as I sought to explain the perils of unwarranted secrecy and the importance of continued disclosure. Audiences seemed generally receptive, sometimes even enthusiastic. The response that moved me most was a rising ovation, after a commencement address at the University of Arkansas, by the gowned graduates massed on the steeply banked seats of Razorback Stadium. The feeling that I was being understood by many people around the country helped to sustain me during a trying time.

The most trying aspect of this period in limbo was trying to maintain the façade of common ground with CBS. Between out-of-town trips, I visited my office, reading my mail, chatting with friends and parrying questions about when I expected to be back at work. My communication with CBS News executives went entirely through Califano, who sought to mediate recurrent charges of "truce violation." When Salant was quoted in *Newsweek* as saying he had not been consulted about publication of the Pike report, I cried foul, and Califano was advised that Salant had been misquoted. When I responded to a questioner at the University of Florida that I was "busting" to tell what had happened inside CBS about the Pike report, but couldn't until the congressional investigations were over, the Orlando *Sentinel-Star* headlined, "Schorr Hints CBS Knew of Leak Plans" and Small called Califano to charge an armistice infringement. Califano replied that I could not be held responsible for what a newspaper deduced.

When Small heard that I was to be interviewed for an hour on the NBC "Tomorrow" program, he telephoned Califano to express the suspicion that I was going to unleash an attack on CBS, threatening that, if I did, he would spill some "dirt" about me. The "dirt" presumably had to do with the allegation that I had tried to implicate Aaron Latham and Lesley Stahl in the transmission of the Pike report. This allegation, never raised by my superiors in their talks with me, was just beginning to percolate in unattributed comments to the press. Califano reported that Small subsided after my NBC appearance where, in fact, I responded to Tom Snyder's question about my CBS problems by saying that it was hardly appropriate for me to discuss them on NBC.

The greatest threat to the shaky façade of harmony came in a CBS leak that exposed the secret agreement for delayed resignation. I had decided, despite my ambiguous status, to attend the annual dinner for the President and other government officials given by the Association of Radio and Television Correspondents. Ostensibly a journalists' function, the dinner is actually a television industry showcase, permitting corporate executives to rub shoulders with those in Congress and the administration. Correspondents are encouraged to invite, at company expense, the highest-ranking officials on their beats to be their guests.

The featured entertainment of the black-tie dinner on March 25 was a lampoon of President Ford's maladroitness by the comedian Chevy Chase — followed by President Ford lampooning himself by pretending to trip, misreading a speech and putting his pipe in his eye. The evening's unlisted attraction was the presence of a suspended correspondent with his guest — former CIA Director William Colby. It caused mouths to drop and heads to spin in double-takes. Months before, I had invited the retiring director to be my guest. After my "suspension," and before I could call to release him from his obligation, Colby had telephoned to say that he was still looking forward to coming. To those — like Congressman Pike — who came up to us in astonishment to ask what we were doing together, Colby replied casually that we were simply two friends who had shared many interesting experiences — now two professionals on the shelf. After dinner, I took Colby up to the hotel suite where CBS was having its own crowded party and introduced him to CBS executives, including the corporate president, Arthur Taylor. They exchanged intelligence about the Soviet Union, where Taylor had been visiting, trying to negotiate CBS rights to cover the Moscow Olympics. Colby, fully aware of the sensation he was causing, was making an extraordinary gesture — but one that made CBS look a little foolish.

The next afternoon, Nina Totenberg, a reporter for National Public Radio who had been at the dinner and the CBS private party, telephoned to ask my comment on a story she had from a CBS executive. It was that CBS had "bought out" the remaining three years of my five-year contract and that I would be dropped at the end of the congressional investigation. Appalled at the breach of confidence, I declined comment. Ms. Totenberg said she planned to broadcast the story that evening.

The problem was erased from my mind a few minutes later when a physician called from New York to say that my long-ailing mother, eighty-four years old, had died in the hospital after a heart attack. My wife and children were in Aspen, skiing. My brother and sister-in-law were on their way to Little Rock, Arkansas, to visit their son. As I telephoned to assemble my scattered family and organize a funeral in New York, I was constantly interrupted by calls on my second line. Nina Totenberg's broadcast had been picked up by the wire services, producing a rash of reporters' requests for verification. Late at night, Califano arrived unexpectedly at my home, asking if he could help. Blessing him for his thoughtfulness, I said, "I'll handle my mother's funeral, and you handle mine." I talked to relatives and rabbis; Joe talked to reporters.

My mother, widowed when I was five, had struggled through poverty to bring up my younger brother and myself. In her later years, along with her devotion to Israel and good works for the deprived in her own community in the Bronx, she had found her fulfillment in Alvin's success as a social worker, professor and author, and in mine as a television newsman. After a series of disorienting heart attacks, she had not understood much of the drama in which her older son was embroiled. It was perhaps as well. Our early life of privation had left her permanently anxious about job security for her sons.

•   •

During the week of mourning I canceled lectures and public appearances. One was at Tulane University, where I had been scheduled to debate against William Colby. He defended me perhaps better than I could have done myself, telling the New Orleans audience that "Schorr carried out his obligation to the First Amendment and to himself as a newsman and should not be punished for the publication of the Pike report." Colby's remarks seemed surprising enough to make newspaper headlines. He was soon joined by Secretary of State Henry Kissinger.

At the annual dinner of Washington's Gridiron Club, the first public event I attended after the mourning period, I was applauded by an audience of newspaper publishers and reporters and lampooned in a skit in which Clark Mollenhoff, the veteran correspondent of the Des Moines *Register and Tribune,* sang, "I want a leak just like the leak they gave to dear old Dan." Secretary Kissinger sought me out to say that in attacking the publication of the Pike report, he had not meant to criticize me.

"I think you got a bum rap," said Kissinger. "The blame should fall on whoever leaked the report, not the journalist who received it."

These remarks — with Kissinger's express authorization — were released to the press by Califano. A furious Bill Small called him demanding to know why he was cooperating in an attack on CBS. In amazement, Califano replied that he had understood the "bum rap" phrase to apply to the congressional investigation, not to CBS. CBS was clearly uncomfortable at finding itself in the position of being less supportive of its reporter than two such symbols of secrecy as Kissinger and Colby. In the *New York Times,* Les Brown reported CBS splitting into "factions" over my reinstatement. He wrote on April 1, "To some degree, close observers say, the divided sentiment within CBS can be affected by the drift of public opinion on Mr. Schorr, the feelings of affiliate stations and the trend of press comment. Lately, the press comment, at least, has been heavily in Mr. Schorr's favor."

In mid-May, I began chafing at three months in limbo that threatened to stretch out indefinitely. The fabric of the truce arrangement with CBS had worn increasingly transparent. "Suspension" and leaks about a "contract buy-out" had done most of the harm to my position that could be anticipated from discharge or resignation. Califano warned that the longer the cover-up went on, the worse it would look when it ultimately ended. At my suggestion, Califano proposed to Small that, in the interests of both parties, we should tear up the agreement of February and replace it with a current immediate resignation. After examining a draft exchange of letters that would accomplish this, Small rejected the proposal, suggesting instead that the February document be simply scrapped, without my resigning. I declined to give up the settlement that had been so weirdly forced upon me in February, and we remained in our strained stand-off position.

• •

My role as a controversial figure developed almost into a full-time occupation while the House Ethics Committee dragged on with the preparations for its investigation. Califano jokingly commented that if CBS wanted me to go back to work, I might not have time. Lecture offers multiplied, and various awards were conferred. In the type-casting that characterizes television, I found myself being invited to appear on panels as a protagonist on First Amendment issues and an antagonist in national security debates. Princeton University featured me in a "debate" with William Colby despite my advance warning that we agreed on a great many matters. The head of the University of Cincinnati broadcasting department suggested (without consulting me) that I be invited to give some lectures, and found himself embroiled in a local newspaper controversy.

A point comes when one is a sufficiently recognizable symbol to break through from the news world into the entertainment world. I was told that gags were being made about me by the satirist Mark Russell and on the Johnny Carson show on NBC. A fictional CBS reporter in Norman Lear's situation comedy "All's Fair" joked about being short-handed since my departure. An Art Buchwald column on a completely unrelated subject concluded with the punch line that something was as inconceivable as "the night Daniel Schorr replaces Walter Cronkite as anchorman on the CBS News." I found myself depicted in Gary Trudeau's comic strip, "Doonesbury."

The next step was invitations into the entertainment world itself. Three Hollywood producers offered me roles as a newsman — in one case even an anchorman — in independent productions. Not quite ready to break with reality, I declined. Marlon Brando called to consult me about an idea for a film about the CIA. Robert Redford invited me to his Burbank, California, studio to screen the almost-completed film *All the President's Men,* with the proposal that I record a few additional lines in the climactic scene to underscore my real-life role in the story of Woodward and Bernstein. It became a gossip column item for Maxine Cheshire when CBS vetoed my participation in the film. Perhaps the ultimate sign of having become a "household word" was finding myself a crossword-puzzle word in the Sunday *New York Times.*

This fleeting and fortuitous fame struck me as having a certain real significance. Americans select their role figures on the basis of their own concerns. Deservedly or not, I could see that I was being perceived as having done something defiantly individualistic in an age of suffocating conformity. For some the symbolism seemed to be a willingness to brave both overbearing government and overweening news media in the interest of public enlightenment. These themes were reflected in my mail, which, by May, had turned overwhelmingly favorable.

A couple in Missoula, Montana, wrote, "We turn in desperation to the press, and if we don't get it there, the game is over." A scrawled note from Zephyr Hills, Florida, said, "If it were not for men of courage like you, this would be worse than Russia." A woman from Nashville, Tennessee, said, "You restore, however singly, my feeling that the media need not be the monolith of bland, well-paid, unthinking, success oriented employees of giant corporate enterprises."

As the target of a bureaucratic investigation, I appeared also to be enjoying some windfall benefit from the anti-Washington feeling evidencing itself in the presidential primary campaign. If all this could be brought home to Congress, Califano and I agreed, there might still be hope of averting a bruising confrontation. In June, after some four hundred interviews with officers of Congress and the Executive Branch had failed to turn up the source of the leak, a motion was made in a closed session of the committee to wind up the investigation. It was defeated. So was another motion to limit the investigation to congressional personnel.

The committee staff, recruited from retired FBI officers, turned for the first time to reporters, asking several from the Washington *Post,* the *New York Times,* the *Village Voice,* the Reporters' Committee and myself to appear for interviews. All of us refused to testify without subpoenas, except, inexplicably, Clay Felker of the *Village Voice* and his subordinates. Unable to find the source of the leak, the committee decided to hold public hearings, starting with congressional and other government witnesses, leaving until later the decision whether to go outside the domain of government and subpoena journalists.

I left with my family for five weeks in Aspen. Observing the Democratic convention on television, I heard Walter Cronkite report that "my colleague, Dan Schorr" received one Oregon vote in the balloting for the vice-presidential nomination.*I worked on the lecture that I annually gave at the Aspen Institute of Humanistic Studies. This one, scheduled for July 22, in the midst of the Ethics Committee hearings, was prepared with great care, discussed at length on the phone with Califano's associates in Washington and distributed in advance to news organizations in the capital. Our purpose was to try to head off a subpoena by making clear that it would not produce answers from me.

"If subpoenaed," I said, "I shall not give any testimony about the source of the House Intelligence report, or the source of any other confidential information. I use categoric language not to appear defiant or uncooperative, but to avoid any possible misunderstanding on what, to me, is a vital principle . . . I hope there will be no confrontation with Congress over sources . . ."

The speech was warmly received in the crowded auditorium high in the Rocky Mountains. I waited to see what effect it would have on Capitol Hill, meanwhile getting daily telephone reports from Califano's office and from reporter friends about the progress of the eight days of Ethics Committee hearings. The chief investigator, David Bowers, reported that the staff's 420 interviews had revealed chaotic security procedures in the hectic final days of the drafting of the Pike report. He went into considerable detail about how copies were being circulated during the weekend of January 25, when the draft became available to John Crewdson of the *Times* and myself.

*It was cast by a university student, Scott Bartlett, of Eugene, who wrote me that it "stemmed from both my appreciation of your resolve to share the CIA information with the American public and from my disappointment in CBS's apparent subservience."

He established that Crewdson had only made notes from the report and the only missing copy was the one that I had. Bowers testified that "we are quite a bit closer" to knowing the source, but would not say, in open session, whether he believed the source to be in Congress or in the Executive Branch. I found it hard to gather from summaries of the public testimony how close the committee was really getting.

The CIA testified that it could not have been the source because it had not even been given the final draft. Then, however, Congressman Les Aspin admitted on the witness stand that he had unofficially slipped the final draft to Mitchell Rogovin, the CIA's special counsel. Both Aspin and Rogovin testified about an accidentally missing page in that copy — a page printed in the *Village Voice* — and claimed that this absolved them of responsibility for the leak. They were not asked whether there was any proof, other than their testimony, that the page had actually been missing.

On the last day, July 29, Congressman James V. Stanton of Ohio, a member of the Pike committee, caused a stir by testifying, "I talked to Mr. Schorr on one occasion in the Speaker's lobby of the House in regard to the report, and Mr. Schorr indicated on that occasion that he had received the report from the CIA, and he volunteered that to me, and I indicated to him surprise, and he said, 'Of course, I would deny that if anybody ever asked me.'"

John Kuhns, in Califano's office, called me in Aspen, expressing fear that Stanton's testimony would make a subpoena for me almost inevitable. We agreed to tell the press that I recalled no conversation of any kind with Stanton and that, if there had been one, I could not conceivably have discussed my source with him.*

On July 26, in the midst of the hearings, I was jarred to hear from Califano that CBS, which had been emphasizing its stalwart financial support of my legal fight, had told him it would pay no further fees unless I was actually called to testify. The CBS attorney, Joseph

---

*In early 1977, Stanton, now in private law practice after having run unsuccessfully in the senatorial primary, still insisted that he remembered such a conversation with me, but said he was unable to fix it on any approximate date that would help me check with my calendar as to whether I was in the Capitol at the time. Needless to say, I still recall no such conversation.

DeFranco, also demanded an advance estimate of what that might cost. His letter added, "If Schorr is cited for contempt by the Committee, CBS will, of course, pay for your legal services on behalf of Schorr in connection therewith on an hourly basis." Califano replied that "it could be devastating to Mr. Schorr to have us immediately stop all work" and denounced the CBS position as "a clear breach of CBS's legal and moral commitment."

Califano urged CBS to consider the effect on other CBS reporters if support was withdrawn from one in the midst of his fight to protect his source. He asked, "What would you do in terms of reliance on CBS if you were a reporter for it?" Privately, Califano told me that if CBS pulled out, he would continue my defense without reimbursement.

Adjourning until after the Republican convention, the Ethics Committee gave no indication of its future plans. The air of uncertainty that surrounded the investigation led me to hope that it might be fizzling out. When the committee's counsel, John W. Marshall, came up to introduce himself to me before my speech at a convention of the American Bar Association in Atlanta, I told him that I was glad to have him hear me in this forum — and I hoped he would not hear me in any other. Marshall smiled.

I proceeded with my prepared speech, not looking up for his reaction as I said, "If the committee's delay in deciding its future course reflects a hesitation to subpoena journalists, that is to be applauded. Clearly a decision to try to compel testimony by journalists about matters involving news gathering and sources would mean crossing the First Amendment Rubicon. I hope that the committee will find some way of discharging its difficult task while remaining on its side of the constitutional great divide."

Because my speech was sponsored by the Bar's section on "Individual Rights and Responsibilities," I had another message to deliver, this one aimed at my CBS employers. It was the assertion that a journalist in "a large news enterprise, subject to its disciplines when engaged in its process, still retains personal freedom of expression outside it." Furthermore, I said, reporters in television have "a right and perhaps a duty" to criticize their own industry, and a duty as well to get information to the public that they cannot provide through their own organizations.

"When did freedom of the press evolve into a franchise to be exercised only through large enterprises?" I asked. "What has happened to the basic concept of freedom of expression as a freedom for every American? . . . I hold that the purpose of the First Amendment is to promote the broadest dissemination of legitimate information through all channels, and not only established, authorized channels."

Believing my problems with Congress were about over, I wanted to have my conflict with CBS clearly drawn before my resignation was announced. However, my problems with Congress weren't over. Far from giving up, the Ethics Committee was preparing for a head-on confrontation.

XI

UNDER SUBPOENA

In Los Angeles with my family, visiting my wife's parents, I met the Democratic nominee for President, Jimmy Carter, at a reception on August 22. He recalled my having interviewed him during the 1972 convention in Miami Beach and said pleasantly that I was missed in this campaign. I replied that my future seemed to depend on what his Georgia compatriot, Congressman John J. Flynt, Jr., chairman of the House Ethics Committee, might have in mind for me. Not about to get involved in this controversy, Carter murmured, "I never have been able to figure out what Jack Flynt has in mind."

Three days later I was lunching at the Beverly Wilshire Hotel with Stanley Sheinbaum, president of the American Civil Liberties Union in Southern California. In the midst of explaining to him that the House investigation appeared to be fading away inconclusively, I was called to the telephone. My wife relayed a message from Washington. The Ethics Committee had just voted, eight to four, to issue subpoenas summoning Clay Felker, Aaron Latham and Sheldon Zalaznick of the *Village Voice,* and me to testify at a public hearing on September 15.

The word "jail" suddenly materialized from a mist of abstraction. Stanley offered the ACLU office for a press conference, but I decided that if there was ever a time for a low profile, this was it, and I would be better off simply responding to queries. When I returned to the home of Fred and Lotte Bamberger, my in-laws, there were already two-dozen messages waiting.

My wife, on such occasions, tends to sublimate apprehension by pitching into tasks at hand. She got the children occupied elsewhere, explained which messages had priority, suggested that I talk to Joe Califano at his summer home in Martha's Vineyard before returning any of the calls and asked where to put an NBC camera crew on its way to interview me.

It was my parents-in-law, refugees from Nazi Germany, where Fred had been in the Dachau concentration camp, whose faces showed alarm.

"Don't worry," I reassured them. "This is a long process. Even if the House votes against me, there will be a series of tests in the courts — maybe up to the Supreme Court — before anything can happen to me. It can be years."

I assumed that the lopsided committee vote to authorize the subpoena, in the face of my proclaimed refusal to identify my source, amounted to a decision to recommend a citation for contempt. I assumed also that, despite an improvement in the climate of opinion since the pursuing posse days of February, the House would support the committee in an investigation it had ordered. Yet, to the surprise of my family, I found myself being more glad than scared about the subpoena. "I think they may have helped to bring the real issue into focus," I said. "It isn't a matter any more of what I did with the Pike report, but where I got the report. It's a clear-cut issue of protection of sources, and I think the press will see it that way. Maybe, after all my mistakes, this won't turn out to be a net minus — if we don't blow it in the hearing. I'm glad to see it come to a head." I'm not sure I convinced any in the family that I wasn't just whistling in the dark.

Jonathan and Lisa didn't seem to perceive the reality of the situation until they saw it on television. I had been invited to the studio of KNXT, the CBS-owned station, to be interviewed live by the anchorpersons of the local news, Connie Chung and Joseph Benti, with whom I had worked in network news. The interview came immediately after the Cronkite show, where Congressman Flynt was seen announcing the subpoenas, in ominous-sounding tones.

"Are you prepared to go to jail?" asked Connie.

"I don't contemplate the prospect with any joy on the eve of my sixtieth birthday," I replied. "I hope it won't come to that, but I cannot betray a source."

It was then, my wife later told me, that Lisa asked, "Do they really want to put Daddy in jail?"

•   •

At the end of August, when I returned to Washington, the Ethics Committee was asking the House for $100,000, in addition to its original $150,000, to complete its investigation. Chairman Flynt told reporters he thought he knew who had provided me with the Pike report, but was not yet in a position to announce the name. I hoped that this was only the customary "appropriation bait," but wondered how close the committee was getting and what surprises it might have in store when it confronted me in the public hearing.

With the end of the Labor Day weekend on September 7, Califano was back from his vacation, and we started strenuous preparations for the hearing the following week. It struck me that this was my first legal contest; I had survived sixty years without ever before having had the need to retain a lawyer. The whole procedure fascinated me. When lawyers prepare to fight a case, the client becomes the object rather than the subject of the exercise, like a patient in a surgical operation, to be consulted over, "prepped" and wheeled into position.

Around Califano's office there was a swirl of activity as he conferred with his associates — John Kuhns and Benjamin Heineman, Jr. (Heineman replaced Robert Barnett, who had joined the Mondale campaign.) They pored over research papers and greeted me with vaguely encouraging words and a preoccupied air. These were some of the impressions of an encounter with a legal dynamo in motion:

First, Califano directed me to shut myself up in an unused office with the twelve-volume transcript of the July hearings of the Ethics Committee, familiarize myself with the testimony and make notes for him on any special problems the testimony might raise for us. When I emerged, Califano and his associates had completed drafting their legal brief, which I asked if I might see. It argued cogently, but in narrow terms, that there was no justification for encroaching on the confidentiality of news sources in the specific circumstances of this case — a House committee report previously approved, most of its substance already known, with no demonstrable harm to national security. I remarked that I would also like the brief to say that in circumstances less favorable, I would still assert the right to protect my source. Califano, a little impatiently, said that this brief was not designed for a television talk show, but for an anticipated judicial test. The Supreme Court had already held that a reporter enjoyed no absolute right of confidentiality in the face of grand jury demands, and what it might decide about congressional demands was very uncertain. If the case could be won on the unreasonableness of the Ethics Committee action without testing the broader constitutional issue, that would still be a victory.

I was sent back to my cubbyhole to draft an opening statement for the hearing. Where, I asked, was the one I wrote last May when Califano had wanted us to be ready for any sudden contingency? *That needs rewriting. Make it direct! Make it personal! Don't try to make any constitutional arguments. That's what you have lawyers for. This is where you state your credo as a reporter.*

On September 13, two days before the hearing, we assembled in Califano's conference room. Containers of coffee were brought in, and Califano told his secretary to hold all calls. Now the surgeon had turned into the shirt-sleeved editor. Pencil in hand, he read my draft statement aloud, very slowly, to Kuhns and Heineman. Each word was weighed and, while the basic substance was accepted, many verbal changes were made. Then I was asked to read the statement aloud, trying to imagine myself at the hearing. Finally, in exasperation, I said, "Why don't you fellows handle the law and let me worry about the broadcasting?"

On September 14, we were back in the conference room. Now the lawyers were playing Ethics Committee, throwing questions at me and testing my answers. Some basic guidelines emerged. *You will* not *testify about how you got the Pike report. You will* not *testify about how the report was handled within CBS.* We worked out specific language to be used in refusing to answer questions: *Respectfully decline . . . Feel that my rights in this matter are protected by the First Amendment . . .* We discussed the categories of questions I would have to answer lest we appear, in court, to have pressed the limits of First Amendment protection too far. *You* will *answer fully all questions about your dealings with the Reporters' Committee and the arrangements for transmitting the report to the* Village Voice. Kuhns explained that these were essentially noneditorial matters that had happened outside my own news organization and could not be validly covered by the First Amendment.

The subject that occupied more of our time than any other was the tricky "waiver problem." It was explained that answering some innocent-sounding question could lead to a claim that I had waived any right to silence on related questions. *Watch for the "Jim Stanton waiver booby trap." They'll ask you to comment on his testimony that you told him you got the Pike report from the CIA. You deny it, and they then start asking you about conversations you had, or didn't have, with everyone on the Pike committee and staff, right down the list.* We deliberated on how I would handle such a question, whether I could say that I had already publicly denied any conversation with Stanton. *No good, they'll say they want you to repeat it under oath.* I said that I didn't want to refuse to answer, which might be taken as confirmation of Stanton's bizarre story. *Say you talked to* nobody *about sources, but don't repeat Stanton's name.* That wasn't precisely accurate. I had discussed my source with Califano, and also with my wife. Would the conversation with my wife be privileged? Califano asked to have a research memorandum quickly drawn up on the subject, and we returned to it after lunch. The memorandum was inconclusive; it was not known whether the husband-wife privilege, which would apply in a criminal court, also extended to a congressional hearing. Finally, Califano said we would simply have to act on the assumption that it did apply, and trust that, in any event, politicians would not be likely to demand that a wife betray her husband. It had taken three hours to work out a prospective scenario on the Stanton question, and we rehearsed it this way:

Q: Did you tell Congressman Stanton, as he has testified, that you received the Pike report from the CIA?

A: I talked to no one about my source other than two privileged persons.

Q: Who are those two persons?

A: My lawyer and my wife.

Califano said his instinct warned him that the "Stanton thing" would be crucial. *Be very careful! I have a funny feeling they may pin their strategy on trying to get you to comment on Stanton, and then claiming waiver.* He impressed on me that the outcome of this test might hinge more on how we picked our way through the minefield of technicalities than on how eloquently we stated our position.

•   •

As we emerged from the conference room to look through ac-cumulated telephone messages, we became aware that enormous press and public interest in the hearing had been building up. Public Television stations WNET, New York, and WETA, Washington, were arguing with the Ethics Committee staff over authorization to arrange live coverage, and wanted our support. Califano told the committee we would welcome it. Advised that they would be limited to one camera, without special lighting, the television producers responded that they would "go live" with a single miniature elec-tronic camera. Nothing like this had been attempted before; if it worked, it would mean that Congress could not effectively prevent live television coverage of any open hearing.

I found myself also basking in the unaccustomed warmth of gen-eral support. In New York, a press conference was held to announce the formation of a Citizens' Committee Concerned with Freedom of the Press, including educators and labor leaders. A petition campaign had been started by Randy Furst, a young reporter for the Minneapolis *Star,* which was taken up nationally by the Newspaper Guild of America. Within two weeks, 5500 signatures were collected in newspaper and television newsrooms around the country. The four reporters of the Fresno, California,

Bee, themselves under a sentence for contempt involving refusal to disclose a news source, signed in their jail cell.

On the eve of the hearing, while I was closeted with my lawyers, a press conference "in defense of Daniel Schorr" was being held in the House Office Building, the room arranged by Congressman H. John Heinz III of Pennsylvania, who led a bipartisan group of thirty-five House members backing my position. Reporter Furst brandished telegrams from Walter Cronkite, John Chancellor, Barbara Walters and Jack Anderson. He introduced union leaders, members of Congress and an array of journalistic stars including Dan Rather, Carl Bernstein, Seymour Hersh, Mary McGrory and I. F. Stone.

I listened later, with unalloyed pleasure, to a tape of the press conference, hearing Rather and Bernstein impersonally support the First Amendment and Hersh and Stone upbraid them for not backing me more directly. Hersh, praising me in his own fashion as "a competitor I had great respect for," stated, "I'm wholeheartedly for the issue, and I'm wholeheartedly for Dan Schorr." Izzy Stone, in magnificent fury, roared, "I cannot understand how respected journalists who are my friends should have allowed themselves . . . to engage in a campaign of denigration and character assassination." Mary McGrory, who hates to speak in public, was there to say, "Dan Schorr's brothers and sisters can remind the House that all he was doing was finishing the job that they had begun and lost their nerve about." Then Charles Perlik, Jr., president of the American Newspaper Guild, led a delegation down the hall to deliver the petitions and telegrams to the House Ethics Committee. Chairman Flynt called Califano to complain of the "pressure" being put on the committee. Califano told him that it wasn't our pressure.

The Ethics Committee had clearly not reckoned with the reaction that its subpoena to a reporter would produce — a belated backlash against the antisecrecy backlash, a surge of sentiment for an unfettered press. On the eve of the hearing I was buoyed by the hope that House members who had voted "their American Legion posts" in January might now be getting different signals from home.

●   ●

My wife awoke on September 15 with a severe headache — I assumed more because of tension about her husband's position as a potential jailbird than her impending position in the "Maureen Dean spot" behind the witness. We met Califano and his associates at his office and proceeded to Capitol Hill in two taxis, Califano observing, on the way, that perhaps we should have let CBS pay for a limousine — a reminder of the summer of CBS discontent about paying the bills. At the Rayburn Building, we heard that the line of spectators for the ten o'clock hearing had started forming inside at 6:30 A.M. As Califano and I mounted the marble steps in a drizzling rain, he turned to me, saying, "Hey, isn't there something terribly wrong with this picture? Isn't it always the *Jewish* lawyer with the *Italian* gangster?"

Entering the huge hearing room of the Education and Labor Committee, I had, more vividly than ever, the sense of role reversal that I had first experienced in 1972 testifying before Senator Ervin about the FBI investigation. Having covered many a hearing from behind the same bank of cameras now pointed my way, I had often wondered what a principal witness thought about in the waiting period while flashlights clicked and reporters stared from the press table. Now I knew: being the center of attention quickly became a normal condition. The sense of theater stilled the sense of anxiety. One nodded to colleagues no longer colleagues, one consulted one's lawyer about matters that didn't matter. One even asked one's wife how her headache was.

Then the event itself took over. The first witnesses were Felker, Latham and Zalaznick to testify about the *Village Voice* part of the episode. They could say how *they* got the Pike report; they did not know how *I* had gotten it. Yet, when Latham was asked by committee counsel John Marshall if he had "any knowledge whatsoever" of how or from whom I had received the report, he refused to answer and persisted in his refusal after being formally warned by Chairman Flynt that he could be held in contempt of Congress. To many in the hearing room it seemed incomprehensible that Latham would risk jail for refusing to provide information he did not have.

Then I heard Marshall saying, "Mr. Daniel Schorr to the witness stand." I felt, oddly, no anxiety, only the same kind of tension that came with an important broadcast in prime time. The statement I had rehearsed twenty times came easily:

"Mr. Chairman, I appear before this committee today under protest, in response to a subpoena whose issuance I deeply deplore . . ."

Addressing myself first to the materials the subpoena had demanded of me, I stated that I would not supply the copy of the Pike report in my possession because examination could conceivably help to determine its source. The statement concluded:

"Mr. Chairman and members of the committee, we all build our lives around certain principles, and without these principles our careers simply lose their meaning. For some of us — doctors, lawyers, clergymen, and, yes, journalists — it is an article of faith that we must keep confidential those matters entrusted to us only because of the assurance that they would remain confidential.

"Now, for a journalist the most crucial kind of confidence is the identity of a source of information. To betray a confidential source would mean to dry up many future sources for many reporters. The reporter and the news organization would be the immediate losers, but I would submit to you that the ultimate losers would be the American people and their free institutions.

"And, if you will permit one last personal word . . . to betray a source would for me be to betray myself, my career and my life. And to say that I refuse to do it isn't quite saying it right. I cannot do it."

I could tell from the hush and the faces of the committee members that the statement had made an impression, but Marshall plunged ahead with his prepared scenario. He insisted that I produce the copy of the Pike report and the notes I had taken during coverage of the Pike committee. When I refused, Chairman Flynt read a form statement warning me that "willful refusal" would "subject you to prosecution and punishment by a fine or imprisonment or both." After which, according to the ritual, I had to refuse again.

Next came the "Stanton waiver booby trap," almost exactly as forecast.

MARSHALL: Did you have that conversation with Congressman Stanton?

SCHORR: I have never discussed with anyone anything relating to the source of that report other than with two privileged persons.

MARSHALL: Do you mean by that response that your answer is no, you did not have that conversation?

SCHORR: My response must speak for itself.

MARSHALL: Who were the two privileged persons that you discussed the report with?

SCHORR: My counsel, Mr. Califano, and my wife.

Marshall continued to press for a more direct reply, accusing me of being nonresponsive, but I held my ground. Chairman Flynt demanded, on pain of another contempt citation, that I respond.

FLYNT: The question was: did you have such a conversation with Representative James V. Stanton? That question is very clear. Your answer does not appear to be responsive to the question. You are therefore again directed to answer the question.

SCHORR: I find it sufficiently responsive, and I find that I cannot answer it in precisely the terms that you put it, because I have no intention of starting down a list of people to whom I may or may not have spoken . . .

FLYNT: And you refuse to answer the question?

SCHORR: In the terms in which it is now stated, I refuse, although I consider my answer sufficiently responsive.

Few in the hearing room understood that, of nine threatened citations for contempt, this one was the most perilous for me. Infinitely worse than a confrontation over First Amendment rights would be the appearance of having "blown" the case on a technicality. At the luncheon recess I was relieved to be told by Califano, Kuhns and Heineman that I had "done fine." Chairman Flynt courteously invited us to have lunch sent up to his committee's office, where we might have some rest and privacy, sitting around his conference table as we prepared for the afternoon session. Marshall looked in to express admiration at the "professionalism" with which we had handled ourselves.

In the afternoon, Marshall set what looked like one more "waiver trap." He asked whether I had paid any money to the person who had given me the Pike report. Warily, I said that I did not want to open up a line of questions directed to my source, but would be happy to say that "no money ever changed hands in any way in any connection with the report." Marshall made one further stab at narrowing my answer to the point where he could claim I had opened the door to questions about my source. He asked whether my general reply "also refers to specifics" — whether it represented a reply to his specific question. As coached, I refused to apply my general answer to a specific question, and Marshall gave up, turning the questioning over to committee members.

Suddenly, the feeling in the hearing room changed, and the hostility that had accompanied nine accusations of contempt began to evaporate. The accusatory atmosphere in which the investigation had been launched seven months before seemed almost palpably to be lifting. On live television, my nemeses acted curiously defensive, almost apologetic at the climax of their long pursuit. They seemed now more frustrated than angry, and they phrased their questions in courteous tones.

The South Carolina Republican Floyd D. Spence, who had been one of my most ardent critics, asked me to understand the problem of Congress in trying to keep its secrets.

Conceding that "policing your house . . . is a perfectly legitimate and necessary function," I sought to define the limit. In trying to recover information, "you cross that very delicate, fragile, important line that has to do with what is your legitimate function and what is our legitimate function."

To the hypothetical question of whether I would disclose a source if a life depended on it, I said that I was not an absolutist, though I had never in forty years of journalism encountered a case where any other consideration had outweighed the need to protect a source. "That's the answer I wanted," said Spence with satisfaction.

James H. Quillen, the hard-bitten Tennessee Republican, wanted me to explain why the internal handling of information in a news organization should be protected by the First Amendment. I said that "when a subpoena is issued to try to compel the production of information about the specifics of that process . . . the element of compulsion involved in this is a chilling element for future consultation." After a further colloquy, I was amazed to hear Quillen say, "I understand your sincerity, Mr. Schorr, and I respect it."

My inquisition was turning into a seminar, and I was beginning to enjoy myself. Broad questions provided opportunities to make some of the points that had ripened along the lecture trail.

> *On secrecy:* "There have been situations in which a President of the United States has cloaked the cover-up of illegality with the invocation of national security . . . While I do have great respect for national security, I have very little respect for the system of classification . . . I would be given pause if I thought it [disclosure] would do harm."

> *On defying the House:* "I emphatically do not agree that the House has the right to . . . try to enforce its rules by reaching out to the press and establishing, in fact, a gag order . . . This House was created to be responsive to the political will of its constituency . . . The press was given a different function. The press, as I see it in the Constitution, was given the function of monitoring what the government does, of giving people information, even information which may at that moment not be popular . . ."

> *On the role of the press:* "There is a necessary tension between what you do and what I do . . . Once a secret is out, if you go and try to chase it down, and call it back, and punish the one who has published it, then I think you have gone too far . . . How in God's name can we expose the secrets of government and let the people know what the government is doing if we can only expose what you say we can expose?"

As the hearing neared its close, Thad Cochran, Mississippi Republican, said, "I support you a hundred percent — or if the vogue is a thousand percent, or whatever it is — in your refusal to disclose your source." Charles E. Bennett, Florida Democrat, who had made the original motion to subpoena me, said the committee's intention was not to harm me, but it felt obliged to get my testimony. He was sorry if I "took a little umbrage."

Some sort of miracle had happened: the confrontation had turned into a classroom — for Congress and for the nation. The First Amendment seemed alive and well.

"Mr. Schorr," said Chairman Flynt, "you and your counsel, Mr. Califano, may step down. You are excused from your subpoena." Marshall leaned toward him and whispered urgently in his ear. Flynt corrected himself. "Strike that! We do *not* excuse you from your subpoena because we continue to demand the answering of questions which you have previously refused to answer."

Flynt had almost forgotten his own contempt warnings. By the time we were back in Califano's office, informal nose counts showed at least six out of twelve committee members opposing a contempt citation — meaning that it already lacked the needed majority. We were also told that the House leadership was warning the committee that a recommendation for contempt would probably fail on the floor and damage the investigative authority of all committees.

I went home and took a nap, which is my favorite way of releasing tension. A telegram from Salant, resuming a contact broken in February, said, "Congratulations. Your appearance today was superb and an immense service to all your fellow journalists, to the Constitution and to the public's right to know. I am grateful."

An impish history ordained that Salant would that day be in Williamsburg, Virginia, attending the convention of the CBS radio affiliates who had wanted me fired. He told them that I had spoken before the committee "courageously, eloquently, brilliantly, but not arrogantly," immediately adding, "Now, let's separate that out from all the other difficult issues which may be on your minds, and are on my mind — the questions of what he did with the report afterward, the question of turning it over to the *Village Voice,* the question of whether he had any right to do it, since our position is that it was our property."

Also in Williamsburg was Arthur Taylor, who later said that he thought of me as he paid tribute in a speech to the Virginia patriots who had run risks for freedom two centuries earlier. His speech concluded, "They took those risks for all of us, and, in a sense, we owe it to them and to the future to take further risks to insure that the principles they fought for continue to flourish." Taylor recalled to me that these were his last public words as a CBS officer, coming less than a month before Paley fired him.

A week later, in a complicated series of votes, the House Ethics Committee formally decided to abandon any effort to have me cited for contempt. Its final report stated, "This committee did not recommend that Mr. Schorr be held in contempt, but it does consider his action in causing publication of the report to be reprehensible." It noted approvingly that "the journalism profession itself exposed the involvement of Mr. Schorr."

On the basic issue of control of information, the committee was unyielding: "Newsmen, just like anybody else, are not infallible in their judgment of what is right or wrong, good or bad, for our Nation. The mere assertion by a newsman that he revealed some Government secret 'for the good of the country' does not insure the country actually will benefit. Nor is the assertion that the Government overclassifies much information a guarantee that the revealed secret will not do great harm. The fact is, the news media frequently do not possess sufficient information on which to make a prudent decision on whether the revelation of a secret will help or harm . . ."

One could not expect this committee of Congress to be persuaded that information which has reached a news reporter is, by simple virtue of that fact, no longer secret. It was in character for a security-oriented panel to demand that reporters caulk the leaks sprung by government officials. Perhaps the failure to resolve the debate about "who decides?" was itself a part of the "necessary tension" between government and the press.

What mattered to me was that the seven-month investigation had not tracked down my source nor compelled me to reveal it, and I felt encouraged to hope that Congress would be more hesitant in the future to engage in such a confrontation. It had cost the taxpayers $450,000 for the Pike committee to prepare a report to the public on intelligence operations, and another $250,000 trying in vain to discover how that report had actually reached the public. It had cost $150,000 in legal bills that CBS balkily and complainingly paid to Califano to defend the confidentiality of news sources. It would be left to history to determine how much of the expense, the time and the trauma were justified.

I listened to my children making their own recapitulation. "Daddy had a secret," said six-year-old Lisa, "and got into trouble because he wouldn't tell anyone his secret."

"No, dumdum," said Jonathan. "Daddy had a secret, and he gave it to a newspaper, and Congress got mad, and wanted to put him in jail, but the consumers of America thought Daddy was right, and they wouldn't let Congress put Daddy in jail."

I explained to them that they were both right. Daddy had two secrets — one that he had to tell and one that he couldn't tell. And it was true that the "consumers of America" had saved him from jail.

• •

With the end of the congressional investigation on September 22, a strange CBS minuet began. Formally, the time had finally come to conclude that I was no longer under investigation* and to accept my long-pending resignation. Instead, CBS stated to the press, "He is not reinstated as of this moment. We will address ourselves to the problems between us promptly." Socolow telephoned to ask me to meet with Salant in New York the following Monday.

CBS News Correspondent Marya McLaughlin interviewed me for the Cronkite show, asking what was the next step between me and the network. Not mentioning the scheduled Monday meeting with Salant, which Socolow had asked me to keep confidential, I said simply, "The ball is in the CBS court."

In the *New York Times* next morning, Les Brown wrote, "High-ranking officials of the network were reported so impressed with Mr. Schorr's presentation before the committee last week, and with the public reaction to it, that his chances for reinstatement appeared markedly improved." It was as though CBS was reconsidering the cancelation of a program in the light of an unexpected surge in ratings.

---

*Technically, I was still under the scrutiny of the Justice Department, which did not advise me until April 6, 1977, that "our investigation of this matter has now been completed and we do not contemplate taking any further action in this case at this time."

The next day Salant interviewed eight CBS News executives and correspondents — mostly anchormen — separately, seeking their views on whether I should be reinstated. Mike Wallace and Dan Rather told me later they had advised reinstatement. So did George Herman, who reported that, when asked by Salant if Schorr's presence would demoralize the Washington bureau, he replied, "No more than it always did." I could not ascertain the views of Walter Cronkite and others.

CBS seemed to be proceeding on the assumption that I would gladly waive the well-compensated resignation it had forced upon me in February. I resented having been abandoned under fire, when I was being widely damned, and being considered for reinstatement now, when I was being widely applauded. I disliked what looked to me like a smear tactic in the late-blooming "issue" of my alleged effort to implicate Lesley Stahl and Aaron Latham in the transmission of the Pike report, which had only begun surfacing in CBS-inspired press reports when other complaints about me had started losing their persuasiveness. Furthermore, in the seven months of adjusting my sights to the assumption of separation, I had started making plans for lecturing, teaching and writing, and had found the withdrawal symptoms of removal from television reporting less painful than anticipated.

Yet, for all my Byzantine experiences, a quarter century of my life was bound up in this organization, and I vacillated about what I would say on Monday. "It depends," I told Califano, "on what they say. If they want me to come back, I'll ask, 'To do what?' I haven't thought beyond that."

"You're mad!" he said. "There's nothing to go back to. They just want to get rid of that awful February agreement and have you back until people forget you're a hero, and dump you then."

The next day Mike Wallace called and said he wanted to interview me for the "60 Minutes" program. "You're news!" he said. "You're the man of the week after that great performance before the Ethics Committee. We want you for our show. It's my idea, and we haven't asked any executives about it." I agreed to tape an interview in the

CBS Washington studio on Saturday evening for broadcast on Sunday.

When we met, Wallace and Don Hewitt, the executive producer of "60 Minutes," expressed hope that I would be back at work soon. They knew — though it had not been announced — that I was seeing Salant on Monday.

From the control room — actually a truck parked outside the building — Hewitt gave the cue to "Roll tape!" Wallace began, "Dan, you have my profound admiration and that of your colleagues here and elsewhere, I know, for the eloquent and persuasive case that you made for the protection of a reporter's sources." Twice, because of technical problems, Hewitt asked Wallace to start over. The third time, while waiting for the cue to begin again, Wallace jocularly voiced impatience with the interruptions: "I'm going to have this line down about my profound admiration pat by the time — as a matter of fact, what I'm going to say is: 'I think you're a shit, Schorr, and most of your colleagues do, too, and . . .' " Hewitt came in over the loudspeaker and said he was ready to start.

The interview itself dwelt at length with the issue of leaks versus security, the problem of disclosure of grand jury testimony and a variety of other general subjects. Finally, Wallace asked me if I knew why I had been suspended by CBS. When I replied that I was not sure, he said, "I think I do. Correct me if you think I'm wrong. You denied to the CBS management that you supplied the Pike papers to the *Village Voice* . . ."

Depressed at the turn the interview had taken — so incestuous a dialogue at so delicate a moment — I sought to explain my actions, and finally said, "I'm not sure how much further I want to discuss this because it kind of hurts to be involved in a discussion which is so basically trivial."

The Stahl matter was one of three complaints that Wallace said would be raised with me on Monday. A second was the question of property right in the Pike report — "that you offered the material, which arguably belonged as much to CBS News as to Dan Schorr, to another publication." A third was my speech at Duke University criticizing the CBS handling of the Nixon resignation.

"What am I addressing?" I asked. "Am I addressing the CBS position?"

"No," said Wallace, "you're addressing my questions. As I told you before I went on the air, this interview was my notion."

The hour-long interview was cut to twelve minutes. Deleted were Wallace's thrice-stated expression of admiration and the general discussion of secrecy and disclosure. This was like retribution for all the interviews I had ever persuaded public figures to give against their own interests and all the complaints of tendentious excerpting that had ever been directed to me. It struck me that I had permitted Wallace to serve as an instrument for television's vengeance against one of its own who had fallen from grace.

When Wallace asked, during the Saturday night taping, if I wanted to return to CBS I replied, "While I haven't determined exactly what my future is, I have learned one thing: I don't need broadcasting as much as I thought I did." I was still temporizing. On Sunday a procedural snag forced me to stop wavering. I had stated that I was bringing Califano with me for the Monday meeting in New York, determined not to repeat the February experience of facing a CBS tribunal alone. Socolow advised that Salant objected to the presence of a lawyer. When I phoned Salant at his home in Connecticut to ask the reason for his objection, he explained that no lawyer was needed for a purely internal discussion between employer and employee involving no legal problems.

I interrupted him, "Dick, I've known you too long to leave you in the dark until tomorrow. It's my intention to resign."

There was a long silence at the other end of the line, and then a gasp of consternation.

I suddenly felt depressed. I realized that he had been totally unprepared for this development and that he clearly had personally not wanted this outcome. We had both been propelled toward a final break, my boss in no more control of the situation than myself.

I said I could not understand his surprise since my resignation had been made inescapable by the agreement we had signed together in February. Salant said he had not understood at the time what was in the agreement, drafted by corporate lawyers from Black Rock; that when he realized a few weeks later how it foreclosed all options, he wanted to tear it up. It had always been his real intention to keep the door open to my possible return, he said. It didn't make much sense, but I didn't argue.

"I planned my life on the assumption that people mean what they say and do," I said.

"I guess you're right," replied Salant. "I simply goofed on this."

I paid him some warm and sincere words of tribute and told him I was aware of the enormous pressures he had been under. It was hard to close the conversation. At one point, we lapsed into silence, broken when Salant groaned, "Oh Christ!" Finally, feeling as dismal as he sounded, I said, "See you tomorrow."

Monday afternoon in Salant's office was the final act of the drama of the two February meetings. Califano was with me, and Salant had brought in John Prettyman, of Washington, to replace the CBS corporate lawyers whom he blamed for much of his problem. Califano started by presenting my one-sentence letter of resignation "in accordance with the letter agreement of February 23." My journal notes, made that evening, describe what happened next:

Salant says he won't accept resignation under the February 23 agreement. Prettyman notes timing of resignation is at CBS discretion. I say yes, but discretion only to determine when investigation over, which it obviously is. Salant says let's talk about reinstatement. I say, "But you fired me in February." He says, "Then I'm rehiring you now." I say it won't work — would be impossible situation for Small, and difficult for Socolow. Those two sit stonily silent.

Califano and Prettyman go next door to Small's office to work out something, leaving rest of us talking uncomfortably. Socolow leaves, without goodby, apparently no longer needed if we're not going to hash out who said what about Stahl and Latham. After a while Salant says, "Let's see what the lawyers are doing." Turns out that, to save CBS' face, they are negotiating a new resignation agreement. Califano advises me to go along with this, saying they're so desperately anxious to destroy the February 23 letter that they're willing to improve terms of resignation, giving me greater freedom to work — even on television on occasional basis — while still on CBS payroll. Califano asks me to start drafting a letter to Salant to go with my resignation.

Outside Salant's office, CBS News Correspondent David Culhane is staked out with cameraman Herb Schwartz, hoping for something to break in time for the Cronkite show. CBS News staking out the president of CBS News to find out what happens to a correspondent of CBS News! I tell Culhane I understand his problems, but in this situation I can't leak — he'll have to wait for the final communiqué. Finally, the lawyers have the papers ready, but there is an unexplained delay. Salant leaves, returns later in the evening and says he's very embarrassed, but can't sign tonight. There are two "clearances" he can't get. One is Arthur Taylor, celebrating his wife's fortieth birthday and refusing to take calls. Salant doesn't mention the other. Paley?

We signed next morning. My new resignation letter said, "At sixty, it may well be that my best contribution can be made in other ways than daily broadcasting. Furthermore, aware of the polarizing effects within CBS News of the controversy involving me, I would doubt my ability to function effectively if reinstated. I believe that my reinstatement would be a source of tension within an organization whose future success I still care about . . . I leave CBS News with sadness, but without rancor."

Salant's reply said, ". . . I share your sadness. Your many years of reporting for CBS News have been unusually distinguished and a major contribution to American broadcast journalism." He concluded with renewed praise for my testimony before the House Ethics Committee.

As Salant and I shook hands and he jokingly invited me to join him in a tennis match with Arthur Taylor, it seemed to both of us a reasonably elegant close to a stormy chapter. After my return to Washington, Small had dinner with Califano and told him that Salant had been "really ready to take Schorr back" after going through a three-point agenda that included the disposition of the Pike report, the suspicion that fell upon Lesley Stahl and my criticism of CBS at Duke University — precisely the agenda that Mike Wallace had predicted. Small also said that had I been reinstated in the Washington bureau, Eric Sevareid would have been furious; Socolow would have found his position in Washington "impossible" and would have probably been transferred; Stahl might have resigned.*

Having spared CBS an internal upheaval, I hoped that the détente we had reached could be sustained. I talked warmly of CBS News as I was interviewed on tape for CBS Radio on leaving Salant's office, and on film for the Cronkite show on my return to National Airport in Washington. The filmed interview was not used, and my heart sank when, instead, I heard Cronkite giving his own version of my resignation — using the smear that I had considered to be part of a discarded CBS contingency plan. Citing the reference in my letter to not wishing to be "a source of tension," Cronkite said, "That is an allusion to the reason for his original suspension — not, as the public generally believes, for giving a newspaper the House Intelligence Committee report, but for, among other things, letting a colleague be suspected for a time as the source of the leak."

When I protested to CBS that this had not even been mentioned at the time of my "suspension," Cronkite agreed to broadcast a correction. The next night, he conceded on the Evening News that he "misspoke," but went on to say that letting a colleague be suspected "was the reason for the tensions within CBS News that he said led to his resignation — not the suspension itself." He was wrong again.

Perhaps it is in the nature of an escapist medium to trivialize its conflicts, personalize its disputes and construct its own consoling realities.

As to the tensions I had in mind, I submit that I am the best authority. They were the tensions that resulted from my inability to accept the standards of the media establishment, my unwillingness to squeeze news exclusively through television's narrow funnel, my suspicion that news decisions were sometimes steered by corporate tugs at the reins — and, most of all, my heretical position that a vast

---

*A possible solution that Salant discussed with Arthur Taylor and John Schneider in preparation for the meeting with me was my being assigned to New York or a foreign bureau "until the dust settled," Taylor told me in a postmortem a year later.

media enterprise with profound impact on American society was as valid a subject for examination as the government.

Out of television now, I returned in a reporter's role to work on a story as fascinating as Nixon's White House and Helms' CIA — Paley's CBS.

XII

THE SOLE PROPRIETOR

SIX MONTHS after leaving CBS, I asked the chairman of the board, William S. Paley, what part he had played in forcing me out. None at all, he said, and advised me to talk to Richard Salant, "a truthful and honest man [who] will tell you that he never had any instructions from William S. Paley."

"What was Paley's role?" I asked Salant.

"Never spoke to me about it," was his crisp reply, and then he added, teasing, "Come on, Dan, you're a better reporter than that. What's your next question?"

The Harvard-trained lawyer who had hopped off the corporate ladder out of his attachment for news was nearing retirement as head of the news division and in an impish mood. Behind him lay years of defending the integrity of information in a great entertainment enterprise, jealously fending off the encroachments of the Kingdom of Dreams and Profits on his little Duchy of Reality and Deficits. He himself had been abruptly removed as president of CBS News in 1964 to make way for Fred W. Friendly and as abruptly restored in 1966 after Friendly's departure. Among the occasional painful tasks that Salant had had to perform was to fire his effervescent deputy, Gordon Manning, because Paley had taken an inexplicable dislike to him as companion on his 1973 trip to China, and replace Manning with the soft-spoken Washington bureau chief, William Small, to whom Paley had taken a liking. Salant had seen his own mentor, CBS President Frank Stanton, forced into retirement by Paley and, most recently, had seen Stanton's successor, Arthur Taylor, suddenly fired by Paley. At the corporate peaks Paley's actions were visible, if not comprehensible. Viewed from below they seemed obscured in mist.

"My next question," I said, "is to repeat my first question: What was Paley's role?"

"Well," said Salant, "Paley dealt with Taylor and Schneider. I kept getting calls from them — 'Paley says this . . . Paley says that . . . Paley wants you to . . . He thinks so and so.' When people talk from over there, you never know whether they are really passing along what the guy said or whether they are just using his name. All I can say is that I got all sorts of messages about what Mr. Paley thought." After the *Village Voice* publication of the Pike report, the message was that "he was jumping all over the lot."

When I asked Taylor about it, he said that he had had very little discussion with Paley about specific decisions — he suspected, in fact, that Paley had been going around him directly to Salant or through Schneider. As president of the CBS Broadcast Group, Schneider reigns over Paley's empire within its original borders, before it expanded into records, books, toys and a baseball club. Schneider personified the new echelon interposed between the News Division and top management in 1966 that had spurred Friendly to resignation. As to the decisions concerning me, Schneider said that he had been "in the stream of deliberations," had been a link in "the chain of consideration," not in any very active way. But Paley? Far, far removed, said Schneider, whatever the people lower down might surmise.

Schneider volunteered an anecdote about the folly of trying to project the boss's desires. "They were preparing for the opening of 'Who's Who' [the program about personalities, spun off from '60 Minutes' in early 1977 and terminated at the end of that season]. Somebody said, 'Gee, why don't we open with Leopold Stokowski? I just know Paley would love that. It probably isn't the right interview to open with, but Paley's going to be seeing the first episode, and he'll like that one.' Well, there were two things wrong with that decision. First, it wasn't good programming; we've got to have more popular appeal. Secondly, Paley saw it and hated it. He said, 'What are we putting on those old guys for? Whoever heard of Leopold

Stokowski?' So, people worry about little things that will please Paley or displease Paley, or please Schneider or displease Schneider. And it's just the wrong way to live!"

The anecdote, aside from putting Schneider on the side of those who see Paley as young in heart, had a reminiscent ring. It stirred recent memories of Washington investigations that had mired down in talk of overzealous subordinates overreacting to the President's ambiguous words. I was back with the Senate Intelligence Committee, seeking the reasons for the derailment of decision-making — if that, indeed, is what it was — and finding itself awash in "circumlocution and euphemism," "plausible deniability," "differing perceptions" and "floating authorization."

It was much the same as I embarked on my inquiry into Paley's CBS — the strangest inquiry of my career. I wanted to know more about the relationship between the two-billion-dollar-a-year world of prime time, courtship of affiliates and fear of government, and its brash little appendage of news, which filled less than 5 percent of the prime-time hours, in ways that sometimes irritated the affiliates, infuriated the government and gave Bill Paley a stomachache.

Explaining that I was impelled not by vindictiveness but inquisitiveness, I asked to interview old bosses — and *their* bosses. All of them talked to me — most of them on tape. Often they were in startling contradiction with each other about the course of events, and about the role of Paley. Paley himself sat with me for almost four hours over a two-day period, his tape recorder alongside mine — once "taking a feed" from his former employee when he accidentally erased part of his tape. We spent more time in direct conversation in February 1977 than during all the twenty-three years I had worked for him.

For most of those years, Paley had been more legend than person for me — the practical visionary who had built both a successful entertainment network and, with Edward R. Murrow as his conscience, the finest and most pampered news organization in the industry. My first direct communication from Paley came in 1956 when I was stationed in Moscow. He wrote asking me to look after his "favorite niece," Kate Roosevelt, the stepdaughter of Jock Whitney, whose wife was the sister of Paley's wife. For courtesies easy to extend to the charming young tourist, I was rewarded, on my return to New York, with house seats for *My Fair Lady,* the vastly successful Broadway musical that Paley's uncanny sense about entertainment had acquired for CBS, and with an invitation to a Sunday supper-musicale at the Whitney estate in Manhasset, Long Island.

Stationed in Germany from 1960 until 1966, I joined other European correspondents who were summoned to Paris during Paley's biennial trips for a leisurely lunch, with faultless service and exquisite wines, in his suite at the Hotel Ritz. These meetings had no visible purpose other than to display Paley's continuing interest in the old Murrow news organization. The unstructured conversations, under the influence of cocktails, wine and after-lunch cognac, had sometimes unexpected results.

At lunch in the spring of 1962, Paley complimented me on the recently aired "CBS Reports" documentary on East Germany, "Land Beyond the Wall." Its dramatic climax showed Walther Ulbricht, the East German Communist leader, upbraiding me for my questions and finally storming out of the room in full view of the camera. "What I admired most," said Paley, "was the coolness with which you sat there and looked at him while he was yelling at you."

Breaking into laughter, I said, "Surely you understand that the shots of me looking cool were 'reverses,' filmed after Ulbricht had left the room!" No, Paley had not understood that, and had not known about "reverses" and he wanted all this explained. Feeling as though I was betraying some company secret — albeit to the head of the company — I proceeded to explain in detail the conventional postinterview procedure for shifting the camera and focusing it on the correspondent to repeat the principal questions, plus a gamut of absorbed and skeptical poses, all of this to be spliced into the interview to add variety and facilitate editing. Paley was fascinated.

"But isn't it basically dishonest?" he asked finally. "Aren't you in a position to sharpen your question the second time around? And can't you arrange your reactions the way you would have liked to have them?"

"Absolutely! And that temptation will be there unless you're willing to go to the expense of having two cameras each time." With a sense of plunging deeper, I went on:

"The deception goes much further than that. Let's talk about your friend, General Eisenhower. He recently filmed a series of interviews with Walter Cronkite. I happened to see how a transcript was being edited. At one point, Eisenhower was made to appear to be answering a question he had actually been asked several pages earlier. The producer explained to me that Ike was sometimes so diffuse that questions had to be rearranged to match his replies."

Paley looked deeply shocked. By the time I was back in Bonn that evening, I heard reverberations from New York. Paley had ordered the summary abolition of subsequently filmed reactions and questions, and any editing that attached answers to the wrong questions. His sweeping order, which had film editors wringing their hands, was later quietly eased to permit "reverses" when approved by the interview subject. Since 1962, however, CBS News policy had reflected the Paley rebellion against the creeping deception that his news people had, almost unconsciously, slipped into. That was one kind of Paley intervention into news precincts — as the watchdog of honesty.

Another side of Paley was displayed at a subsequent Paris luncheon. The CBS Radio Network, trying to keep its fingernail-hold on solvency, had begun requiring correspondents to "billboard" commercials — that is, to mention the names of the sponsors. I argued that the tawdriness of the practice harmed the prestige of the correspondents and of CBS News. With a flash of irritation, Paley said that if I was not happy with the commercial requirements of radio, I could give up doing the broadcasts. That was Paley, the businessman.

My real troubles with Paley, however, stemmed from his involvements on the American scene. In my interviews with him I sought answers to a series of questions resulting from these entanglements.

•   •

Why did Paley react so vehemently in 1964 to my broadcast about Senator Goldwater?

There was a side to Paley I discovered for the first time in my interviews with him — the dabbler in presidential politics. "I was an FDR man during FDR's time. I was very neutral on Truman. Eisenhower and I were very close friends. I was very, very strong for Eisenhower. And I got pretty close to Nixon."

Close enough not only to play golf with him and contribute money to his campaign, but to try to become his adviser. In 1960, after studying figures indicating successive Nixon gains in the four television debates, Paley became convinced that Nixon could beat Kennedy if he accepted his opponent's challenge to two more debates. He tried to make the point at a strategy meeting in New York's Waldorf Astoria Hotel, but an exhausted Nixon left before Paley could get his ear. He then tried to arrange to accompany Nixon on a trip to Newark, but Nixon said only on condition that there be no discussion of the debates. Paley gave up — convinced forever afterward that his advice could have won the election. At a luncheon after the election, where Nixon first raised the question of running for governor of California, only Paley and former Secretary of the Treasury Robert Anderson advised him against it.

"You'd be a fool to do it," Paley remembers saying. "You don't have to worry about being forgotten. Adlai Stevenson didn't do anything for four years, and he got the presidential nomination again. And, if you run for governor, there's always a chance you might lose." Paley recalls with satisfaction the chorus of protests, and someone's admonition, "How can you even think that?"

Against the background of his deep involvement in Republican politics, I could better understand Paley's chagrin in 1964 when he found himself embroiled in controversy with Senator Goldwater over my broadcast from Germany. At the Republican convention in San Francisco, he was, because of his friendship with Eisenhower, assumed to be a supporter of Governor William Scranton of Pennsylvania. ("I had never met Scranton at the time, though I knew his brother-in-law, Jim Linen, the publisher of *Time,* and Scranton's sister quite well.") Paley denies that anyone advised him against going to San Francisco. (Frank Stanton, however, says, "I can remember urging him not to go. Bill had a way of getting into things and really screwing up the works at the last minute.")

Paley also does not remember what Fred Friendly vividly recalls — that, for four days running, after the Goldwater eruption, he demanded that I be fired. That, said Paley, was "absolutely untrue"; he had "never once" said to an executive of CBS News that "I think so-and-so ought to be fired." What Paley remembers is disappointment. "I put it down as one of the few occasions when I thought CBS had not lived up to its traditions that I was so proud of."

Was it then also untrue — as Arthur Taylor had told me — that during the controversy over the Pike report in 1976, Paley had said I should have been fired, as he had wanted, in 1964? "No, no. I said, 'I've had this thing about Schorr in my mind for a long time.' I was a great admirer of yours, but . . . under fire you failed me, so to speak." Whether Paley specifically talked of firing me in 1964, as Friendly once again reaffirmed, and, in 1976, as Taylor remembers, may, perhaps, not be crucially important. When the chairman says, "I've had this thing" about someone, no one misses the message.

Salant said he inherited the problem when he returned to the CBS News presidency in 1966. "Paley would bring up the Goldwater controversy, and I would say, 'Mr. Paley, I don't know the facts. I can't discuss it.' And regularly he would say, 'How do you feel about Dan Schorr?' And then he'd go through the whole damn thing, and it would get to be a more and more embellished story all the time And my mission in life then was to keep you on the payroll."

It was easier for the chairman to hold a twelve-year grudge against a correspondent who had unwittingly embarrassed him than to analyze his ambiguous position in San Francisco as the head of a network and a dilettante in Republican politics. Paley was not conspiring against Goldwater, as the candidate charged, but he *was* against Goldwater, which made him vulnerable. It took him another few years to understand that vulnerability.

In 1968, Governor Nelson Rockefeller, a good friend, was Paley's favorite candidate. He believes that Nixon knew it, "and I don't think he ever forgave me for that, and, since 1968, I was in his bad books." In 1970, the chairman finally decided it might be wise for him to get out of politics. "The electoral process had become so closely tied to the affairs of broadcasting that I said to myself that I don't think it's fair to be a partisan anymore." He had never exerted influence through CBS to help a candidate, but he thought that even appearances might be harmful. So he would go to the polls and cast a secret ballot, like any other citizen, and make no more political contributions. Herbert Kalmbach, President Nixon's private lawyer and fund-raiser, came to see him before the 1972 election, and Paley told him of his new attitude. He found Kalmbach quite understanding. "He seemed like a very nice guy. He said, 'I agree with you a hundred percent. I think you're absolutely right.' "

"From that time onward," said Paley, "I've been absolutely impartial. I haven't given a nickel to anybody. So I stand today clean, so to speak, as far as appearances are concerned."

The irony was that had Paley made the decision to steer clear of politics a few years earlier — in 1964 — the Goldwater incident would undoubtedly not have escalated to the proportions it reached.

• •

Did Paley, fearing Nixon's reprisals, intervene in the CBS coverage of Watergate in 1972?

Presidential pressures and fear of presidential reprisals were real enough, said Frank Stanton, who advocates putting all White House–network communications on the public record to minimize threats. He remembered brushes with President Kennedy, and squabbles with President Johnson, "who would raise hell one minute and next minute ask what you were doing for the weekend." But it was nothing like the experience with Nixon, which caused Stanton to be "plenty worried" in a very concrete way. He actively feared a government attack on the economic underbelly of the network. "The place where we were most vulnerable was in our ownership of stations because of periodic licensing." Contests over licenses, even when won, could be damaging. The CBS fight to retain control of Station WCAU in Philadelphia lasted almost three years and cost millions of dollars. Sometimes Stanton wished he were running a newspaper instead of a network so that he could tell a President to go to hell — and Congress too.

"My job was to make the news department feel they could say

that," said Stanton. "But in my own heart, I knew we could go up to a certain point and we couldn't go any further."

In the evening of his career, his network lagging in the ratings race, Paley looked troubled and care-worn. He worried about his wife's health, and less immediately about his own. As we lunched at his circular desk on weight-watching boiled beef from his private kitchen, sometimes he seemed to be concentrating with difficulty on the business at hand. But he displayed an infectious warmth and occasional flashes of a famous boyish smile. With a Murrow silhouette on one wall of his suite amid a collection of priceless art, Paley was clearly deeply concerned that he should not be remembered as having put fear for his network over the integrity of his network. He had once — so Stanton told me — had a brochure printed to counter the allegation that he had wavered on Watergate but had unaccountably decided not to distribute it, and had left thousands of copies stacked in a warehouse. Now his wish to justify himself was reflected in his willingness to spend time with a former employee — keeping waiting, on one day, John Backe, his new chief operating officer, and, on the other, Robert Wussler, the head of the television network.

Paley's version of the conflict over the two-part Watergate series on the Cronkite show in October 1972 differs mightily, as could be expected, from Charles Colson's, but it also does not square with the recollections of CBS participants. One must make some allowances for the occasional lapses of memory that Paley acknowledges. One must also take into account the disillusionment of disowned heirs apparent. Stanton, who had confidently expected to succeed to the chairmanship on Paley's retirement, was instead retired by Paley, who stayed on as the sole exception to the sixty-five-year limit that he himself had set. Stanton, whom Paley used to scoff at for being "always in his office," worked until the precise moment of his retirement — midnight, Sunday, March 31, 1973 — and left the office key on the desk for Arthur Taylor, with a note that said "Good luck. F.S." Stanton left a lot more at Black Rock — a broken heart. Taylor, fired in October 1976, seemed more stunned than heartbroken. His discharge was to him the best evidence that he had not made the progress he had thought in modernizing and decentralizing the management of CBS. He had found what so many had found — that, ultimately, CBS was still run by a sole proprietor.

Paley seemed nonetheless distressed to find that Stanton and Taylor were not witnesses friendly to him. When he had to address himself to what Colson had said, it was with contempt: "He's a goddamn liar! . . . a monster!" But, when he found himself contradicted by his own former associates, he seemed surprised: "I'm flabbergasted!"

Paley's version of what happened on Saturday, October 28, 1972, when Colson telephoned to complain about the Watergate report on the Cronkite show the night before, relies mainly on notes which he said he dictated on that day at his home in Manhasset. It quoted Colson's charges that "CBS had completely overblown the Watergate affair" and had overlooked allegations against the Democrats. Colson wanted to know about the second installment that Cronkite had announced. He charged that the whole thing had come about — so a woman friend of Cronkite's had said at a party — because President Nixon had refused Cronkite an exclusive interview, so now Cronkite was out to "zing" the President. One sentence in Paley's summary of Colson's tirade rang ominously, "He said that if the President is reelected, which he thought very likely, that it would be very hard for them to establish good relations with us."

However menacing Colson may have sounded, Paley's memorandum contained evidence that he had not acted in response to this pressure because he had already made up his mind, quite on his own, that the Watergate wrap-up was too long, "could not be classified as completely objective" and "did show bias against the administration." The proof of that was in the memorandum — it said he had told Colson of having just expressed his own feelings about the Watergate report to Frank Stanton. According to his memo, Paley then called Stanton again, this time to ask about Colson's specific allegations that CBS had wanted to turn the Watergate report into a special, had tried to find a sponsor and had been turned down by a large corporation. Paley had been assured by Stanton that all this was nonsense.

The important point was the sequence of conversations, and the memorandum, dated that day, emphasized it in its conclusion: "This is a rough sum-up of the telephone call between me and C.C., and me and F.S. right before the call from C.C. and right after the call from C.C."

If Paley told Colson that he had just talked to Stanton, Colson does not recall it. Colson had the impression that Paley was listening to his complaint and reacting to it.

Stanton says positively that he had no conversation with Paley "right before" and could not have had. He had come home in the afternoon, having been out of touch since morning, to learn from his wife that Colson had been trying to reach him. When he returned the call to the White House — at 4:50 P.M., his calendar shows — he was told that Colson had spoken to Paley and no longer needed to talk to him. Only then, said Stanton, did he speak to Paley for the first time that day.

Not "right before" but the previous evening, Stanton *had* talked to Paley. Even then pressure from Colson was already being felt. Colson had called Stanton at noontime to ask menacingly about the rumors of a Cronkite "Watergate special" and had been told by Stanton that no special was planned. Stanton had alerted Paley, on the private line to his New York apartment, to watch the potentially troublesome report on the Evening News and had heard from Paley shortly afterward. "Paley talked about the amount of time that had been given to the Watergate story," Stanton recalled. "I don't think he raised any questions about the substance of it. He said that this was really going to create some problems — problems unspecified. Not vis-à-vis any particular person, but I assume that he was concerned about the White House's reaction."

In any event, Paley had every reason to have Colson on his mind when he met at eleven o'clock Monday morning in his office with Stanton, Taylor, Schneider and Salant. Yet, at that meeting there was no mention of White House pressure or Colson strictures. Paley says that was deliberate on his part. Colson's job, "looking back on it now, was to try to intimidate us," and it was best that this be kept from Salant and the news people "because we didn't want them to know what kind of pressure we were living under from time to time."

He needn't have worried about scaring Salant. The head of CBS News said that had he known about the White House pressures, he would probably have overreacted in the other direction — refusing to make any changes in the Watergate report even if they seemed otherwise warranted, rather than even appearing to be yielding to administration demands. Another thing that Salant might have done — which Paley never dreamed of doing — was to make sure that the White House pressure was publicly exposed.

Paley said that he talked about the Friday night report without any reference to a second installment on Watergate still to come. Early in our interview, Paley thought he had not even been aware at that meeting of an impending Part II until I reminded him that it had been announced by Cronkite on Friday and discussed with Colson — according to Paley's own memo—on Saturday.

In any event, Paley recalled that meeting simply as a detailed critique of Part I — too long as one segment of a news broadcast, presumptuous in shrugging off White House disclaimers on Watergate simply because they had not been made directly to CBS News. He had said not one word to Salant about Part II, about "cutting it down, or editing it, or anything else." I asked Paley why it was necessary to call together all these important people for an hour-long critique that could have been accomplished by memo if there was no pending action involved. "I was very upset by this thing," he said. "I wanted to get my own feelings expressed as soon after the event as possible."

At that meeting, Paley remembered, he had said he was expressing Stanton's viewpoint as well as his own. Stanton, however, said he had not shared Paley's view. He had offered criticism of such details as illegible graphics. He had wished the two parts had been split into four shorter installments for more symmetrical programming. "But I wasn't upset with the content, and I was captivated by the way the whole Watergate thing was pulled together."

Furthermore, said Stanton, Paley *did* specifically talk about Part II. "I think Paley was pressing Salant to find out what was going to be in the second part, and I think there was discussion about the length of the second part. There was discussion about when it was coming up — whether it would be that evening. And Dick said that it depended on what sort of a news day it was, and whether there would be a hole big enough to accommodate it . . ."

"How far," I asked, "did Paley go in that meeting toward actually insisting that something be done about the second part?"

"I guess he didn't have to," replied Stanton. "If he says he doesn't like this first part, and asks what's in the second and how long it is, then the message is clear, isn't it? If I had been Salant, that's the way I would have read it."

To Salant, the message was indeed clear. "Paley did not tell me not to do Part II. He didn't tell me there was any specific thing I should do or not do. He reviewed all the problems he had had with Part I — inconsistent with our policy of fairness and balance . . . reliant on hearsay and what other people had reported, and we didn't clearly enough identify that. He felt that to do this kind of thing short-changed the rest of the news . . . I had never had a session with him in which he was so critical."

Nonetheless, Salant apparently did not get the full message. He had Part II delayed a day and cut in half, with the result that Paley invited him to a private lunch and hauled him over the coals. The chairman denounced the handling of Watergate as "unfair, a hatchet job, one-sided . . . In effect, he said, 'Never do anything like that again.' I didn't agree with him. Ah, hell, all you have to do is look by hindsight." By hindsight the Watergate report needed no justification.

After that luncheon, Salant started keeping his own file on Paley's criticisms and his own possible responses "in case it ever came to further push and shove." One item in that file was an attack on CBS News by Colson before the New England Society of Newspaper Editors a few days after the 1972 election.

"There was a remarkable parallelism between what Colson said and my recollection of some of the things that Paley had said," Salant observed. "That was the first time my antennae started getting attuned."

•　　•

*Was Paley influenced by White House pressure when he banned in-
stant analysis of presidential statements on television in 1973?*

"No," said Paley.

He had not focused so much on the question of "instant analysis"
as on the proposal to institute a policy of opposition replies to presidential broadcasts on controversial issues. He had records to show
that this question had been discussed in the News Executive Committee fourteen times since September 1970 — not connected with
Vice President Agnew's attack on "instant analysis" the previous
November, or any White House pressure. In April 1973, before Paley
left for China, a "presidential reply" policy had been worked out, but
held in abeyance until his return from Peking in the hope that other
networks would join in it. The decision to abolish instant analysis,
said Paley, was "way at the end, tucked in there, before I went to
China and when I came back. And I swear I had little to do with
that. Nor did I give it much thought."

To the extent he had thought about it, he remembered that the
analysis was sometimes done poorly, and that Eric Sevareid was
opposed to it because it had to be presented too hastily to be thoughtful. Paley had thought, "My God, that's not doing a good job or
serving the American people!" He had believed it would be much
better to consider the analysis overnight and then come up with
something meaningful that could be put on the Morning News or the
Cronkite show. That would not be the same audience, of course, but,
then, "you never can quite get the same audience." Nothing had
happened that Salant had not known about, "putting aside whether
Salant ever talked against it or not — I don't remember his having
done so." Then, on June 6, 1973, a statement was submitted to "a
well-ordered meeting" of the committee, and Salant "had every opportunity to read it, completely and wholly, before it was given to
the Public Relations department." Paley had been amazed at the
reaction to the abolition of instant analysis, overshadowing the whole
new policy of opposition reply to the President. In November, he had
come to a meeting and said, "Boys, it isn't working! I think people
expect some reaction right after the President's speech, and I think
we have to change the policy."

It was Stanton who had set up the CBS News Executive Committee — CNEC — back in the 1950s to enable CBS News, newly endowed with the status of an independent division, to join as an equal with the radio and television networks in meeting with top management. It was only in the last six months before Stanton's retirement on March 31, 1973, he said, that Paley had started attending CNEC meetings with any regularity. "What I thought was that Bill was never comfortable with instant analysis, and after I left — maybe this is my ego coming out — he finally decided he could push it through."

Salant did not know of the April decision until it was finally sprung at the June meeting. He had been aware that instant analysis had been troubling Paley. "He has this habit of raising things that are bothering him, sometimes over a period of years." Abolition of instant analysis had been discussed from time to time, and Salant had not fought it very hard, partly because the ground had been cut from under him by Sevareid's widely known opposition. But when the new policy statement was suddenly brought up at the June 6 meeting, Salant was taken by surprise. He did not argue it — he knew from experience the futility of trying to change Paley's mind "in a group situation."

"There was no real discussion," said Salant. "That is so whenever we come to a tough issue about which Paley feels strongly. You know how it is in CNEC. Seven nays, one aye, the ayes have it."

The sole proprietor had decided against instant analysis, and no one knew exactly how or why, or based on what. Shortly before April, when the decision was made, there had been the private meeting with Haldeman — a meeting that Salant had never known about until I told him in 1977.

"Are you convinced," I asked Salant, "that Paley's abolition of White House analysis was not a reaction to White House pressure?"

"I'm not!" said Salant. He paused, enjoying my surprise, and went on.

"Once the Watergate documents came out [disclosing White House threats against the networks], and once Colson made that speech to the New England publishers, where many of the points that had been made by Mr. Paley suddenly appeared as Colson's, I became suspicious of everything."

• •

What was the Paley-CIA connection?

Even without my presence, the luncheon that Paley held in his private dining room on the thirty-fifth floor on February 4, 1976, for George Bush, the new CIA director, did not go as he had hoped. What was to be a sociable welcome for the son of the late Senator Prescott Bush, warmly remembered as an early CBS board member, turned, after dessert, into an argument about CIA agents posing as reporters. It was started by Walter Cronkite, angry because he had been identified by a former television newsman, Sam Jaffe, as having appeared on an alleged White House list of journalists who had purportedly worked for the CIA. To remove the stain on him and on journalism, Cronkite demanded that Bush disclose the list of news people who actually had been CIA agents. Bush was sympathetic to Cronkite's complaint, and ready to consider ending the practice (which he subsequently did). He flatly refused to uncover those who had served the CIA in the past under a promise of eternal confidentiality. At the height of the argument, Paley stepped in, graciously supporting his guest and suggesting that it would be best to bury the past.

A week later it looked as though Paley may have had reason of his own for wanting to bury the past. That was when it had been my lot to go on the Cronkite show with the story, based on the disclosure of Sig Mickelson, former president of CBS News, that at least two former part-time correspondents for CBS News in the 1950s had been CIA agents. The story's most startling aspect had been that Mickelson had learned about one of them, Austin Goodrich, from two CIA officers right in Paley's office, introduced by Paley who listened while they identified Goodrich as one of their men.

Paley denies the story; Mickelson sticks to his guns. When CBS took me off the air in the controversy over the Pike report, William Safire wrote in his *New York Times* column that the fuss over the

Village Voice was a smokescreen for the CIA story — that my real offense had been "exploring Paley's big secret on CBS."

I undoubtedly contributed to the tension, during my summer in limbo, with my own article on the Op-Ed page of the *Times* saying that the institutional arrangements made by news media executives with the CIA were a more important subject for inquiry than the names of reporters who had — for equally patriotic reasons — operated under those arrangements. I noted the circumstantial evidence that Paley, Arthur Hays Sulzberger, the late publisher of the *Times,* and other media tycoons had cooperated to provide cover for CIA agents. William Colby told me that in the 1950s it had been customary to enter into such understandings; sometimes they were even formalized in a written memorandum. "There are executives and retired executives," I wrote, "who could help dispel the cloud hanging over the press by coming forward to tell the arrangements they made with the CIA."

The congressional investigations failed to get to the bottom of the CIA infiltration of the news media. Congressman Otis Pike, chairman of the House committee, asked Colby at a hearing on November 6, 1975, "Do you have any people paid by the CIA who are working for television networks?" Colby murmured, "This, I think, gets into the kind of details, Mr. Chairman, that I'd like to get into in executive session." The room was cleared, and behind closed doors, Colby said that, during 1975, the CIA was using "media cover" for eleven agents, many fewer than in the heyday of the cloak-and-pencil operation, but no amount of questioning would persuade him to talk about the publishers and network chieftains who had cooperated at the top. A CIA director willing to endure the embarrassment of protecting the identity of Mafia collaborators was certainly not going to betray patriotic media proprietors.

When I embarked on my "CBS revisited" project, it was clear that the toughest part would be the Paley-CIA connection, protected by the double cloak of corporate secrecy and intelligence security. The most active period of CIA-media cooperation had been in the cold war days of the 1950s, and there were few — if any — still around in CBS who knew what Paley knew.

One found clues indicating that CBS had been infiltrated. A news editor remembered the CIA officer who used to come to the radio control room in New York in the early morning and, with the permission of persons unknown, listened to CBS correspondents around the world recording their "spots" for the "World News Roundup" and discussing events with the editor on duty. Sam Jaffe claimed that when he applied in 1955 for a job with CBS, a CIA officer told him that he would be hired — which he subsequently was. He was also told that he would be sent to Moscow — which he subsequently was; he was assigned in 1960 to cover the trial of U–2 pilot Francis Gary Powers. Salant told me that when he first became president of CBS News in 1961, a CIA officer called saying he wanted to continue the "long-standing relationship" known to Paley and Stanton, but Salant was told by Stanton there was no obligation that he knew of. Thereafter, Salant had turned down persistent requests for unbroadcast portions of reports and interviews, especially from Eastern Europe. Salant declined to cooperate in setting up a CIA meeting with William Cole, the CBS correspondent expelled from Moscow after filming interviews with Soviet dissidents.

The CIA was the last big item on my agenda with Paley. Earlier, he had casually asked if I knew Bill Safire, and for how long. I had said that Safire was a friend, but that his column "Paley's Big Secret" was entirely his own idea.

"Okay," I said, opening the subject, "the CIA thing."

For the first time, Paley was prepared to acknowledge that he *had* a relationship with the CIA. It had not gone through Frank Wisner, the late head of the CIA's covert operations, who had cultivated media tycoons — though Paley had known Wisner casually, and his wife, Polly, somewhat better. The CIA relationship had been, he asserted, a purely personal matter.

"I cooperated with them — was helpful to them a few times on a very personal basis, and nothing whatsoever to do with CBS . . . I was approached as somebody who could cooperate with them to their advantage. And this was back in the early fifties, when the cold war was at its height and where I didn't hesitate for a second to say, 'Okay, it's reasonable, I'll do it.' "

Paley insisted on keeping off the record the specific nature of his personal service to the CIA. It was a form of assistance that a number of wealthy persons are now generally known to have rendered the CIA through their private interests. It suggested to me, however, that a relationship of confidence and trust had existed between him and the agency.

Paley, in addition, was willing to acknowledge one service he had performed for the CIA through CBS — in fact, it had gone through Mickelson. It had involved permitting the use of the CBS booth overlooking the United Nations Security Council chamber. From there an expert in lip reading would scrutinize the Soviet delegation, hoping to decipher whispered consultations. Paley's point in volunteering this information (which he permitted me to report after I had obtained clearance from the CIA) was that Mickelson might somehow have confused the lip-reader episode with the episode of the Stockholm stringer — a meeting in Paley's office, but for a different purpose.

Mickelson told me that, while he had forgotten about the lip reader, this matter had involved no meeting, only a telephone call from Paley and Mickelson's relayed authorization to subordinates for use of the U.N. booth. Furthermore, said Mickelson, he recalled the lip-reader incident as having occurred during the visit of Premier Khrushchev to the United Nations in 1959 — five years after the meeting in Paley's office about Austin Goodrich, the CBS   or was it CIA? — man in Stockholm.

In March 1976, a month after the Mickelson story broke on CBS, Paley invited him to his office and sought unsuccessfully to convince him that he was mistaken. Mickelson quoted Paley as concluding their talk by saying that he still did not remember such a meeting, but "perhaps your memory is better than mine."

For me, a year later, Paley produced details and documents that added up, as he put it, to "proof positive that Sig's recollection of what happened was wrong." Except that, on scrutiny, what Paley offered proved nothing. He showed me a letter concerning Goodrich, a copy of which had gone to Mickelson, as evidence that Mickelson was mistaken in saying he had not been aware of the stringer's existence until the meeting in Paley's office. However, Mickelson had placed the meeting as having occurred in October 1954, and the letter was dated December of that year, and thus, as I noted to Paley, there was no contradiction. Paley observed that Goodrich had been recommended for Stockholm by his predecessor, Robert Pierpoint, and so must have been legitimate. But Pierpoint said that, while friendly with Goodrich, he had simply not known that Goodrich worked for the CIA.

Paley could have simply forgotten a meeting with Mickelson and CIA officials. What he could hardly have forgotten was whether he had a continuing relationship with the CIA that would have made such a meeting possible. While admitting a personal connection with the CIA and a one-time service — like accommodation for a lip reader — Paley steadfastly denied any relationship involving CBS.

The Goodrich episode provided another way to approach the question of infiltration of CBS. Goodrich's cover had been blown anyway, and while the interdiction on disclosure of "intelligence sources and methods" was formally still in force, I knew enough people in the intelligence community to reconstruct the Goodrich story unofficially.

In 1954, Goodrich was working as a full-time writer on the CBS news desk in New York. Recruited by the CIA, he resigned his CBS job, but arranged to go to Stockholm as a CBS stringer, with a $100 monthly retainer. The arrangement was known to Paley, and to one or two other persons on the business end of CBS, who handled the financial transactions involved.

The agency had similar arrangements with top executives — the *very* top executives — of other news organizations with overseas bureaus. This was the ideal cover for agents because their methods and inquisitive styles of operation were so much like those of foreign correspondents. While the CBS arrangement was essentially a cover for his CIA mission, Goodrich carefully separated the two functions. He was dealing with news editors who had no idea of his other role, and who weighed his suggestions for broadcasts on their merits. It was no part of his job to plant agency-inspired information in the United States. When he worked as a reporter, he *was* a reporter. For people who lead two lives there is such a thing as "controlled schizophrenia"; being sure which hat one has on is essential to successful cover.

Ironically, the 1954 meeting with Mickelson in Paley's office was a security lapse that endangered Goodrich's cover. The two CIA officers wanted to solicit Mickelson's cooperation, and a perfunctory security check on him had been run in advance. But, under the rules, he should not have been made "witting" of the Goodrich arrangement until he had agreed to cooperate. Taken by surprise, Mickelson had not agreed, and thus he represented a potential danger of exposure — deterred only by the obvious involvement of his boss.

Soon after that meeting the CIA apparently decided to change Goodrich's CBS cover. Word filtered down to "unwitting" news executives that Goodrich, whose broadcasting activities had virtually ceased, should be phased out as a stringer. In December, Edward P. Morgan, near the end of his brief term as director of CBS News, wrote to Howard K. Smith, European news chief in London, proposing to cancel Goodrich's retainer as unwarranted. (Almost a quarter century later, Morgan could not remember who so instructed him.) Thereafter, other cover arrangements were made for Goodrich, though he continued to perform occasional nonbroadcasting assignments for CBS. He helped to obtain film for CBS on the Winter Olympics in Helsinki, and he dug up footage on the Russo-Finnish war for Burton Benjamin, producer of the "Twentieth Century" historical documentaries.

I met Goodrich in Helsinki in 1957 when I came from Moscow to cover Khruschev's tour of Finland. He was shooting free-lance film of the trip to be offered to CBS; most of it turned out to be out of focus. Twenty years later I talked to Goodrich, now in the insurance business in Great Falls, Virginia. He liked what I had written about top executives coming forward to explain CIA-media cooperation, instead of letting those lower down get pilloried in a climate of misunderstanding about the motives of those who had served as soldiers in the cold war. Life had been pretty rough after Mickelson had exposed him, and it would be a lot easier for him if the whole arrangement were to be publicly explained by the man at the top who made it. From a continued sense of loyalty, Goodrich would not officially break his own cover — or the cover of anyone else. He had never met Paley. He was sure that Paley had acted out of patriotic motives.

"Maybe, one of these days when Paley retires, I can be of more help," said Goodrich.

•   •

Paraphrasing Walt Kelly's Pogo, I had found the story, and, in part, it was *us*. In probing into sensitive areas of government, I had raised problems inside CBS. It had been self-delusion to believe that one could practice old-fashioned no-holds-barred investigative reporting of the government while representing an organization that felt vulnerable to government pressures, its proprietor ambivalent about his conflicting commitments.

One question remained.

•   •

Why did CBS react so traumatically to my urgent recommendation that it publish the Pike report, and take such drastic action when I went outside CBS to publish it?

As Arthur Taylor, the former chief operating officer of CBS, told me, it had been his impression, from discussions he heard, that CBS involvement in publication had never been seriously considered.

A law firm representing CBS, Cravath, Swaine & Moore, was called and asked for an opinion on whether publication of a secret government document obtained by unknown means would create any legal jeopardy. Not told what the document was, a member of the firm gave the offhand opinion that there could potentially be a problem with the Espionage Act. On the strength of that telephone call the CBS legal department wrote what Salant called "a very sloppy memorandum" that stressed the perils of violations of the Espionage Act, whose extreme penalty is capital punishment. The

CBS publishing division had no trouble deciding it would not get involved.

By contrast, when the *New York Times,* in 1971, received the Pentagon Papers from Daniel Ellsberg, it sought an opinion from its law firm, Lord, Day & Lord. Ignoring the warning of possible jeopardy, the *Times* proceeded to publish. When Attorney General Mitchell threatened to prosecute, the firm abruptly ended its representation of the *Times* on the ground that its advice had been disregarded. The *Times* continued publishing the Papers, and engaged another law firm.

If Ellsberg had given the Pentagon Papers to a network instead of a newspaper, they might never have seen the light of day. Salant told me that during a discussion of the Pentagon Papers at a symposium in Princeton under *Times* and Ford Foundation auspices, he had exploded at the assumption that all a reporter had to do on receipt of such a document was to ask his publisher for a decision. Salant told the participants that for a television journalist it was different than for a print journalist.

"Now, I've got to tell you that I would have brought it to *my* 'publisher,' and I think that he would not have been so courageous, because they have licenses . . . and the government can claim that you have violated the Espionage Act, and so on. And it can also go to the FCC, which knows nothing about the Espionage Act or anything else, and they can revoke your license! And I wouldn't be at all surprised if the chairman of the board and the president of the company might say we just can't risk that."

Salant was talking about *any* television chairman, not *his* chairman, and about the Pentagon Papers, not the Pike report. He may have underestimated the risks that the *Times* took — possible prosecution, loss of advertising and circulation if branded by the Nixon administration with a charge of disloyalty. He may also have overestimated the risk to television of acting in defiance of the government. No license has ever been lost over an issue of national security, and the FCC has taken the firm position that it has no authority over the content of broadcasting — let alone what a subsidiary book company publishes. The important thing is that CBS *perceived* itself as being threatened by this hot potato of a controversial congressional report.

In those circumstances, my conclusion that, with CBS part of the problem rather than part of the solution, I had to go elsewhere to prevent suppression of the report turned into an ultimate showdown between unfettered information and fettered television — and between me and the sole proprietor. A lot of side issues would be raised later about who owned the report, and about the *Village Voice* being the wrong place, and about my initial lack of candor with CBS. But, to my mind, the alacrity with which I was taken off the air and fired stemmed from a conflict much deeper than the complaints about the attendant circumstances.

It was more than I could expect that Paley would tell me clearly — if, indeed, he could see it clearly — why his twelve-year-old grudge against me became suddenly activated in February 1976, with a façade "suspension" and an undated resignation that nobody could later explain. After he had said that it was all "handled by Dick Salant," I pressed on with questions, and Paley said a few more things, which I excerpt, but not out of context:

". . . I never discussed it with Dick. I never discussed it with Dick at all. All I said to Dick once was, 'I think the corporation has to know ahead of time before you make any final decision' . . . I know that Taylor and Salant discussed this matter. He [Taylor] had something to do with the financial aspects of it, which, of course, had to be authorized by somebody — a certain amount of money was involved. And I think Taylor and myself both wanted to be aware of what was happening because the corporation as a whole was going to be affected by what was happening. And I think that Dick through Taylor was put on notice of not making any final move of any kind without at least checking with us or telling us. But at no time did we say to Dick, 'You've got to fire him or you don't have to fire him' . . . We just want to know. It might have been something so disruptive that we might have stepped in and said, 'Hell, you can't do this!' "

If the corporate oversight over Salant was only intended to prevent something "disruptive" from happening, it did not work very well.

One outcome was an undated resignation which Taylor did not learn about until the following week, which hung over CBS for months like a sword of Damocles and for which every executive involved has since disowned responsibility. Someone must have believed it fulfilled the proprietor's wish.

Paley made it appear that it was one of those errors of overreaction — like the mistake of featuring Stokowski to please the boss.

"I know," said Paley, "that Taylor told me he wasn't very happy about that particular statement that had been written. Not because he felt sorry for you, but because he thought it put us in a bad position . . . That was something that was organized and created by Dick Salant, and it came to our attention. We didn't like it. Now the details of why we didn't, I've forgotten."

What Paley clearly remembered was that the situation regarding me had changed, in his eyes, after my testimony before the House Ethics Committee, "one of the finest performances I've ever seen." It had changed enough for Taylor and Schneider to sit down with Salant and discuss possible alternatives to resignation, Taylor proposing reinstatement, Schneider saying that would have a disruptive effect in CBS, all of them finally deciding to temporize by having Salant first discuss with me how I viewed the possibility of my return.

(Paley also telephoned Frank Stanton for advice. To his retired lieutenant the troubled chairman described himself as being on the horns of a dilemma. He explained in detail a situation in which he thought CBS would be damned if it let me go and damned if it didn't. Surprised at being consulted, unaware of the Taylor Schneider disagreement and the undated resignation, Stanton — so he later told me — simply advised Paley to do what was best for CBS News. Paley, for all his pose of arm's length detachment, was clearly deeply involved in deciding what that would be.)

Abrupt discharge, which had seemed such a good idea in February, was clearly out of the question in September. It was as though Bill Paley, the old wizard of programming and scheduling, had seen a rebound in my Neilsen ratings on the strength of an unexpectedly good "performance" and decided not to buck the trend. He told me almost as much:

"I would have been just as happy if this thing had gone on for a while because I didn't know what kind of explosion was going to take place . . . Well, suddenly Schorr is fired, you know! It was a very tricky period we were going through. There were rumors of all kinds flying around, as I understand it."

Eventually, though, had I not taken the decision into my own hands, separation would have been effected some time later, when the dust had settled. The proprietor had long since made up his mind, as he often made up his mind about matters of personnel, policy and programs, on the basis of his personal vision of what was best for his company, its stability and its profits. Paley might find it comfortable to reduce the issues to nagging little matters — in my case going back to 1964 and Senator Goldwater — but the real issues were much broader.

My case, I believe, had come to personify, in a form too accentuated to be tolerated, the conflict between the make-believe world of corporate television and the abrasive world of news.

XIII

THE NATIONAL SÉANCE

AS A RECENT REFUGEE — or is it exile? — from television, I continued my education about its influence on Americans. People would come up to me and say they missed me in a direct and personal sense as though, having entered their living rooms all these years, I had become a part of their lives. Some of them, forgetting the one-way nature of the connection, spoke as though the relationship had been reciprocal. Sometimes, in random meetings, I encountered an assumption of intimacy that was greater than I could handle. Easy enough to manage were the many variations on "You look just like on television" and "You look better than on television." Harder to deal with were such remarks as this one, from an elderly matron, "I used to wake up with you every morning," and, from a man sitting with his wife in a lecture audience, "What made you think you had the right to resign without asking us?"

Frank Mankiewicz, an observer of the television scene in addition to his other attainments, wrote that "Uncle" Walter Cronkite's news team had come to be perceived as "the classic American family," a sort of precursor of the Waltons, "complete with the wayward older son (Daniel Schorr), the sassy little sister (Lesley Stahl), the nephew who is almost accepted as a member of the family (Dan Rather), the solid if independent brother (Roger Mudd) and, to be sure, the wise grandfather (Eric Sevareid)." What I had not fully realized was that my role belonged not so much to me as to the viewers; they had largely fashioned it from their impressions of my reporting of news events and, later, from my involvement in news events. During my travels, parents pointed me out to their children as though I were on display. One businessman pulled me out of my seat in an airport lounge, saying jovially, "Come on over here, I want to show you to my partner. He doesn't believe it's you." It is surely not the way he would have treated an ordinary stranger, but clearly I represented to him not so much a human being as an image descended from the screen — one, moreover, to which he had earned part ownership by dint of long and faithful attendance.

In my first months out of CBS, many asked how it felt to be off television, as though they feared that I was suffering some kind of cosmic withdrawal symptoms. I finally grasped that underlying their questions was the concern that since I had derived my identity from being on the air, I might now, in some existential sense, be in danger of vanishing altogether. This experience struck me as one of the symptoms of a great American malady induced by too much exposure to television — the substitution of images for reality. The illness had progressed beyond the previous stages of image-making and image-manipulation employed in the selling of products and politicians. The perceived world was beginning to crowd out the real world, with consequences often odd and sometimes ominous.

I thought back to various episodes observed over a period of a decade that, at the time, had given me pause because they demonstrated some of the effects of television — generally accidental, even unwitting, but having significant influence on people's perception of events and sometimes decisive impact on the outcome of events.

The Electronic Additive: In May 1972, CBS News was video-taping a preconvention Democratic platform hearing on foreign policy in New York City. Several persons in the audience wandered from their seats to where I was working and peered in fascination at the witness, Averell Harriman, on our tiny black-and-white monitor. When I pointed out that there was nothing on the monitor they could not see in the flesh only twenty feet away, a middle-aged man replied, "Yes, but it's more interesting when you see it on television."

Fine Tuning: In early 1968, Senator Robert Kennedy told a group of reporters on Capitol Hill that "under no foreseeable circumstances" would he run for President. The quotation was running on the news wires when I arrived at his office to film an interview on a different subject. Confirming to me the accuracy of the quotation, the senator smiled, but adamantly refused to repeat it on camera. Three months later, when Kennedy had announced his candidacy, his press aide, Frank Mankiewicz, explained that he had counseled this strategy. While Senator Kennedy was still undecided, such a statement could be made for newspapers, but not directly on television, which would have given it too much impact — and, incidentally, might have come back to haunt him when he finally decided to make the race.

Arbiter of the Senate: In the spring of 1971, the staff director of a Senate committee dealing with poverty problems urged me to bring CBS cameras to a scheduled hearing. He outlined the "visual appeal" of the panel of witnesses he had arranged, which would include a black, a poor white and an Indian in full headdress. When I expressed regret that a conflicting assignment would prevent me from covering it, the staff director, seeing me as his last hope for network coverage, said, "I'll get to the chairman and ask him to postpone the hearing." Then, when I objected to being put in the position of influencing the Senate's legislative calendar, he replied that it was not realistic to hold the hearing without cameras — most members of the committee would simply not turn up until informed by their aides that television was present.

At another time, in the corridor of the Senate Office Building, I ran into Senator Hubert Humphrey trying to round up a quorum for a hearing of the Joint Congressional Economic Committee. Half-jokingly, half-despairingly, he asked if I could install dummy cameras and turn on some bright lights to attract truant members of his committee.

Political Upstairs, Downstairs: A strange media accident helped to launch Senator Edmund Muskie in 1970 as the early front-runner for the Democratic presidential nomination. Sharing a half-hour television broadcast with President Nixon on the eve of the congressional elections, Muskie delivered a reassuring, moderate chat against the homey background of a fireplace in Maine, contrasting starkly with a strident tirade by Nixon denouncing student protestors, which his lieutenants refused to withdraw even after being advised that defective recording had made it almost inaudible. Fifteen months later, the television-propelled Democratic front-runner found the fickle medium starting him on the downward slope toward becoming a rear-runner. During the New Hampshire primary campaign, CBS cameras caught him, on a Saturday morning outside a newspaper building in Manchester, shedding tears of chagrin over an insult to his wife. The exclusive film, almost lost in shipment to New York, was located barely in time to be developed and rushed, unscreened, onto the Saturday Evening News. Another few minutes' delay and Senator Muskie might have been spared the political damage of being seen crying on television — considerably more potent than the newspaper accounts and pictures. What one television accident had fortuitously given Muskie — an appealing image — another had begun to take away.

Lunar Double Vision: In July 1969, when platoons of CBS personnel were deployed around the world to report reaction to the first lunar landing, Producer Robert Chandler and I set up electronic cameras in a picturesque café in Hilversum, Holland, to transmit interviews with *burghers* witnessing the momentous event. As the cloudy picture came on the screen and Houston Control went wild, a stolid Hollander, asked for his reaction, shrugged and said he like the landing better the first time when the picture was clearer. It turned out that he had taken an earlier simulation for the real thing. So had others present, who apparently had no sure idea of the difference between the actuality, the real moment of history, and the studio enactments. Nor did they seem concerned about the distinction.

Special Effects: In January 1976, I showed the unreleased report of the House Intelligence Committee on television four times, the last time stating that it might be suppressed. None of the millions who saw me hold up the document wrote or telephoned to ask, "How come?" Several of those I later asked about the singular lack of reaction explained that they had become so confused by the use of graphic effects on television that they had long since given up trying to determine when they were seeing a real thing or a visual aid. Some also said they were uncertain where Cronkite really was when he appeared, during a single half-hour, against a succession of authentic-looking backgrounds. Visual aids had produced a triumph of disorientation.

The Kid's Show: In 1975, a woman wrote to the columnist Abigail Van Buren, telling of being bound and gagged by a robber, who told the victim's four-year-old boy to watch television for a while before calling for help. The child looked at TV for the next three hours, ignoring his mother's struggle to get his attention. To the child, the television show appeared to be more real, or at least more compelling, than his mother's muffled screams.

•   •

Clearly, television had unleashed some tremendous new force. Like nuclear energy, its effects could be beneficent, destructive — and some incalculable. Its exposure potential was reflected in the facts that 97 percent of American homes owned at least one TV set and the typical young American spent more time in its presence than in the presence of a schoolteacher. As fundamentally as nuclear radiation could change matter, television could change minds.

For one thing, the steady beam emitted by television has a kind of greenhouse effect, accelerating the sprouting of new ideas, trends, fads and personalities, and burning them out with equal speed. Warmed by television, the fad of "streaking" swept the country in a few weeks, and disappeared in a few months. John Kerry, an eloquent Vietnam veteran, appeared on television at a Senate hearing to become an overnight national personality — only to be almost forgotten a year later. "Earth Day," to the astonishment of Senator Gaylord Nelson, its originator, took the nation by storm in 1970 and became a relatively minor manifestation a year later. The great national issues — pollution, energy and war — tend to roll over the country in swelling waves, only to ebb into boredom long before much progress has been made toward solutions. The historian Daniel J. Boorstin mourned that the dizzying array of ever-new sensations has all but made the American forget his national history. "By enabling him to be everywhere instantly, by filling his present moment with experiences engrossing and overwhelming, television dulled the American's sense of his past."

This was written before the phenomenon of *Roots,* which did not, however, change Dr. Boorstin's mind. In conversation, he said he regarded Alex Haley's exploration of his slave ancestry more as "an accentuation of the contemporary than an exploration of the past." Academics may well go too far in refusing to see how much history, culture and science are transmitted — albeit in forms that might not pass their professorial standards — to millions not likely to read the professors. Some intellectuals, like the late Jacob Bronowski, found television an exciting way to present our distant past. After his series, "The Ascent of Man," Dr. Bronowski said that television "may yet become as persuasive an intellectual force as the book." There seems, nevertheless, some truth in Dr. Boorstin's observation that "we have enlarged our sense of the contemporary. We are overwhelmed by our sense of where we, and our contemporaries all over the world, are at this moment."

Beyond that, the American's present is being affected in ways that scholars, scientists and writers have been grappling to understand. Some critics see television turning Americans away from good citizenship. Professor Michael J. Robinson of Catholic University in Washington holds that viewers, seeing political news they did not choose to see and are unable to evaluate, tend to become uninterested, angry or alienated. Margaret Mead, the anthropologist, has written that Lincoln's Gettysburg address would not have survived the constant repetition a presidential speech gets on television and that television-generated boredom is creating an ominous "tide of turned-off voters." George F. Will, the columnist, finds, "The discomforting immediacy of public affairs in the television age has left the public enervated and longing for nothing so much as psychic 'breathing space.' "

The problem, I believe, goes deeper than boredom. On television, the often humdrum real world must compete, on unequal terms, with the excitement of the made-up world. The two worlds unfold, in bewildering proximity, on the same screen, using many of the same visual techniques. Generally, reality loses. Sometimes the news is exciting enough — a President slain or driven from office — to rival fiction, and then it may merge, in the minds of many, with all the other thrilling dramas on the same channels. To add to the confusion, the department of make-believe draws some of its plots from the stockpile of reality and reenacts them with stunning realism. When the Israeli raid to free hostages at the Entebbe Airport in Uganda was dramatized in 1977, several viewers told me they had trouble remembering, a few weeks later, whether they had seen the real participants or actors. Time was when a person went to the movies and surrendered, knowingly, to a few hours of fantasy, the walk from home to cinema marking the transfer from world of fact to world of fiction. Now the unreal filters from the "tube" into the home along with the real and, gradually, the thin line between reality and fantasy becomes eroded in the minds of many.

What overexposure tends to do to people, report the psychologists, is to make them more passive, more inclined to sit back, waiting to receive images, slower to respond to stimuli. Marie Winn, in her book, *The Plug-In Drug*, may have gone too far in concluding that television is so addictive and destructive as to warrant shutting down the whole industry. Certainly, television, as a phenomenon, has had an effect on our collective personality that warrants concern. When people witnessing real accidents, muggings and other emergencies fail to respond, it may well be because they have become confused about whether they are perceiving actuality or fleeting images on the screen — like the child who ignored his bound mother for the television show.

By forging a magic electronic circle, coast to coast, television has created a national séance. Millions sit figuratively holding hands as they are exposed together to a stream of images and suggestions, mixed-up facts and fancies, playing more on their senses than their intellects. Television may be on its way to doing in America what religious mysticism has done in Asia — dulling the sense of the objective and tangible and making the perceived more important than the fact. There is at least a superficial similarity in the trancelike state that accompanies both experiences.

E. B. White foresaw the revolutionary effects of television when he wrote in *Harper's* in 1938, after witnessing an early demonstration of the invention, "I believe television is going to be the test of the modern world, and that in this new opportunity to see beyond the range of our vision we shall discover a new and unbearable disturbance of the modern peace or a saving radiance in the sky. We shall stand or fall by television — of that I am quite sure."

So far, it would appear, the score is "unbearable disturbance" over "saving radiance" by a fairly large margin.

•   •

In the "saving radiance" department of television, I put news, by which I mean all communication of real life. Although electronic journalism has been said to have blighted print journalism, it is a fact that, apart from a few metropolitan centers, radio and television bring the outside world to vast areas starved for information by skimpy, bland, semimonopolistic newspapers. At moments of high crisis and tragedy, television news has minimized rumor and panic by a steady stream of information and actuality. Much of the best of television, however, is an uphill battle against its show-business surroundings.

The guardians of reality in television, the news people, fight a valiant rear-guard action. As dealers in substance in the bazaar of shadows, they hang out semantic shingles to express their embarrassment at the company they must keep. It is thus forbidden, under CBS News policy, to say on the air "Cronkite show" or " '60 Minutes' program." "Shows" and "programs" come from the entertainment side of the tracks; CBS News does "broadcasts." Though the news people cling to journalism and try to shun theater, they cannot escape the stage they are obliged to share. An inevitable part of appearing on television is the cut of clothing, the styling of hair, the shade of make-up. As part of the constant experimentation with lighting, camera angles and backgrounds, a director once tried a black backdrop for an analysis I was taping for the Morning News. It had the dramatic effect of making me seem to be appearing from nowhere. Next morning the director received orders from New York not to use the black backdrop again; it was reserved for Eric Sevareid. Some of the memorable moments of television journalism have been essentially theatrical — like John Chancellor signing off from "somewhere in custody" when taken off by police during the 1964 Republican convention, or Walter Cronkite thundering down from his anchor booth, "Those thugs!" when Dan Rather was rudely handled on the floor of the 1968 Democratic convention. Or, for that matter, my reading of the unscanned list of the "Top Twenty" Nixon enemies on live camera, coming upon my own name at "No. 17."

Television news must coexist with its entertainment environment. It is permitted some leeway to operate as a "loss leader," but it must still play the "ratings game" at least against competing news broadcasts. Inevitably, news reporting is overshadowed by the anchorperson rivalry, which sometimes imposes a show-business decision, such as ABC's $5 million contract for Barbara Walters in the quest for additional rating points.

Television news also cannot escape its tools — the cameras, microphones and lights—which often make it hostage to cooperation from its subjects. They are provided with the opportunity to negotiate ground rules and to present their best sides. Television is a medium made to order for those with aptitudes for stage acting and synthetic sincerity. It has encouraged the development of thespian talents where none had been previously known to exist. Twenty years ago, in the early days of television, it was difficult to find people willing or able to provide "man-in-the-street" interviews. (This was before the day of the "person-in-the-street.") The average citizen tended to choke up, stammer or shy away in the presence of a camera. Americans who have been interviewed for television still represent a small minority, but over the years increasing numbers have become ready, willing and amazingly able to perform before the cameras; they have been conditioned to feel that they are potentially a part of the act.

It has become customary, in some communities, to put city council and school board meetings on local television, and President Carter's Cabinet has been observed in action by network television. On television, such a proceeding tends to become a simulation — self-conscious, self-serving and rarely self-effacing. It is presented as an "actuality," but it has lost some of its actualness. To the alterations of reality that television's subjects manage to contrive, television news unavoidably adds some of its own. It selects the interesting over the boring, the simple over the complex, the concrete over the abstract. Its time restraints and demands for pacing oblige it to make the rambling speaker seem pithy, the disjointed debate terse and cogent. The humdrum reality of life is subtly changed into a more exciting television version of reality. Newspapers also condense events, but not as convincingly. More pervasively than the printed press, television reduces issues to confrontations of celebrities and polarizes controversies into extreme positions. The middle grounds, the uncertain people and all the stammerers tend to be left, in the jargon of the trade, on the cutting-room floor. As professionals strive to capture the world in a few exciting words and pictures, there emerges a new semblance of the truth, a kind of allegory of events. Deep in their problems of editing, synchronizing, finding the clearest sound and the most telling picture, and saving precious seconds at every point, the professionals forget — until an occasional controversy arises over deceptive excerpting, as in the case of truncated interviews in "The Selling of the Pentagon" — how far behind they have left their audience in understanding how their capsule allegory of events differs from the actual event.

The reality that television presents, however imperfect, has become, for all practical purposes, the only important reality. Because television is the arbiter of the significant, little can succeed without its blessing. Proposals, programs, grievances, issues and candidates need to be legitimized by the "tube" or they cannot gain votes, popular support and money. Accordingly, television news, which has few criteria for selection other than previous notoriety or inescapable news interest, is constantly confronted by people figuratively waving their hands in its face — cleverly, desperately or menacingly — for attention.

The President of the United States need not wave his hands, but merely snap his fingers. Yet, in the White House, the planning for the use of television is no longer an adjunct to strategy, but a central part of strategy. The timing, format and style of a presidential appearance receive as much attention as the content. President Johnson moved the State of the Union address from its traditional noon hour to evening prime time. President Nixon turned the majesty of "the Presidency" almost into a studio prop. They were, however, amateurs compared to President Jimmy Carter, who has demonstrated an ability to convert almost every aspect of his activities into appealing television scenarios. He has been playing radio and television like an electronic organ — the first total media-age President.

In Congress, where the networks cannot be summoned with presidential ease, more energy is required, and more obeisance is made to the media. Senators and Congressmen release their speeches for quotation on morning broadcasts before they have been made on the floor — something that would once have been regarded as an inconceivable slight to the prerogatives of Congress. The legislators routinely present themselves in the television gallery to provide capsule summaries of speeches while the Senate and House weigh the advantages and perils of allowing television to witness actual debates on the floor. Committee chairmen strive to lure television to their public hearings so that, in turn, other committee members, and eventually the public, may become interested in the issues being studied. In executive sessions, committees devote an increasing amount of their time to planning how they will deal with the news media. Inside the Senate Intelligence Committee, Chairman Frank Church and Vice Chairman John Tower would discuss what to tell the staked-out cameras. On occasion, the committee would rescind a split vote so that harmony could be announced. The transcript of an executive session of the House committee investigating the Kennedy and King assassinations was distributed by accident, revealing that the meeting had been mainly devoted to writing a scenario for the waiting television cameras. Fighting for an appropriation, the committee planned the dropping of hints about some of its investigative leads in order to build up interest in its activities.

Access to television is competitive, but it has always been feasible for those with recognizable names, faces and settled roles in society. For those outside the charmed circle of authority — minorities, advocates of causes, protestors, radicals — access to television was, at first, harder to come by, and often impossible. Impossible, that is, until they learned that television was susceptible to manipulation, if they found the right levers to press. Some groups learned by a process of trial and error that menace worked better than meekness.

In the late 1960s, with urban unrest part of my assignment, I came slowly to realize how the television news process — from which I do not exempt myself — placed a premium on the rhetoric of violence. Black leaders who talked thoughtfully, at press conferences, about hopes and plans for peaceful change tended not to make it on the evening news; those who warned of riots and destruction often had greater success. In the rivalry of rhetoric, H. Rap Brown and Stokely Carmichael had a decided edge over Roy Wilkins and the Reverend Andrew Young. By giving the extremists exposure, we helped to gain them support. There developed, between TV news and black extremists, a tacitly agreed mutual manipulation. To questions of "Do you think this situation is likely to lead to violence?" there were ready and willing answers. On a dull day one needed only to stake out Carmichael's store-front headquarters in the Washington ghetto, and wait to be favored with an assortment of hair-raising threats of ruination.

Just as the "ins" learned to gear their activities to media events — visually appealing episodes arranged in convenient places at times convenient for evening news deadlines — so the disinherited and the disaffected learned their own techniques for media manipulation. At first, they used demonstrations, and developed something called "guerrilla theater." The Poor People's Campaign of 1968, which Martin Luther King planned but did not live to lead into Washington, was designed as a media event. Mule carts brought the poor to an encampment called "Resurrection City" near the Lincoln Memorial. When its novelty began to fade, when its tents began to sink into the mud under dismally steady rainstorms, when television began to turn its back on this microcosm of poverty, the organizers wrote more action into the script of their guerrilla theater. The Reverend Ralph David Abernathy and the Reverend Jesse Jackson led mass sit-ins in government buildings, confrontations with Cabinet secretaries and, finally, a march up Capitol Hill to be met by police with bullhorns and predictable arrests — a sure-fire "winner" for the evening news. With Jesse Jackson as their leader, they chanted over and over again, "I am somebody!" It was an assertion of identity, and one convincing way to get confirmation of identity was to see it recognized on the evening news.

The urban riots of the 1960s presented a serious problem for television. On the one hand, the medium loves the action-packed thud of fists and policemen's clubs. There are few more exciting pictures than a fire-bombed building in living color. Networks found it difficult to resist film of riots until they were forced to take account of the effect of these pictures on the imitative and suggestible. Compelled, for once, to come to terms with its own potency, television belatedly laid down limitations on coverage of riots for fear that the epidemic would rage out of control.

The "I am somebody!" refrain and the mass riots of the 1960s began to turn into a grimmer form of media manipulation in the 1970s. The make-believe violence that had become such a steady diet in television entertainment found its reflection in scenarios of real violence — sometimes written by those acting out their own fantasies. The new manifestation was kidnaping and murder, hostages and hijacking. One of its crucial aspects was the hijacking of television — the arbiter of identity, the greatest prize of all.

In 1975, when the radical Baader-Meinhof gang in West Germany kidnaped a politician as hostage for the release of five imprisoned comrades, they forced German television to show each prisoner boarding a plane and to broadcast dictated propaganda statements. A German television executive stated, "For seventy-two hours we lost control of the medium."

When Arab terrorists seized the Vienna headquarters of OPEC, the organization of oil exporters, in December 1975, killing three persons and taking eleven oil ministers hostage, their timetable called for continuing their siege in the building until the television cameras arrived.

When the so-called Symbionese Liberation Army planned the kidnaping of Patricia Hearst, the exploitation of the media — forcing radio and television to play tapes and carry its messages — was a central part of the plan.

The siege of the Hanafi Moslems in Washington in March 1977, with hostages being held in three locations, was a classic example of media-age terrorism. Their leader, Hamaas Abdul Khaalis, spent much of his time giving telephone interviews and having his wife check on what was being broadcast. When statements were made to which he took umbrage, he issued threats and quickly got apologies and retractions on the air.

"I am a TV camera," wrote Art Buchwald in a column on the Hanafi siege more serious than his custom. "Who knows how long the siege would last if I were not here? Who can predict what these men yelling their oaths of defiance would have done if they had known I wasn't coming?"

Television's diet of make-believe violence had helped to make violence as normal as apple pie. Television had contributed to breaking down the compartments between fact and fantasy, encouraging some to turn their fantasies into facts. Television had established itself as the way to assert identity and as a target for manipulation. All these chickens were coming home to roost. Broadcasting organizations were being forced to become the link between terrorists and their audience — giving the terrorists their greatest triumph and, at the same time, renewing the cycle of emulation.

Television executives agonized about the role they were being obliged to play. Richard Salant, in April 1977, issued guidelines for CBS News coverage. To censor terrorist sieges off the air would be to risk the destruction of credibility; such sieges should be covered, but with restraint, "not sensationalized beyond the actual fact of its being sensational." And, as far as possible, terrorists' demands and statements should be quoted, but they should not be put on the air themselves. The guidelines failed to come to grips with two problems. First, viewers have become conditioned to feed on the excitement of such events. During the Washington Hanafi siege, the one station that broke away from live coverage to avoid oversensationalizing the episode immediately lost part of its audience — precious ratings points. Second, the Salant statement did not deal with the problem raised when terrorists holding hostages present blackmail demands for access to the air.

"Television is a whore," jeered Dr. David Hubbard, a writer on hijacker psychology. "Any man who wants her full favors can have them in five minutes with a pistol." Two incidents in early 1977 provided chilling examples. In Indianapolis, Anthony George Kiritsis wired a sawed-off shotgun to the neck of a mortgage company officer, Richard Hall, led his hostage out to the police and the TV camera crews and yelled, "Get those cameras on! Get those goddamn cameras on! I'm a goddamn national hero!" In a Cleveland suburb, Cory C. Moore, an ex-marine, not only got the attention of television, but, through television, the attention of the President of the United States. Before releasing the diabetic he was holding hostage, Moore had the satisfaction of seeing President Carter, at a televised news conference, promising to talk to him; he watched the President on a TV set he had traded for a second hostage. Terrorists had learned to turn television into their personal megaphones. "These crimes are highly contagious," warned Dr. Harold Visotsky, head of the Department of Psychiatry at Northwestern University. "Deranged persons have a passion for keeping up with the news and imitating it."

A few of the unbalanced had risen from the national séance of television to seize the medium — to *become* the medium in the spiritualist sense. In most cases, the attempt to hijack television would end in prison, death or suicide. This was the terminal reality waiting at the end of the fantasy that impelled such actions, but coming too late for those who had lost sight of reality in the mists of television make-believe. "I think, therefore I am," Descartes had said. "I am seen, therefore I am" was the new version. Television had created a new class distinction of the Visible and the Invisible, and the most extreme were ready to muscle their way into visibility.

The many still joined in the electronic séance were not left unaffected by the violent actions of the few. They learned about these unsettling actions swiftly and vividly through the magic of television, and they reacted in ways not always immediately apparent. In Manhattan, in 1968, Professors Stephen M. Holloway and Harvey A. Hornstein were conducting an experiment in psychology. They dropped wallets on the street and counted how many people returned them. Over a period of time they found the average was 45 percent.

On the night of June 4 they were dropping wallets when Senator Robert Kennedy was fatally wounded in Los Angeles by an assassin's bullet. To their astonishment, not one of the wallets dropped that night was returned. This set the professors off on a new piece of research to discover the connection between an assassination and refusal to return lost wallets. They concluded that people who had learned from the dismaying television scenes and other news media about the slaying of the senator were no longer inclined to be helpful to each other. A social bond that ties people together had, for the moment at least, been severed. "When people hear bad news," the scientists wrote, "they are likely to become more competitive and less cooperative."

Another side effect of television, with its conditioning of audiences to fantasy, excitement and personalities, is to create a market for a kind of "real life" adventure that might be called "semifiction." The semifiction celebrity may be a real person, sometimes a person from the news media, inflated by the multimedia build-up into a figure larger than life. For audiences living in the borderline zone between reality and fantasy, it hardly mattered whether Alex Haley's ancestor was literally Kunta Kinte, as described in *Roots,* or whether Nixon and Kissinger literally knelt in prayer, as described in *The Final Days* by Woodward and Bernstein. In the film of *All the President's Men,* did Ben Bradlee play Jason Robards or was it vice versa? To thousands who saw the reenactment of the Entebbe raid, the late Peter Finch will forever be former Prime Minister Yitzhak Rabin of Israel. I can even confess to a fact-fiction lapse of my own. In Los Angeles one night, on first meeting Edward Asner, who played the television news director in the late-lamented "Mary Tyler Moore Show," I asked what his future plans were. It was after a late dinner and a lot of wine, and I hope he didn't perceive that for a fleeting moment I saw him like myself, as a displaced newsman. (To add to my confusion, his next television role was as a newspaper city editor.)

The appetite for adventure linked to the stirring events of our times has brought large rewards for books written about these events by chroniclers and participants, in fact and fiction. Since the appetite is for the excitement of conflict and cabal in high places, the rewards are shared impartially by accuser and accused — by Samuel Dash, Leon Jaworski, Richard Ben-Veniste and George Frampton, Jr., as well as by Nixon, Haldeman, Ehrlichman, Colson, Dean and Magruder. I wonder when someone will determine, on a cold cost-benefit calculation, that the multimedia wages of sin have grown so high as to warrant deliberate malfeasance in office and a few well-publicized months in jail before contrition and contract for the book, the paperback rights, the movie rights, the television rights.

We are in an era when events hardly have meaning except as they are packaged. Daniel Boorstin, in his perceptive book *The Image,* warned that made-for-media "pseudoevents" might crowd out "spontaneous events." *The New Yorker* made the point, in its own way, with a cartoon showing a man transfixed by television, his wife explaining to a friend, "Richard takes the news very seriously. To him, they are all real people."

This is a melancholy world for an old-fashioned newsman to contemplate, but I believe the real world will overcome in the end. Television will yet be tamed, as nuclear energy and genetic engineering must be tamed and harnessed to peaceful uses. For television, the seeds of salvation may lie in itself — its tendency to burn out by overexposure the very forces it helps to generate. Oversaturation may arrest America's obsession with escapist fantasy. When the fascination of the séance palls, America, I am confident, will come back from dreamland seeking an old-fashioned answer from an old-fashioned reporter to an old-fashioned question, "What's the news?"

NOTES AND SOURCES
INDEX

NOTES AND SOURCES

Abbreviations of names and materials frequently used in notes:

AR Report of the Senate Intelligence Committee, "Alleged Assassinations Plots Involving Foreign Leaders—An Interim Report," 11/20/75 (Assassinations Report)

CSR Staff report to the Warren Commission by lawyers, William T. Coleman, Jr., and W. David Slawson

Con. Rts. hearing Subcommittee on Constitutional Rights of the Senate Judiciary Committee, "Freedom of the Press," Sept.–Oct. 1971 and Feb. 1972

DS Daniel Schorr

FS Frank Stanton

HEC House Ethics Committee

HIC House Select Committee on Intelligence

HJC House Judiciary Committee, Impeachment Inquiry

HJC transcripts "Transcripts of Eight Recorded Presidential Conversations," May–June 1974, House Judiciary Committee

NPP "Public Papers of the Presidents, Richard Nixon," Vols. for 1969–74

NYT *New York Times*

Presidential transcripts "Submission of Recorded Presidential Conversations," April 30, 1974

SIC Senate Select Committee to Study Governmental Activities with Respect to Intelligence Activities

SWC Senate Select Committee on Presidential Campaign Activities (Senate Watergate Committee)

WC Warren Commission

WH White House

WP Washington *Post*

WSP William S. Paley

Quotations from and descriptions of meetings and activities participated in by individuals cited in the text are taken from personal conversations, interviews, letters and memoranda to which DS was a party.

I. THE ACCIDENTAL INVESTIGATOR *(Pages 1–16)*

page

3fn   "utilize SCHORR" and "derogatory information." Material received under Freedom of Information request: CIA memo, 8/26/58, and ONI-FBI-MID "confidential" entry, 3/19/42.

4   Item: . . . 1948. DS scripts, 6/15 and 6/18/48.
Item: . . . 1952. DS original draft for *Life* magazine, "The Queen and the Faith Healer."

4–5   Item: . . . 1957. "Face the Nation," CBS Television Network, 6/2/57; Eisenhower news conference, 6/5/57.

5   Item: . . . 1959. DS script, 4/15/59.

5   Item: . . . 1960. DS script, 10/24/60.

6   Item: . . . 1962. DS script, 8/29/61.

6   Later, in a closed. DS script, 5/9/62.

7   From Munich. DS script, 7/10/64.

10   On hand, as *Newsweek* noted. 5/3/65.

10   In his 1970 book. Barry Goldwater, *The Conscience of a Majority* (Englewood Cliffs, N.J.: Prentice-Hall, 1970), p. 184.

10   Sally Quinn, in her book. Sally Quinn, *We're Going to Make You a Star* (New York: Simon and Schuster, 1975), p. 40.

10   Appearing on Dinah Shore's. "Dinah!" CBS Television Stations, 12/10/76 (aired).

10   The "Dinah!" show producer. "Dinah!" 3/8/77 (aired).

14fn   In a memorandum. Hunt memo, 11/72 (introduced 11/4/74).

15   It actually followed. DS script, 8/23/72.

15   The *Post* was reporting. WP, "New Name Drawn Into Bugging Case," 8/25/72.

II. STAND-UPS AND STAKE-OUTS *(Pages 17–34)*

page

20   "ironclad procedures." DS script, 8/28/72.

20–22   E. Howard Hunt. DS script, 8/29/72.

21fn   Hunt. DS script, 10/29/74.

22   Charles Colson. DS scripts, 8/29 and 8/30/72.

22–23   John Mitchell. DS scripts, 9/1, 9/2, and 9/5/72.

23   Hunt and Liddy. DS scripts, 8/31 and 9/11/72.

24   O'Brien. DS scripts, 9/7, 9/8, 9/11, and 9/12/72.

24–25   Baldwin. DS scripts, 10/5 and 10/17/72; Los Angeles *Times,* 10/4/72.

25   As John Dean. HJC transcripts, p. 7.

25   The Democrats' counsel. DS scripts, 9/21 and 9/22/72.

26   When Judge John Sirica. DS script, 10/6/72.

26   In the Oval Office. HJC transcripts, p. 13 (9/15/72 conversation).

26   It would be disclosed. Sen. Rules and Administration Comm. hearings, 11/1–11/14/73.

26   In any event. DS script, 10/3/72.

26   On our program. "Face the Nation," 10/15/72.

26   William E. Timmons. SWC hearings, Bk. 3, pp.960–62; John W. Dean, *Blind Ambition* (New York: Simon and Schuster, 1976), pp. 142–44.

26–27 Robert Stephens. Marjorie Boyd, *Atlantic Monthly,* April 1973, p. 44.
27 Brasco himself . . . In July 1974. Conviction 7/19/74, Federal District Court, New York.
27 As a final gesture. DS scripts, 10/10, 10/12, and 10/13/72.
28 Common Cause suit. Filed 9/6/72 in Federal District Court; DS scripts, 9/6, 9/29, 9/30, and 10/10/72.
28–29 Hugh Sloan, Jr. DS script, 10/25/72; WP, "Testimony Ties Top Nixon Aide to Secret Fund," 10/25/72.
29 As recorded in the book. Carl Bernstein & Bob Woodward, *All the President's Men* (New York: Simon and Schuster, 1974), pp. 183–84.
29–30 Common Cause suit. DS scripts, 10/30 and 11/1/72.
32 Cronkite's script. "CBS Evening News," CBS Television Network, 10/27/72.
33 Watergate Part II. "CBS Evening News," 10/31/72.

III. White House and Black Rock *(Pages 35–64)*

page
37fn Alexander P. Butterfield. HJC hearings, Bk. I, p. 32. William Safire. In his book *Before the Fall* (Garden City, N.Y.: Doubleday, 1975), p. 287.
37 1952 "Checkers" speech and 1960 election defeat. Richard M. Nixon, *Six Crises* (Garden City, N.Y.: Doubleday, 1962), pp. 129, 422.
37 On November 3. NPP, #425, pp. 901–9.
37 Correspondent Marvin Kalb. "CBS Television Network: Analysis by CBS News Correspondents," 11/3/69.
38 Dean Burch-FS. FS affidavit, U.S. District Court, Central District of California, *United States of America* v. *Columbia Broadcasting System Inc.,* 4/25/74.
38 Later, in response. FCC statement, 11/20/69.
38–39 October 17, 1969, White House memo. SWC Final Report, "The Shot-gun versus the Rifle," pp. 267–68.
39fn Public Television network. "Thirty Minutes with _____" program, 5/4/72.
39 Nixon read it. *Before the Fall,* p. 352.
40 The ominous character. FS speech to the International Radio and Television Society, 11/25/69.
40 The next time President. NPP, #486, pp. 1025–28.
40 Morton summary. CBS Television Network, "Commentary Following Nixon Speech on Vietnam," 12/15/69.
41 On January 21. SWC hearings, Bk. 8, pp. 3325–26.
41 On February 4. SWC hearings, Bk. 10, p. 4112.
41 Colson . . . walk over his grandmother. Theodore H. White, *The Making of the President—1972* (New York: Atheneum, 1973), p. 275.
41 Manager of special assignments. SWC hearings, Bk. 9, pp. 3669–814.
42fn "supplied Presidential authority." SIC Report, Bk. II, pp. 114–15.
42 "talking paper." SIC hearings, Vol 2, p. 86.
42–43 By the next month. 7/17/70 memo made public by SWC.
43 When the FCC ruled. 8/26/70 memo made public by SWC.
43–44 In the Senate Watergate. 9/25/70 memo made public by SWC.
50 Antitrust suits. *United States of America* v. *Columbia Broadcasting System Inc., U.S.A.* v. *American Broadcasting Companies, Inc., U.S.A.* v. *National Broadcasting Company, Inc.,* U.S. District Court, Central District of California.

50   The conversation went. HJC Statement of Information, Bk. V, Pt. 1, p. 314.
50   Buchanan television interview. NPACT "Thirty Minutes with ———,"
      5/4/72.
51   Stanton of CBS. FS affidavit, *U.S.A.* v. *CBS Inc.,* 4/25/74.
51   Leonard Goldenson. Goldenson affidavit, *U.S.A.* v. *A.B.C., Inc.,* 5/14/74.
51   Julian Goodman. Goodman affidavit, *U.S.A.* v. *N.B.C., Inc.,* 5/13/74.
51–52 On September 15. HJC transcripts, p. 15.
52   License challenges. Competing applications for license renewals were filed
      with the FCC against WJXT on 12/29/72 and on 1/2/73, and against WPLG
      on 1/2/73.
53   Cronkite came on. "The CBS Evening News," 10/27/72.
56   President Nixon's news. News Summary, 11/2/72.
57fn   Caulfield. SWC Final Report, pp. 124–25.
58   On December 18. Speech to Indianapolis Sigma Delta Chi.
59   On March 13. HJC transcripts, pp. 74, 47, 69.
61   On June 6. WSP statement, 6/6/73.
62   Two weeks before. NPP, #162, p. 547.
62   *Variety.* 6/20/73.
62   Senator John Pastore. *Television Digest,* 7/2/73.
63   In the year-end. "CBS News Special: 'The Correspondents Report,'"
      12/23/71.
63   In one "post-Nixon analysis." CBS Television Network, "Commentary Fol-
      lowing President Nixon's State of the Union Address," 1/22/71.
64   On November 12. WSP statement, 11/12/73.

IV. "A REAL MEDIA ENEMY" *(Pages 65–90)*

page
65   In a March 1971. NPP, #110, p. 457.
65   During the same month. 3/30/71 Drury interview, *Newsday,* 11/12/71.
66   On the CBS Morning News. DS script, 1/3/68.
67   A few days later. NPP, #23, p. 53; NPP, #48, p. 99.
67–68 Patrick Buchanan. *Before the Fall,* p. 346.
68   Disapproving White House attention. DS scripts, Feb.–July, Sept.–Nov. 1969;
      Apr.–June 1969; (Carswell) 3/16–3/20/70; (Haynsworth) Sept.–Nov. 1969;
      May–July 1970; 4/21/70.
69   In June 1970. DS scripts, 6/1 and 6/2/70.
69   Senator Robert Dole. Dole floor statement, 6/3/70.
69   In March 1971. DS scripts, 3/8–3/10/71.
69–70 Press Secretary Ron Ziegler. WH news conference, #955, 3/10/71.
70   On the same day. Transcript made available from WH.
70   On August 17. NPP, #268, pp. 893–98.
71   There appeared to be. DS script, 8/18/71.
72–73 In early November. DS scripts, 11/2–11/9/71.
73   The underlying truth. DS scripts, 11/17–11/22/71.
73   The *Post* headlined. WP, "FBI Probes Newsman Critical of Nixon," 11/11/71.
73   Press Secretary Ron Ziegler. WH news conference, #1239, 11/11/71.
73   The Chicago *Tribune.* "Why Did the FBI Investigate Schorr?" 11/18/71.
74   The President's counsel. Con. Rts. hearing, 2/1/72, pp. 425, 988–89.
74   But Senator Ervin. Con. Rts. hearing, 2/1/72, p. 423.

74fn Train, induced. WP, "White House Weighed Job for Schorr," 2/1/72.
74   There was also. Con. Rts. hearing, 2/1/72, pp. 424–25, 989–90.
74–75 "I am Daniel Schorr." Con. Rts. hearing, 2/1/72, pp. 416, 419–20.
75   Senator Ervin. Con. Rts. hearing, 2/1/72, p. 426.
75–76 Patrick Buchanan. ABC "Dick Cavett Show," 3/22/73.
76–77 When, for example. Sen. Judiciary Comm. hearings, 3/1/73, p. 276.
77   The following August. NPP, #276, p. 829.
77–78 Mitchell. DS script, 4/14/73.
78   "And so he said." WH transcripts, p. 691–92.
78   This would later. DS scripts, 7/10 and 7/11/73.
78   As Washington reeled. NPP, #125, pp. 289–99.
78   This began. *Blind Ambition*, p. 270.
79   He wrote. *Blind Ambition*, p. 285.
80   Dean viewed it . . . Dean agreed. *Blind Ambition*, pp. 285–86.
80   Dean-Cronkite interview. "CBS News Special Report: 'Watergate: An Interview with John Dean,' " 5/17/73.
80   The Caucus Room. SWC hearings, Bk. 3, pp. 1021–94.
81fn Dean had testified. SWC hearings, Bk. 4, pp. 1511–15.
81fn In his book. *Blind Ambition*, p. 325.
81   Dean related. SWC hearings, Bk. 3, p. 1071.
82   Senator Herman Talmadge. SWC hearings, Bk. 4, p. 1490.
82   "in connection with." SWC hearings, Bk. 8, p. 3156.
82   Haldeman-Montoya. SWC hearings, Bk. 8, p. 3157.
82   Higby, who had. HJC Statement of Info., Bk. VII, Pt. 2, p. 1123.
82–86 DS-FBI investigation. HJC Report, pp. 150–51; FBI materials from a collection of thirty documents released 7/1/74 under Freedom of Information request of 3/19/74; HJC Testimony of Witnesses, Bk. III, pp. 238–41; HJC Statement of Info., Bk. IX, Pt. 1, p. 204 (6/14/73 tape), and HJC transcripts, pp. 56–57 (3/13/73 tape).
86fn Safire wrote. *Before the Fall*, p. 356.
87–89 Dean memos. SWC hearings, Bk. 4, pp. 1349–50, 1689, 1692–96, 1692–1753.
89   "I want the most." HJC transcripts, p. 10.
90   With White House agents. SWC Final Report, Ch. III, pp. 361–444.
90   The "Plumbers." SWC Final Report, Chaps. I and II, pp. 1–360.

V. COLLISION COURSES *(Pages 91–120)*

page
91   The magazine of journalism. *MORE*, 12/73.
92   Khrushchev. "Face the Nation," 6/2/57.
94   Most events on. Daniel J. Boorstin, *The Image: A Guide to Pseudo-Events in America* (New York: Atheneum, 1972).
94   In May 1971. DS scripts, 5/20 and 5/21/71.
95   On the Cronkite show. DS script, 10/23/72; presidential news summary, 10/24/72.
95   When Gray testified. SWC hearings, Bk. 9, pp. 3462–554.
95   There was a succession. DS scripts, 10/19 and 11/22/73, 5/8/74.
96   A tribute I. "Security of Rough Draft Report," 5/7/74.
96   At the outset. DS scripts, 10/5–10/7/72.

96   In December. DS script, 12/18/72.
96   I was the only. DS script, 10/17/72.
97   An early 1973. Newton N. Minow, John Bartlow Martin, and Lee M. Mitchell, *Presidential Television* (New York: Basic Books, 1973).
97   Nixon-Haldeman. WH transcripts, p. 643.
97   Contrary to Haldeman's. SWC hearings, Bk. 1, p. 3.
100   Morrie Ryskind. Los Angeles *Herald-Examiner,* "Liberal Dilemma," 8/8/73.
100–01 Nixon statements. NPP 1973, #126, p. 299; NPP #134, p. 330; NPP #233, p. 695; NPP #312, p. 900; NPP #334, p. 956. NPP 1974, #25, p. 55; NPP #122, p. 397.
101   He made embarrassing. NPP, #334, 11/17/73, p. 952.
102   On April 30. "Analysis by CBS New Correspondents: President Nixon's Address to the Nation on the Watergate Affair."
102   President Nixon. News Summary, "The President's April 30, 1973 Speech," 5/1/73.
102–03 On October 23. "CBS News Special Report: The White House Tapes—The Nixon Decision."
103   On November 17. "Analysis by CBS News Correspondents Following 'The President and The Editors.' "
103   My only other. CBS Radio Network, "President Nixon's Address."
104   And Victor Lasky. Syndicated column, North American Newspaper Alliance, 12/9/71.
105   Howard Baker. SWC Final Report, Ch. 11, pp. 1105–66.
105   There were transcripts. HJC transcripts.
106   July 18-CBS. "CBS News Special Report: 'The Impeachment Hearings: Wiretaps and Plumbers.' "
106   Nixon statements. NPP 1973, #162, p. 547; NPP #236, p. 723; NPP #246, p. 740; NPP #312, pp. 900 and 905. NPP 1974, #83, p. 295.
107   Haldeman's and Ehrlichman's letters. NPP, #133, pp. 327 and 328.
113   At nine o'clock. NPP, #244, p. 627.
113–14 Cronkite, Sevareid, Rather. "CBS News Special Report: 'President Nixon Resigns.' "
115–16 Denver *Post.* "Schorr Feels Nixon 'Lived and Died by Television,' " 8/19/74.
117   An inaccurate summary. *Duke Chronicle,* "Duke Fellows Discuss Media," 1/20/75; *Media Report,* "Inside the Media," 1/31/75.
117   When *New York.* "Dan ('Killer') Schorr—The Great Abrasive," 6/16/75; "Letters: 'No Soft Line at CBS,' " 7/14/75.
118fn   Bazelon address. "F.C.C. Regulation of the Telecommunications Press," The 1975 Brainerd Currie Lecture, Duke University School of Law, 4/5/75.

VI. TRANSITION *(Pages 121–129)*

page
122–24 Ford's pardon testimony. HJC Subcommittee on Criminal Justice, 10/17/74.
125   The President had hinted. HJC transcripts, pp. 94 and 118.
25   During his first. SWC Final Report, Ch. 8, p. 940.
126   He told Haldeman. Presidential tape from files of the special prosecutor, 6/23/72.

128   In progress. "CBS Reports: 'Prescription: Take With Caution,'" 1/10/75 (aired).

VII. SON OF WATERGATE *(Pages 130–152)*

page

130   In the *New York Times.* 9/8–10/21/74.

130–31   Cline, who had. DS script, 10/17/74 (aired).

132   Hersh, on top. NYT, "Kissinger Said to Rebuke U.S. Ambassador to Chile," 9/27/74.

133fn   A staff report. SIC, Vol. 7, "Covert Action in Chile," pp. 170–73.

134   Two months later. NYT, 12/22/74.

137   "Why did you resign?" DS scripts, 12/23–12/24/74.

137   Colby wrote. Colby letter, 12/24/74.

138   President Nixon. Presidential transcripts, pp. 318–42.

138   Hardly back in Washington. CIA Commission Report, 6/75, pp. 271–74.

138   McClellan and Stennis hearings. DS scripts, 1/15–1/16/75; Colby statement, 1/15/75.

139   Seventeen months earlier. SWC hearings, Bk. 8, pp. 3232–89.

139   "Well," he had. 6/23/72 presidential tape made available by the special prosecutor's office, 8/74.

139–40   Four months later. DS script, 12/23/74.

140fn   In September 1971. HJC Statement of Information, Bk. VII, Pt. 2, pp. 1029–80.

140fn   In March 1976. SIC, 3/11/76.

140fn   Ehrlichman's 1976 novel. John Ehrlichman, *The Company* (New York: Simon and Schuster, 1976).

141   Three days later. DS script, 1/13/75.

141   Helms' testimony/Stennis. DS script, 1/16/75; Helms statement, 1/16/75.

142   Further trouble. DS script, 1/22/75; Senate Foreign Relations hearings, 2/5 and 2/7/73, pp. 1–2, 17, 13, 26.

143   "Memorandum for all CIA." 5/9/73.

143   In August 1973. 8/29/73.

145fn   Lumumba. AR, pp. 13–67.

146   I sat down. DS script, 2/28/75.

146   On a rainy Sunday. DS script, 3/17/75.

147   Indeed, President Johnson. DS script, 4/25/75.

147fn   Thomas Powers. "The Rise and Fall of Richard Helms," 12/16/76.

148   "I must say." DS script, 4/28/75.

148–49   Prouty/Helms. DS script, 4/29/75.

149   Church came out. DS script, 5/7/75.

149   On May 22. DS scripts, 5/22 and 5/23/75.

149   Suddenly, President Ford. DS scripts, 6/5 and 6/6/75.

149–50   "Can I conclude." DS script, 6/6/75.

150–51   The Rockefeller commission. "Report to the President by the Commission on CIA Activities Within the United States," June 1975, pp. 130, 141, 28, 111, 226–27, 32–33, 228.

150fn   CIA file. Released 4/5/77.

151   "The Rockefeller report." DS script, 6/11/75.

VIII. THE ASSASSINS *(Pages 153–178)*

Page
153   Even though. Hugh Davis Graham and Ted Robert Gurr, "Violence in America—Historical and Comparative Perspectives."
154   Plots against eight leaders. AR, pp. 260–64, 13–70, 191–215, 217–23, 225–54, 4 fn.
158   "Simple retaliation." CSR, p. 7.
161   "We were hysterical." AR, p. 142 fn. 1.
161   Between 1960 and 1965. AR, p. 71.
161   They started. AR, p. 72.
161fn The CIA disclaimed. AR, p. 71 fn. 1.
161   Speaking of. AR, p. 142 fn. 2.
162   *The Accident Plot.* AR, pp. 72–73.
162   *Poison Cigars.* AR, p. 73.
162–63 *Mafia, Phase One.* AR, pp. 74–82.
163   *Mafia, Phase Two.* AR, pp. 82–85, 85 fn. 1–4.
163–64 *Seashell and Diving Suit.* AR, pp. 85–86.
164   *The Inside Man.* AR, pp. 86–90; NYT, "Havana Accuses Seven of Plotting With CIA Agents to Assassinate Castro," 3/6/66.
164   Dr. Cubela. SIC Final Report, Bk. V, p. 13.
164   On Saturday. SIC Final Report, Bk. V, p. 14.
164–65 Castro speech and interview. SIC Final Report, Bk. V, p. 41, 14, 14 fn. 18.
165   "Cuban Coordinating Committee." SIC Final Report, Bk. V, pp. 15–16.
165   His CIA contact. SIC Final Report, Bk. V, p. 17.
165   Major Cubela. AR, p. 87.
165   Instead. SIC Final Report, Bk. V, pp. 17–18; AR, p. 87.
165   Fitzgerald/counterintelligence. SIC Final Report, Bk. V, p. 17 fn. 32.
165–66 Accompanied/The Major/He also/CIA technicians. SIC Final Report, Bk. V, pp. 17 fn. 32, 18; AR, pp. 87 fn. 3, 88.
166   It took. SIC Final Report, Bk. V, p. 19.
166   Kennedy speech. SIC Final Report, Bk. V, pp. 19–20.
166   Cubela/An air drop. AR, pp. 89, 88; SIC Final Report, Bk. V, p. 20.
166   A chillingly. AR, p. 89.
166   In Dallas/Paris/Havana. AR, pp. 72, 89, 174; SIC Final Report, Bk. V, p. 21.
166–67 (For pages 166–67). AR, pp. 153, 266–67, 268, 269, 150, 173, 131–34, 178, 89–90; SIC Final Report, Bk. V., pp. 77–80.
167fn Castro allegations. WP, "Cuba Voids Hijack Pact," 10/16/76.
167   Johnson/Helms. AR, p. 179.
167   Cubela confessed. NYT, "Cuban Admits Plot to Murder Castro—Asks Death Penalty," 3/8/66.
168   Helms' testimony. AR, pp. 148–50, 119–20.
168   McNamara testimony. AR, p. 158.
169   McCone/Helms testimony. WC hearings, pp. 122–24, published by the Government Printing Office, Washington, D.C., November 1964; Bk. V, p. 77.
169–70 Morgan/Helms. Bk. V, p. 70.
170   Oswald. Bk. V, p. 91; CSR, p. 90.
170   Oswald/Mexico/Kennedy. SIC Final Report, Bk. V, pp. 4, 24, 25; CSR, pp. 91–92, 94–95, 90.
170   Katzenbach/Moyers. SIC Final Report, Bk. V, p. 23.
171   CIA/Helms/desk officer. SIC Final Report, Bk. V, pp. 24, 25, 27–28.

171   Helms cable/"coordinator." SIC Final Report, Bk. V, pp. 29, 31.
171–72   Angleton/FBI. SIC Final Report, Bk. V, pp. 31, 49 fn. 15.
172   Angleton group/Senate report. SIC Final Report, Bk. V, pp. 57–59.
172   Nosenko report. CSR, pp. 44–45, and appendix "Statement by Yuri Ivanovich Nosenko."
172–73   Warren Commission. SIC Final Report, Bk. V, pp. 60, 67.
173   CIA officials. SIC Final Report, Bk. V, p. 71.
173   But in 1965. SIC Final Report, Bk. V, p. 78.
173   Warren Commission conclusions. President's Commission to Investigate the Assassination of President John F. Kennedy Final Report, September 1964.
173   The Warren Commission's. SIC Final Report, Bk. V, p. 2.
174–75   Liebeler/Rankin. 9/16/64 memo, "Quote from New Orleans *Times-Picayune* of September 19, 1963, concerning Fidel Castro's Speech."
175   In May 1975. 5/30/75 memo, "Review of Selected Items in the Lee Harvey Oswald File Regarding Allegations of the Castro Cuban Involvement in the John F. Kennedy Assassination."
175fn   In a June 1977. ABC Television Network, "Fidel Castro Speaks," 6/9/77.
175   In July. CSR, p. 96.
175   In August. SIC Final Report, Bk. V, p. 91.
175   On September 17. CSR, p. 106.
175   On September 23. CSR, p. 96.
175–76   Instead, in great secrecy. CSR, pp. 91, 92, 76, 78.
176   Silvia Duran. CSR, pp. 93–96; SIC Final Report, Bk. V, p. 125.
177   Castro July interview. *National Enquirer,* "Fidel Castro Says He Knew of Oswald Threat to Kill JFK," 10/15/67.
178   Former President Johnson. King Features Syndicate column, 4/24/75.

IX. The Leak Age *(Pages 179–207)*

page
183   The first public hearing. SIC hearings, Vol. 1, pp. 4–51; DS script, 9/16/75.
183   Details of the twenty-year. SIC hearings, Vol. 4; Schwarz. SIC hearings, Vol. 4, p. 27; DS scripts, 10/21–24/75.
183–84   National Security Agency. SIC hearings, Vol. 5; DS script, 10/29/75.
184   Cong. Bella Abzug. House Subcommittee on Government Information and Individual Rights hearings, 10/23/75, p. 2; DS script, 10/23/75.
184   One big story. Los Angeles *Times.* "CIA Reportedly Contracted with Hughes in Effort to Raise Sunken Soviet A-Sub," 2/8/75.
185   Within hours. DS scripts, 3/18 and 3/19/75.
187fn   For example. *Time,* 7/28/75, p. 42.
188fn   CIA payments. WP, "CIA Paid Millions to Jordan's King Hussein," 2/18/77.
188fn   Hussein quote. *Newsweek,* "Hussein on His CIA Money," 3/7/77.
191   Welch was on a list. *Counter-Spy,* summer 1975.
191fn   Only when. SIC Final Report, Bk. 1, p. 458.
192   One bizarre footnote. HIC Draft Final Report, 1/76, p. 83 fn.; DS script, 1/20/76.
192fn   The *New York Times.* "Intelligence Budget Totaling $6.2 Billion Is Reported Sought," 4/1/77.
193   January 26. NYT, "House Committee Finds Intelligence Agencies Generally Go Unchecked," 1/26/76.

196   It was Bellon. Daniel Schorr, *Don't Get Sick in America* (Nashville: Aurora Publishing Co., 1970); "CBS Reports," 4/21/70.

202   The following Tuesday. WP, "CIA Balks at Listing Reporters," 2/10/76; DS script, 2/10/76.

203   That night. NYT, "An Ex-CBS Writer Is Linked to C.I.A.," 2/11/76.

204   *Village Voice* was out. 2/16/76.

205   Next morning. WP, "Part of Intelligence Report Published in N.Y. Tabloid —'Voice' Melodrama," 2/12/76.

205   The White House. WH press statement, 2/12/76.

205   Secretary Kissinger. Kissinger briefing, 2/12/76.

207   They would also. CBS public release, 2/13/76.

X. THE OTHER SIDE OF THE BARRICADE *(Pages 208–236)*

page

208–09   NYT editorial. 2/15/76.

209   In dismay. NYT, "Of Secret Documents," 2/22/76.

209   The Chicago *Tribune.* "Clear conscience reaps a tidy profit," 2/20/76.

209   Buffalo *Evening News.* "Breach of Journalistic Ethics," 2/20/76.

209   Peoria *Journal-Star.* "Will CBS Cover Up?" 2/18/76.

210   In quick succession. DS scripts, 2/15 and 2/16/76.

210   The Justice Department. 2/17/76 statement.

210   Philip Buchen. 2/13/76 news conference.

210   I was meanwhile. DS script, 2/17/76.

211   A brief chat. Washington *Star,* 2/18/76, p. 1.

212   Which came out. *Broadcasting,* "Schorr suspended from reporting—CBS will go only part of the way in defending him," 3/1/76.

213   "Not freedom." WBTV, 2/24 and 2/25/76.

213   "We don't think." WSAU, 2/24/76.

213   "It could well." WISN, 2/19/76.

213   WCSC. 2/26/76.

213   Word of my removal. WP, "Schorr Taken Off His Assigned Beat," 2/20/76.

214   When word leaked. NYT, "Affiliates Committee of CBS Radio Urged Dismissal of Schorr," 3/11/76.

214   Rising to offer. *Congressional Record,* 2/19/76, pp. H1178–87.

216   We read together. WP, 2/20/76.

222   The first leading. NYT, 2/24/76.

222   In more satiric. NYT, "Secrets, Anyone?" 2/16/76.

223   Appearing with me. WTTG, "Panorama," 4/2/76.

223   A. H. Raskin. NYT, 2/25/76.

223   "Panic in the House." St. Louis, *Post-Dispatch,* 2/23/76.

223   "House in Disgrace." San Jose *Mercury,* 2/26/76.

223   "A lunatic course." Washington *Star,* 3/15/76.

227   When Salant. *Newsweek,* "News Media—'Daniel in the Lion's Den,'" 3/8/76.

227   When I responded. Orlando *Sentinel-Star,* "Schorr Hints CBS Knew of Leak Plans," 4/14/76.

227   "Tomorrow" program. NBC, "Tomorrow," 3/11/76 (taped).

229   He defended me. WP, "Colby Backs Schorr on CIA Report," 3/30/76.

230 These remarks. St. Louis *Post-Dispatch,* "Kissinger Agrees With Colby That Schorr Got a Bum Rap," 4/6/76.
230 In the *New York Times.* "Schorr, CBS and the Vow of Silence," 4/1/76.
231 A fictional CBS reporter. T.A.T. Communications, "All's Fair," 10/19/76 (taped).
232 Perhaps the ultimate. NYT, 7/11/76.
233–34 Bowers testimony. HEC hearings, pp. 11, 18, 20–27.
234 CIA testimony. HEC hearings, pp. 116, 121, 296.
234 Stanton testimony. HEC hearings, p. 392.
235 If the committee's. DS speech, 8/10/76.

XI. UNDER SUBPOENA *(Pages 237–258)*

page
239 Chairman Flynt. 8/30/76 statement.
242 In New York. 9/11/76 press conference.
244 The first witnesses. HEC hearings, pp. 506–31; Latham. HEC hearings, p. 515.
245–49 DS testimony. HEC hearings, pp. 531–67.
249 An impish history. "Speech to CBS Radio Network Affiliates Convention," 9/16/76.
249–50 Also in Williamsburg. "Speech to CBS Radio Network Affiliates Convention," 9/15/76.
250 Its final report. HEC "Report on Investigation Concerning Unauthorized Publication of the Report of the Select Committee on Intelligence," p. 43.
251 In the *New York Times.* "Schorr's Job Status Uncertain Despite Gain Over Ethics Panel," 9/23/76.
252–54 "60 Minutes." 9/25/76 (taped); 9/26/76 (aired).
257 The filmed interview. CBS Evening News, 9/28/76.

XII. THE SOLE PROPRIETOR *(Pages 259–284)*

page
262 "CBS Reports." "CBS Reports—'Land Beyond the Wall,' " 1/4/62.
274–75 Safire. NYT, "Paley's Big Secret," 3/2/76.
275 I undoubtedly. NYT, "The CIA Cloud Over the Press," 7/20/76.
275 Cong. Otis Pike. DS script, 11/6/75.

XIII. THE NATIONAL SÉANCE *(Pages 285–301)*

page
285 Frank Mankiewicz. WP, *Potomac* magazine, "The Great Certifier," 10/31/76.
289–90 The historian. Daniel J. Boorstin, *The American: The Democratic Experience* (New York: Random House, 1973), p. 395.
290 After his series. Jacob Bronowski, *The Ascent of Man* (Boston: Little, Brown, 1973), p. 14.
290 There seems. Daniel J. Boorstin, *The Exploring Spirit, America and the World, Then and Now* (New York: Random House, 1976) p. 69.
290 Professor Michael J. Robinson. Robinson and Paul Weaver, ed. Richard Adler, *American Political Legitimacy in an Era of Electronic Journalism— Reflections on the Evening News* (New York: Praeger, 1975).

290   Margaret Mead. NYT, "David From Goliath, Doze in the Arena," 10/25/76.
290   George F. Will. *Newsweek,* "To the Survivor," 11/15/76.
291   Marie Winn. *The Plug-In Drug,* (New York: Viking, 1977).
297   In 1975 and When Arab terrorists. *TV Guide,* "The Medium in the Middle," 7/31 and 8/7/76.
298   "I am a TV camera." WP, "Live and In Color With No Questions . . . and No Answers," 3/15/77.
298   Richard Salant. NYT, "CBS Curbs on Terror," 4/15/77.
299   "Television is a whore." *TV Guide,* 7/31 and 8/7/76.
299   In Indianapolis. *Newsweek,* "Kidnappings: Three Days of Rage," 2/21/77.
299   "These crimes." *Time,* 3/21/77.
299–300   In Manhattan. *Psychology Today,* 12/76.
301   Daniel J. Boorstin. *The Image: A Guide to Pseudo-Events in America,* 3rd ptg., (New York: Atheneum College Ed., August 1972), p. 39.

INDEX

and alleged anti-Nixon bias, 52

and analysis of presidential statements, 61–64

and contempt charges against Stanton, 47–49

correspondents who worked for CIA, 202–4, 274–80

and coverage of Watergate hearings, 97–98

deterioration of Schorr's relations with, 126–29

efforts to mend relations with White House, 56–57, 60–61

and "Goldwater Affair," 7–11

and impeachment debate, 107

in-depth report on Watergate, 31–34, 53–56

Khrushchev interview, 4–5, 92–93

and "The Loyal Opposition," 41, 43, 49

Nixon White House's grudges against correspondents, 65

and Nixon's enemy lists, 88–89

and Nixon's resignation, 108–16

and Paley's connection with CIA, 274–80

pays legal costs to Califano, 251

and publication of Pike report, 204–7, 216

and question of reinstatement of Schorr by, 251–58

reaction to Schorr's Duke speech, 117–18

relations with CIA, 198, 201–2

request for Schorr's resignation, 216–17, 219–22

and Schorr's assignment in Moscow, 2–3

and Schorr's cable on "prestige poll," 5–6

and Schorr's discovery of evidence incriminating Liddy and Hunt, 23

and Schorr's efforts to publish Pike report, 195–98, 200

Schorr's inquiry into Paley's, 258, 259–84 *passim*

seeks to withdraw financial support from Schorr, 234–35

shaky façade of harmony with Schorr, 227–28, 230–31

threatened with antitrust suit, 50–51

traumatic reaction to publication of Pike report, 280–84

war between Nixon and, 35–38, 42, 43–47

CBS News Executive Committee (CNEC), 272, 273

"CBS Reports," 127–29

Chancellor, John, 13, 62, 67, 243, 293

Chandler, Robert, 216, 217, 288

Chapin, Dwight, 19

Chase, Chevy, 228

Chase, Sylvia, 128

Cheshire, Maxine, 232

Chicago *Daily News,* 67

Christian Science Monitor, 1, 4

Chung, Connie, 238

Church, Frank, 149, 150, 166–67, 295

and administration proposals to tighten security, 211

chairman of committee investigating assassinations, 149–50, 153, 154–61

opening of mail of, 183

on Rockefeller Commission report, 151

Subcommittee on Multinational Corporations of, 193

Church, Wells, 2, 10

CIA, 99, 105, 142

assassination plots, 144–52, 153, 154

attempts to kill Castro, 154–61 *passim,* 161–69

CBS journalists who had worked for, 202–4, 274–80

Church's committee investigating assassinations by, 149, 150, 153, 154–61

development of deadly poisons, 183

and Ethics Committee's hearings on Pike report leak, 234

and House Intelligence Committee, 186–93

and link between Castro and